THE EASY GUIDE TO REPERTORY GRIDS

THE EASY GUIDE TO REPERTORY GRIDS

Devi Jankowicz

Graduate Business School
University of Luton, UK

WILEY

Reprinted with corrections April 2013

Other Wiley Editorial Offices

John Wiley & Sons Inc., 111 River Street, Hoboken, NJ 07030, USA

Jossey-Bass, 989 Market Street, San Francisco, CA 94103-1741, USA

Wiley-VCH Verlag GmbH, Boschstr. 12, D-69469 Weinheim, Germany

John Wiley & Sons Australia Ltd, 33 Park Road, Milton, Queensland 4064, Australia

John Wiley & Sons (Asia) Pte Ltd, 2 Clementi Loop #02-01, Jin Xing Distripark,
Singapore 129809

John Wiley & Sons Canada Ltd, 22 Worcester Road, Etobicoke, Ontario, Canada M9W 1L1

Wiley also publishes its books in a variety of electronic formats. Some content that appears in
print may not be available in electronic books.

Library of Congress Cataloging-in-Publication Data

Jankowicz, Devi.
    The easy guide to repertory grids / Devi Jankowicz.
        p. cm.
Includes bibliographical references and index.
    ISBN 0-470-85404-9 (pbk. : alk. paper)
    1. Repertory grid technique.   I. Title.
    BF698.8.R38J36 2003
    155.2'8–dc21   2003006941

British Library Cataloguing in Publication Data

A catalogue record for this book is available from the British Library

ISBN 0-470-85404-9

Typeset in 10/12pt Palatino by Dobbie Typesetting Limited, Tavistock, Devon

CONTENTS

LIST OF FIGURES

LIST OF TABLES

ABOUT THE AUTHOR

Devi Jankowicz is Professor of Constructivist Managerial Psychology at the University of Luton. He has been using repertory grids in a variety of occupational and managerial applications for 30 years. He used to specialise in psychometric testing until it was suggested to him that talking to people in their own language might be more valuable than talking to them in psychologists' language, and this book is written in that spirit. As well as being useful in his work as a Chartered Occupational Psychologist, this perspective has been particularly fruitful in his personal research on knowledge transfer across cultural boundaries between the West and the post-command economies of Central Europe.

PREFACE

This book is the result of some experiences I've had during the last 10 years, teaching repertory grid technique to a variety of audiences. There have been two main kinds of trainee. The first has comprised my direct students at Luton Graduate Business School, managers studying for MBA and MSc degrees on a part-time basis, and young graduates on the full-time masters programme. There have also been undergraduates, here and there, from the education and the management departments. All par for the course, one imagines, for a technique which presents itself as a mental-mapping and decision-making aid.

The second group, you might feel, is rather surprising. It comprises members and affiliates of the Occupational Division of the British Psychological Society, as part of their continuing professional development programme; psychologists and counsellors in some UK and Irish universities; and psychologists working for the Employment Service. Shouldn't psychologists, the very people who ought to be well informed about cognitive structures, mental maps, and decision-making technique, already know all this?

You could be right, but by and large they don't, and for two reasons: academic attitudes and simple availability.

ACADEMIC ATTITUDES

There's a certain approach taken to repertory grids, and especially to the theoretical underpinning, personal construct psychology, in university psychology departments. The theory tends to be offered, at a rather basic level, as part of course on personality, and the technique, where it's made available, in a two-hour seminar workshop in which the bare bones are practised but the applications, variants, and solutions to practical problems – 'how do I present the grid results of a large sample of people rather than the single person on whom I practised?' being the most common – are never addressed in any detail.

The attitude stems from a preference for positivist epistemology within the psychological profession, even where the more recent constructivist approaches are known about, and the related techniques understood. (If you're curious about all this, you might like to glance at Jankowicz, 1987a; Neimeyer, 1983, or the fuller treatment in Neimeyer, 1985.)

The result has been that the repertory grid technique is little used beyond its specialist adherents, and the central value of personal construct psychology as the basis for understanding all epistemologies in the first place has been scandalously neglected – often in favour of a pointless argument between proponents of qualitative versus quantitative methods, statistical versus experiential approaches, all of which is largely irrelevant. And so, people like myself, part of an international network of personal construct psychologists numbering no more, I would guess, than a thousand worldwide, are approached to train those who should already be trained. One does what one can, and this book is part of it.

SIMPLE AVAILABILITY: TO MANAGERS IN PARTICULAR

To focus on the other, and broader, audience for this guidebook, the managers and practitioners. Forget all that about epistemologies. From your point of view in particular, there simply hasn't been a simple practical guidebook to offer you for many years, ever since the Stewarts' *Business Applications of Repertory Grid*, published in 1982, went out of print. There have been many books outlining the basic theory, and one or two on the technique itself, but none have gone into the kind of practical, procedural detail which a user, bereft of a decent introduction in the psychology departments or isolated as a practitioner, needs to see if s/he is to become comfortably proficient in repertory grid technique.

The second edition of the *Manual of Repertory Grid Technique* by Fransella, Bell & Bannister will appear in 2004 (also published by Wiley). That gives a more detailed and in-depth coverage of repertory grids, as did the first edition (1977) by Fransella & Bannister, which has been out of print for several years. This guidebook has been seen in its entirety by the senior author, who has shared details of the planned contents of the Manual with me, all within the constraints of our respective publication schedules.

Between the two, it may be possible to ameliorate, if not reverse, the neglect of this technique in the universities, and in the meanwhile provide the user with a solid foundation for practice.

It remains to thank my kind collaborators. Fay Fransella has already been mentioned; her spirit resides in the comments made by the 'second voice' of this book, though the responsibility for its embodiment in print is, of course, my own. Tom Ravenette provided examples of early forms of grid analysis and much moral support! Thanks, too, to Ms Marianna Pexton of the Analytical Services Division of the Department of Social Security (DSS), now Department of Work and Pensions (DWP), for facilitating departmental permission to reproduce Table 7.1. My special thanks go to my colleagues and students, who have seen earlier drafts of this guide and contributed their valuable comments and ideas.

Devi Jankowicz
Professor of Constructivist Managerial Psychology
Graduate Business School
University of Luton
February 2003

CHAPTER 1

INTRODUCTION

This small volume is intended as a convenient and user-friendly introductory guide to the various procedures involved in eliciting and analysing repertory grids. It isn't an academic treatise but a guidebook which provides you with instructions on

• how to elicit grids

• how to analyse them to an accepted and rigorous standard.

It isn't a book about the theoretical background, personal construct theory (PCT), since there are many of those: the bare bones of the theory are outlined, just for reference, in Appendix 6. It isn't an academic treatment of repertory grid technique, with a comprehensive review of the research on grids and their use. That job is done by its companion volume, Fransella et al. (2004): see below. It is a practical workbook and guide, using which you can teach yourself how to elicit and analyse repertory grids. By the time you finish it, going through all the examples and exercises, you will be proficient in grid technique. Think of it as an introduction which teaches you the basics, and refers you to more advanced information as required.

1.1 HOW TO USE THIS GUIDEBOOK

The purpose of this section is to provide you with some suggestions on how to make the best use of the material which follows. The first thing to notice is that it's been written by two distinct persons.

The first is a technician. He knows about grids, and he wants to tell you, as clearly as possible, how you can use them. One of life's definitive techies, he takes the reasons for his knowledge for granted, and in order to provide clear procedural instructions, he doesn't stop to examine his ideas or his rationale in any great detail. He knows his stuff, and all he cares about is to help you understand what you're doing with grids, as clearly as possible. He often uses relatively short, declarative sentences, since his purpose is clear and simple instruction. He writes like this, using the full width of the page.

> The second person is a theorist. She, also, knows about grids, and has used them extensively herself. As a result, she knows that the simple use of a procedure does not guarantee success; indeed, she believes very strongly that simple technique, bereft of ideas, concepts, and the *reasons for* doing things in a particular way, is often misleading and occasionally dangerous. There's no such thing as a simple procedure, uninformed by a set of assumptions for doing things one way rather than another, and if you're unreflective, and don't learn a good set of reasons, your use of grids will be inaccurate and, ultimately, ineffective. Because she deals in theory, justification, and rationale, her sentences are often a wee bit longer. She writes like this, in indented text.

Occasionally, the two argue with each other in order to make a point.

Secondly, it follows that the best way of reading this book is to read it in stages. There are five simple steps.

- Skim-read it, just running your eyes over the text as you turn the pages. See what's on offer and, more importantly, how it's laid out, with text, exercises at the end of each chapter, and answers to exercises and supplementary information in the appendices.

- Read it from start to finish, in order. This isn't a textbook that you can dip into, and the various bits of technique build on each other. Take your time, and master each section before moving on to the next.

- At the outset, you should ignore the theorist, and read only the material written by the technician. Avoid all the indented material. Get your head round the procedures, and focus on the examples.

- When you have grasped the bit of technique that's involved, and perhaps practised it on yourself *only*, read the indented material which accompanies the technique.

- Don't use the procedure with another person until you've read *both* sets of material.

> Consequently, this book is a dialogue between two voices. It will be up to you as the reader to put the two voices together; to make your own sense of the two sets of

information. Reading has to be an active process if the material which you read is to be retained, and procedures which encourage people to talk to themselves as they're reading are a particularly good way of learning! (see Thomas & Harri-Augstein, 1985: 16–17).

Pace yourself, and don't spend too long at any one time with this guide. It's not a novel that you can read in one gulp, nor is it something you can pick bits out of. Some of the procedures may look complicated, and it may take you a little while to get up to speed. *They're actually very straightforward*, as you'll realise as soon as you've carried them out. Each one takes a bit of explaining in written text, but as an activity in itself, is very easy – as you'll see as soon as you do the relevant exercise. And so, steady does it. Plan on reading a section at a time, do the exercise(s), practise the technique, and come back to the next section another day.

If you have a friend with whom you can spend time trying out each technique as you learn it, that would be very helpful, though a lot of the grid activities can be done by yourself, on yourself.

Towards the end of each chapter, you'll find the following:

- A set of 'Things to Do'. The best way to learn a technique is to practise it, and the exercises under this heading provide you with the opportunity to do so. If you want to learn how to use grids, you have to tackle each exercise at the point in the text where it's suggested.

- Occasionally, some suggestions for 'Further Reading' are provided, highlighted where relevant.

At the very end of the book, you'll find a set of appendices. Of these, one is particularly comforting, and that's Appendix 1. It provides you with the 'Answers to Exercises'. Take them on board, look again at your own attempt at the exercise and, when you're happy to proceed, read on from the appropriate part of the chapter.

The other one I want to mention here is less cuddly, but you'll appreciate it because it's very practical. Appendix 7 is a 'Summary of Grid Procedures'. This will be your *vade mecum* after you've learnt the basic techniques. Every procedure presented in the guide is collated here in note form, to be used as an *aide-mémoire* when you're carrying out a grid interview and need to refresh your memory about one of the steps. You can expect to use it a lot at first, dispensing with it when you feel ready.

This book is meant to be entirely self-contained, and so it is, so far as the basics of grid technique are involved. You can be up and doing without any other reading. However, name–date references and a reference list in the usual form are provided, so that you can develop your knowledge of the background theory, advanced points of technique, further details on procedures, and some applications.

You'll need these in any case if you're using grids to obtain empirical material for an assessed project or dissertation that forms part of a course of study you're following. If so, you may have encountered repertory grids before, for they form part of Chapter 13 of Jankowicz (2000a), a research methods textbook for management project and dissertation work.

Finally, if you want further guidance on points of technique, resource materials, and a gateway to additional resources, you might like to log in to *The Easy Guide to Repertory Grids* website. There are further details on this at the end of Chapter 9.

1.2 WHAT THIS BOOK CONTAINS

We start off in Chapter 2 with a description of what a repertory grid is, what it consists of, and why you would want to use one. A completed sample grid is provided so that you can see the beast for yourself, while the exercise gets you used to the basic constituents of a grid, which are called 'constructs'.

Chapter 3 provides you with the procedural steps involved in conducting a grid interview (or eliciting a grid; the terms are synonymous), how to prepare for it, and what the different design options might be. The exercises have you eliciting a grid, and experimenting with the options available to you.

Chapter 4 is a refresher and problem-solving facility. I have tried to anticipate the kinds of questions you might be wanting to ask after you've attempted your first grid, and have provided you with what I hope will be helpful answers – plus some further resources, including electronic ones, where you might find further assistance. The exercises seek to develop your ability to resolve issues that arise in grid technique. Partly, this depends on becoming sensitive to the grid interview as a delicate interpersonal and social process, and, to that end, you are referred to Appendix 2, which provides a detailed transcript of a grid interview session keyed to the exercises.

Once you've got that far, you've come a long way! You know a lot of what there is to know about elicitation, and the next step is to examine the rich information that a grid provides, and to see how it might be analysed. Chapter 5 addresses the basic analysis of a single repertory grid, encouraging you to take account of the process by which you arrived at your interviewee's meanings, as well as describing what's to be seen, and how it might be interpreted. By the end of this chapter, you should know how to get at the meanings being expressed in a single grid. The exercises are designed to give you practice at doing just that: process analysis, simple eyeball analysis, and some construct categorisation.

Chapter 6 takes you a step further, looking at the informational relationships within the grid. Where the previous chapter was largely descriptive, and you made relatively little use of all the numbers, Chapter 6 outlines ways in which you can examine relationships within the grid, using the numbers.

- 'Is it really true that this person likes his best friend better than himself?'

- 'I got the feeling in the grid interview that the interviewee described her boss in terms very similar to those she uses when she talks about her main competitor's MD. Can I see any particular evidence for that?'

- 'If I understand the interviewee correctly, this company's unique selling proposition is practically the opposite of those used by its competitors. Have I understood that accurately; how can I check it?'

- 'Whenever this student says he's confident about a subject he's studying, he also says he had to rely on other people to learn it properly. Is there a relationship between his social support and how effectively he learns?'

Some simple, and some more complex, procedures are outlined by which relationships of these kinds can be examined. The exercises provide an opportunity to practise different components of the analysis procedures.

One of the criticisms that can be levelled at existing ways of teaching repertory grid technique is that relatively little time is spent in teaching people how to analyse *sets* of grids. A grid is a very rich and complex description of one person's views (in fact, it's been designed as the individual assessment device par excellence!) and, perhaps as a result, the analysis of *samples* of repertory grids is rather neglected. Chapter 7 is an attempt to put that right. It provides two different forms of content analysis for the aggregation of grid materials, advocates the use of differential analyses within very simple research designs, and emphasises the importance of reliability in the analysis process. The exercises give practice in all of this.

Chapter 8 provides an introduction to what is, arguably, the most important and powerful activity associated with grid work: the description and self-assessment of the interviewee's personal value system. Along the way, it tackles the issue of social desirability responding ('faking good'), and, as an outcome, provides you with a credible and powerful way of addressing the problem. The exercises encourage you to consider your own values in a given situation, prioritise them, and examine what might be required for you to change them!

Finally, in the last chapter, we confront the major issue of change itself. Change and difference: how can you tell when someone has changed their mind? And how can you assess how well one person understands another person's mind? Is it really possible to get into the other's head and see the world through their eyes rather than your own? The examples check how well *you* have understood the procedures involved.

1.3 WHAT THIS BOOK MISSES OUT

Firstly, it doesn't talk to you like a textbook. At least, I hope not! The point is to learn how to do something in the here and now, rather than to understand it conceptually. There will be times when you think that I'm spoon-feeding you, and, no doubt, academics who review this book will feel that it's far too basic. Never mind: that is a sacrifice well worth making if it creates some clear space in which you can concentrate on learning the basics of technique. You can get round to the more conceptually orientated books once you've mastered this one.

> Always remember the need for a leavening of theory if you're not to misuse the practicalities! There is one text, just one, which you could usefully regard as a companion volume to this one, and as a first recourse when you find that the basics outlined herein are an insufficient basis for your questions. Twenty-five years ago, Fay Fransella and Don Bannister published their *Manual of Repertory Grid Technique*, a text which is to reappear as Fransella et al. (2004). Use that as a conceptual back-up.

Secondly, it needs to be remembered that this is an introduction, and that there's more to learn about more specialized, advanced techniques once you have mastered the basics. There are, for example, a number of index measures (see Section 5.1) based on grid information and sometimes used in therapy. I haven't included them here because they are best used in conjunction with other sources of information (clinical interviews, psychometric tests, *repeated* grid measures, and familiarity with at least one strong theory of cognitive structure), and none of these are included in this guide. (It is rather tempting, for example, after recognising monolithic construing in a single grid, to infer that the individual engages in obsessive thinking in general. I'd rather not make inferences of that kind on the basis of a single grid.)

Thirdly, although I mention computer analysis of grid material, I don't provide a systematic review of the various software packages available for grid elicitation and analysis. This is especially relevant to Chapter 6, in which two of the four procedures rely on some form of software. The introduction to that chapter gives you details of a website through which you can access an online repertory grid elicitation and analysis engine, which is platform-independent and will provide you with any computation facilities you need in working with this guide. (That is a matter of personal preference. Some people like to fiddle with software while they're learning about a procedure that can make use of such software, and some people find it a distraction.)

1.4 A WORD ABOUT THE EXAMPLES

As I've mentioned above, this book provides you with a large number of illustrative examples, worked examples, and exercises, using which you can acquire the various techniques. I wondered whether to base the whole account round a single case, whereby all of the examples would illustrate and develop one particular individual's material on a given topic in a consistent way. I imagine this would have made for a coherent learning experience! I decided against it, though, for two related reasons.

Grids can be used for an enormous variety of purposes, and can deal with any topic under the sun. I wanted to give you a flavour of that richness, by using a variety of examples. Secondly, as you'll see over the page, grids can be used by a great variety of people – undergraduates, teachers, business managers, researchers, and any and all occupational specialists – and it would probably have narrowed interest for the remainder if I'd provided examples pertinent to just one of these groups. If at any point you find that the examples aren't you, then read on. You'll come across something personally relevant shortly after, I'm sure.

CHAPTER 2

THE REPERTORY GRID:
A BASIC DESCRIPTION

We start with a statement of purpose. What is a grid and why would you want one? What does it look like and how is it useful? What, in fact, is it for?

2.1 THE BASIC REPERTORY GRID

'Grid' is actually a generic term for a number of simple rating-scale procedures. They're all used for arriving at straightforward descriptions of how a person views the world, or some smaller part of it, in his or her own terms.

The result of these procedures looks like a set of rating scales printed one above the other, with the ratings arranged in rows and columns into a table or grid. Like a rating scale, a grid can be about anything. Grid procedures result in information which can have an enormous range of applications, and some of these are illustrated in Table 2.1. I shall be drawing on these fields of application to provide examples throughout.

As you can see, they are grouped according to your possible interests; and here I'd like to make a suggestion. While it makes sense to stay focused on your own

Table 2.1 A brief list of applications in which a repertory grid can be used *(there are many more!)*

Some general applications

- Understanding how a person important to you thinks about things that matter to you.
- Forming a fast impression of a person's likes and dislikes.
- The systematic description and exchange of views between two people, as a way of recording and monitoring the process of friendship formation.
- Describing an individual's opinions as part of an attitude survey.
- Gossiping systematically with your partner about your mutual friends.
- Simple problem solving: for example, an artist seeking to resolve a creative 'block'.
- Simple decision making: for example, which model of car to buy.

Some educational applications

- The assessment of a set of teachers by their students, as a course evaluation and feedback device.
- The description of a set of ideas, techniques, examples, or illustrations by the pupils who are meant to be learning them, to discover what the pupils have learnt, and, perhaps more valuably, *how* they have learnt them.
- The systematic recording and assessment of a set of programme components, as part of a programme evaluation.
- The collection of experts', or clients', views about different educational philosophies.
- The description of the ways in which a person thinks about their friends, in order to understand the person, or in support of a counselling relationship with that person.
- Identifying a person's understanding of their options in order to help them to make a career choice.

Some occupational applications

- Knowledge capture and, particularly, the clarification of tacit knowledge.
- Recording the variety of opinions which exist in a group of managers or employees, as part of a team-building exercise.
- Analysing the different stakeholder positions held among a group of employees.
- The systematic description of job responsibilities in order to develop a competency framework for the job in question.
- The development of a performance appraisal scheme for a job in which the preferred ways of doing tasks are initially vague, underspecified, or expressed as 'mother-hoods' rather than as precise performance specifications.
- The development of a new product by building on consumers' ideas about, and preferences for, existing products.
- The training of quality controllers for products, services, and processes where the definition of 'quality' depends on initially underspecified, expert judgement.

Clinical applications

Many and varied: the repertory grid was first devised in the context of clinical psychology. I'm not qualified to make useful statements in that field, but Winter (1992) is the definitive text should your interests lie there.

field of application when working through the examples, it would be wise to attend to the examples in other fields, too. You might be in teacher training, attracted to the examples in education or assessment. Nevertheless, bear with me, and look at the occupational examples, too, since I'll be using them to illustrate points which are relevant to your own use of grids. You might be a manager working under pressure to devise a competency framework; but you should follow the educational applications, too, for the same reason. And you might be a student in these, or related, fields. No doubt everyone will find the 'general' applications interesting and attend to them anyway.

> You should know that there are other types of grid, too (for example, the Implications Grid; Hinkle, 1965); and you should be aware that there are other ways of identifying the ways in which a person sees the world, of which the most important is probably the Self-Characterisation Technique (Kelly, 1955/1991: 323). No numbers or ratings are used in this approach: it's all words! There's more on this in Section 4.3.2.

2.1.1 The Basic Constituents of a Grid

Every grid consist of four components:

- topic
- elements
- constructs
- ratings.

Of these, the most important for the time being are constructs.

Constructs

Our basic unit of description and analysis is called a **construct**. We **construe** things by means of constructs. To construe is to make sense of something; to have a personal understanding of it; to find meaning in it. When I spoke about 'viewing the world' and of 'ways of seeing' earlier on, I was talking about **construing**.

The following are all constructs:

Pleasant	–	Rude
Warm and sunny	–	Cold and windy
A good teacher	–	An ineffective teacher
Ensures I've understood his point	–	Doesn't check if he's made sense

A risky business strategy	–	A safe business strategy
Reliable	–	Unreliable
Usually comes in late for work	–	Always comes to work on time

When you read these examples, insert the words 'as opposed to' in place of the dashes. It's 'pleasant, as opposed to rude'; 'warm and sunny, as opposed to cold and windy'; and so on. A construct always represents a contrast, and you need to spell out the contrast before you can be sure of the meaning intended by the whole construct.

> George Kelly, who first developed repertory grid technique (in a form known as the Role Construct Repertory Test), also developed something rather more important: an explicit theory of human understanding called Personal Construct Theory (Kelly, 1955/1991). One of the central assumptions of the theory is that reality and what we make of it is built up of contrasts rather than absolutes. 'A person's construct system is composed of a finite number of *dichotomous* constructs', is how he put it.

> We simply don't know what 'a good teacher' means unless we are aware what alternatives are possible. To say that a person is 'pleasant' is meaningless unless it's said with some idea that there were other options available; otherwise, so what? And if the person is not pleasant, in what way is he or she not pleasant?

> And so, in expressing a meaning, the most useful comparison to make is the *contrast* rather than the negative: the *particular* opposing or contrasted possibility you have in mind. 'Pleasant' as opposed to 'not pleasant' (the *negative*) is useless! The precise flavour of the word 'pleasant', the precise meaning we intend, can be understood best if we identify the particular *contrast* which is being implicitly conveyed.

> To say someone is 'pleasant as opposed to rude' carries a different meaning of 'pleasant' than to say that someone is 'pleasant as opposed to exciting'. In the former case, 'pleasant' includes politeness, but in the latter, a kind of placidity: 'merely pleasant, maybe even a bit humdrum'.

And so, if you wish to understand how an individual sees the world, in his or her own terms, you need to find out that person's constructs.

It's fatally easy to talk to someone and think that we've understood them, but unless we do so in their own terms – which means finding out what their personal constructs are – we run the risk of simply laying our own thinking on to them. Have you ever filled out a form, done a questionnaire, or taken a psychological test, and felt that *none* of the questions asked, or alternatives offered you, gave you a chance to say what you really thought? Infuriating, no?

The requirement that constructs should always be spelt out in full makes sure that you have captured meaning precisely. Very often, people elicit grids in order to go beyond the obvious and banal; to discover *exactly* what some other person means, or understands, in a given situation. In many of the applications shown in Table 2.1, grids are used in order to avoid the mindless clichés and banalities thrown up by alternative techniques. Think of the last course feedback form you filled in for your lecturer, or the typical performance appraisal questionnaire you had to complete...

Topic

People have constructs about anything and everything. A grid is always conducted about a particular **topic**, with the intention of eliciting just those constructs which the person uses in making sense of that particular **realm of discourse** – that particular slice of their experience. In discovering the constructs, you discover how the person thinks, what meanings s/he usually discerns, about that topic.

Also, while a single construct can be used to make sense of many different people, situations, and events (people may be 'reliable' as opposed to 'unreliable', but so can cars, supervisors, pubs, and interviews, for example), it tends to have a certain **range of convenience**. In other words, it is more likely to be used for some topics, and not for others, by the individual concerned. I might construe lots of people, situations, and events in terms of 'comfortable – painful', but I would normally restrict the construct 'incandescent – luminescent' to a discussion of light sources. (Unless I wanted to describe someone as 'incandescent with rage', I suppose. But you take my point about the relatively narrow range of convenience of 'incandescent – luminescent' compared with a construct like 'comfortable – painful'.)

And there are some constructs that I simply don't possess, for *any* topic, because I don't have dealings with those particular topics. The constructs lie outside my personal **repertoire**. Constructs such as 'distributive – integrative', which I had to look up in a book on industrial bargaining, or 'highly leveraged – unleveraged', which is something to do with management buyouts and similarly beyond my ken.

Which suggests a use in the exploration of *other* people's repertoires. Grids are a very good way of understanding professional and occupational private languages: the technical jargons of teachers, educational administrators, managers, and entrepreneurs, the more specialised languages of tea-blenders and steelworkers; of wine tasters and pilots; of tailors and cutters besides. Bring me a flint-knapper and I'll tell you his language.

In doing a grid on a particular topic, you only discover a *part* of a person's repertoire. Be assured that there are many more constructs, a wealth of different ways of thinking about experience, which the individual no doubt possesses about other topics that you haven't dealt with.

A grid, then, is a highly focused technique, in which the topic must always be clearly specified in advance. Later sections go into this issue in greater depth, in discussing the notion of a person's construct system and the ways in which it is structured and hangs together.

Elements

The way you identify a set of constructs on a given topic is very straightforward. You provide an interviewee with plenty of examples of that topic, and discover the ways in which s/he puts those examples together.

Think of any three people known to you. Can you think of some characteristic which two of them have in common, and in which they differ from the third? 'Well,' you might say, 'Mary is fairly shy, but compared to her, John and Lucy are a lot more outgoing; is that the sort of thing you mean?'

Exactly so. We've discovered that you have a construct, 'shy as opposed to outgoing', which you use when the topic is 'friends'; and we've done this by providing you with examples of the topic: Mary, Lucy, and John. These 'examples of a topic' are known as **elements**.

An **element** is an example of, exemplar of, instance of, sampling of, or occurrence within, a particular topic.

A set of elements is compared systematically to discover a person's constructs.

As you might imagine, choosing the right set of elements is a crucial aspect in doing a grid; it indicates the realm of discourse, and helps to determine the kinds of constructs you'll obtain by hinting at the range of convenience involved.

I shall have plenty more to say on this shortly. For the time being, to give you a flavour of what elements look like, Table 2.2 provides some typical ones. As you can see, practically anything can be an element! I once did a market research activity in which the elements were different cheeses, and the interviewees' constructs about cheeses were obtained by asking them to systematically compare the elements – by tasting them.

Ratings

Grids are very powerful, and for two reasons, the first of which you can anticipate already. They allow people to express their views by means of *their own* constructs, not yours – in other words, to talk about the world in their own terms. No one can object that someone else's assumptions have been laid on

Table 2.2 Examples of elements

If the topic were...	...the elements could be
'Lecturers'	The names of the lecturers who teach you
'My colleagues'	The names of your colleagues at work
'Cars I'd like to buy'	The various models of cars you're thinking of buying
'Effective supervisors'	A list of supervisors you've known in the past (including more, and less, effective ones)
'Government policy papers on education'	A list of the papers, by title
'Competencies required in a particular job'	A list of the main task activities which an employee has to perform (or, alternatively, the names of a set of people who do the job, some well, others less so)
'Perfumes'	A list of perfume brands (or better still, samples of the perfumes themselves)

Usable elements are very varied. In these examples, I've used people's names, car model names, titles of articles, sets of activities, and the actual objects themselves. Instead of people's names I could have used their photographs, or, on the other hand, a code letter if anonymity was an issue. The important thing is not to mix categories: don't combine names, activities, and objects into a single set of elements. The set should be 'all of a kind'.

them; no one has put words into the person's mouth. I'm sure you can think of many situations in which this is desirable.

Secondly, once you as the investigator have discovered a person's constructs, the person's own terms of reference, the grid will allow you to identify *exactly* what the other person means when s/he uses those terms. Each element is **rated** on each construct, to provide an exact picture of what the person wishes to say about each element within the topic.

Between them, the elements, constructs, and ratings of elements on constructs provide you with a kind of mental map: a precise statement of the way in which the individual thinks of, gives meaning to, **construes**, the topic in question.

2.1.2 So What Is a Repertory Grid?

A repertory grid, then, is simply a set of rating scales which uses the individual's own constructs as the subject matter on which ratings are carried out.

No, it's not! That's simply one way of thinking about a repertory grid. Some other ways are as:

- a form of structured interviewing, with ratings or without, which arrives at a precise description uncontaminated by the interviewer's own viewpoint

- an ideal way of conducting a pilot study before using more conventional survey techniques

- a very useful integrating device, that allows you to build bridges between qualitative and quantitative research techniques. The qualitative material is expressed and analysed in a non-woolly, demonstrably reliable way, while quantitative information is obtained which stays true to, and precisely conveys, a person's personally intended meaning.

Actually, I'm not really arguing with you. One of the fundamental assumptions made by George Kelly when developing the Role Construct Repertory Test (Kelly, 1955/1991) is what he called **constructive alternativism**. By this, he meant that different people have different ways of construing the same thing; also, that a single person always has the option of construing the same thing differently on two separate occasions. So you have to grant me that it's possible to accept a variety of different definitions of a repertory grid. To see something as 'nothing but' is to be **pre-emptive** (see Section 5.3.3) – to ignore other options and narrow your focus excessively (Pervin, 1973).

Fair enough. And I'll admit that there are occasions when thinking of a grid in terms of ratings which are numbers, and rating scales made up of words, obscures the fact that all of this is simply a way of expressing underlying *preferences*; in other words, of representing the choices which a person makes in his or her thinking well before they're put into symbols. We'll get on to that eventually.

For the time being, it suits my purposes to teach the essentials of the grid as a simple, but powerful, rating-scale technique.

2.1.3 A Description of the Other Person in Their Own Terms

You'll find that, as a bare-bones procedure, a grid is very straightforward. There's nothing difficult about it. However, there is a substantial amount of skill involved in obtaining an accurate description of the other person's constructs and values, and this book sets out to teach you how to do so. The 'Things to Do' section includes exercises which will help you to practise what I'm preaching.

The end result is a description which stays true to the constructs being offered by the other person, rather than to your own. This involves you in questioning, checking, and mulling over what exactly the other person means – in other words, negotiating your understanding of what the other person means. It's very much a two-way process.

As well as being procedurally simple, the technique is relatively quick. With practice, you'll find that you can obtain all the individual, distinct constructs a person has on a given topic in under an hour. (With practice also, another 40 minutes or so will be sufficient time to arrive at the person's core constructs and personal values, by use of the laddering and resistance to change techniques I describe in Sections 8.1.1 and 8.2.)

Some potential users get worried at this point. 'An hour spent with one person is too long', they'll tell you. Well, that's just too bad! If you want to do something properly, you take the time involved. An hour's structured interviewing isn't a lot to ask for results which are very powerful indeed.

> Quite so. The alternatives which people have in mind when they make this comparison are often (Jankowicz, 2000a: 96):
>
> (a) a conversation lasting 5 to 10 minutes, a procedure which can be informative *but never to the level of detail* obtained by a grid
>
> (b) a semi-structured or fully structured interview which lasts between 30 and 60 minutes: almost as long, but *unlikely to have the same precision* unless it is, in fact, a repertory grid interview!
>
> (c) a psychometric test, which doesn't describe the person in terms of his or her own constructs. It *imposes researchers' own constructs*, their own framework for understanding people, onto the individual, with all the force and energy of a supermarket bread-slicing machine. And many psychometric tests are an hour long, in any case.

2.2 AN EXAMPLE OF A COMPLETED REPERTORY GRID

So, after all this, what does it look like? Let's examine a typical grid in this section, before going on to see how it was obtained in Chapter 3.

Figure 2.1 shows you an example of a completed repertory grid, prepared after a 50-minute interview with a university lecturer (but it could have been a teacher, or an industrial trainer, and so I use the generic term 'instructor').

Subsequent sections will tell you more about how to elicit a grid, how to make sense of what's in it, and how to analyse it; all in greater detail. In the meanwhile, though, you may as well see an example of what you're aiming to produce, and what can be gleaned from it.

The **topic** deals with this instructor's understanding of, and views on, methods of teaching and learning.

The instructor provided nine different teaching methods as his **elements** (some are more situations than methods, but you take my point). They range from the very specific (role-plays and structured exercises) to the more general (learning from life's experience); from the frequently used (lectures and tutorials) to the less common ones (company visits and overseas exchanges).

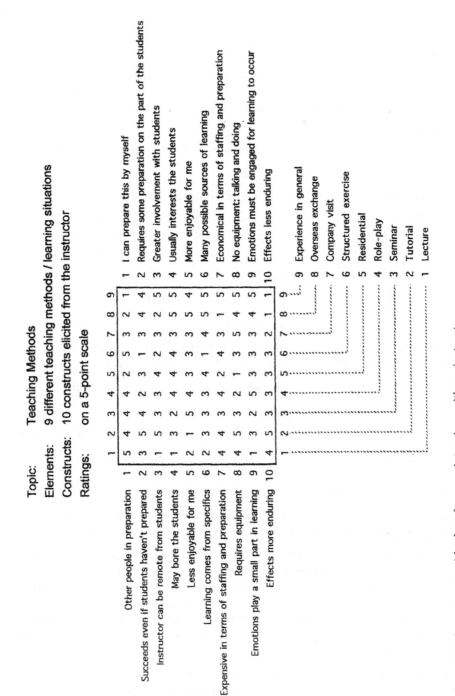

Figure 2.1 A repertory grid taken from an interview with an instructor

They cover the range of possibilities that both he as interviewee and I as interviewer wanted to talk about, and were derived through 5 minutes of discussion. They're numbered 1 to 9 at the bottom right of the figure, each one corresponding with a column in the grid.

The **constructs** were elicited over 30 minutes of concentrated discussion; there they are, numbered 1 to 10 down the figure, each one corresponding to a row of the grid. Notice how each end of each construct is shown, one on the left and one on the right.

This instructor construes (thinks about and views) teaching methods in terms of

- whether he can set up the learning situation by himself, or must involve other people
- the extent to which success depends on the amount of preparation the students have done
- how involved with the students he feels
- how well he thinks the students' interest is captured
- how much he enjoys using the method
- where the learning comes from: specific happenings or actions, as distinct from a less differentiated and more varied set of occurrences
- how much the method costs to use, in staffing and preparation time
- how much equipment is required
- how far the students' emotions need to be engaged if learning is to happen
- the impact on the students in terms of time and, possibly, depth.

So now you know a little of how this instructor thinks.

How do the constructs compare with your own? Are there any surprises? Should he have mentioned other constructs that are perfectly obvious to you?

The answer to this last question is 'no', by the way. The point is to understand the instructor without laying your own views on him. What you do with the constructs you obtain, of course, depends on your purpose. If you were in some advisory or mentoring capacity to the instructor, you might, once you had the constructs, discuss them, examine common ones that haven't been mentioned and explore the reasons why, and so forth. (This issue comes up again in Section 5.2, when we deal with the analysis of repertory grids.)

Turning to the **ratings** and viewing the constructs as rating scales, we follow a general convention that the left-hand end of the construct defines the '1' end of a 5-point scale, and the right-hand end of the construct defines the '5' end of a 5-point scale. Let's see what the instructor has to say about the lecture as a teaching method, by reading back *the ratings in column 1.*

Lectures are seen as something he can prepare by himself; this received a rating of '5' on the construct 'other people involved in preparation – I can prepare this by myself', where 'other people involved in preparation' is the '1' end of that scale and 'I can prepare this by myself' is the '5' end of that scale.

The instructor views lectures as requiring modest preparation on the part of the students (a '3' on the scale which runs from 'succeeds even if students haven't prepared' = the '1' end of the scale to 'require some preparation on the part of the students' = the '5' end of the scale). Lectures are seen by this instructor as putting him into a remote position with respect to students (a rating of '1' on this scale, where '1' = 'instructor can be remote from the students' and '5' = 'greater involvement with the students', with the students possibly being bored).

Reading back the ratings in the remainder of the first column, we find that he doesn't especially like lectures himself. He feels that learning from lectures tends to come from specific points made; the method is, in itself, inexpensive, and requires little equipment. The students' emotions play little part in learning, and he feels that the effects are not especially enduring.

Let's practise reading back what he has to say about another of the elements: the overseas exchange his boss has asked him to organise for students from the next course he's due to teach. Column 8, in fact.

Exchanges are seen as involving a fair number of other people to organise, and a substantial amount of preparation on the part of the students, who may learn even if somewhat separated from the lecturer, while being very interested in what's happening to them. He enjoys them himself, and sees them as providing learning from a varied range of sources; they are, however, expensive to organise and staff. Relatively little teaching equipment is required, and success depends on emotional involvement on the part of the students; the effects, he feels quite firmly, are likely to endure.

You might like to read back what he has to say about some of the other elements (columns) in the grid. There's a lot there, and you'll find that a grid crams masses of information into a small space. It looks as though the 50 minutes was rather well spent in terms of what you've learnt about the instructor's views!

Needless to say, your own views may differ from his – you yourself might have provided different ratings – but that's not the point. Now you know, in detail, what the instructor thinks.

Constructs tell you *how* a person thinks. The ratings of elements on constructs tell you *what* a person thinks.

This should give you an appreciation of the simplest use of a repertory grid: to provide a simple description. How you can arrive at this description – how you agree a topic and elements, how you elicit constructs and ratings – we'll look at in the next chapter, together with some more detailed guidelines on element choice. Later on, we'll consider the issues involved in the elicitation of constructs from groups of people, rather than from individuals.

You can and should go beyond simple description, though, and subsequent chapters will look at a variety of analysis techniques, for single grids, and for sets of grids. The present chapter has just scratched the surface!

2.3 POINTS TO REMEMBER

- Making things explicit is important, but a sense of ownership is equally so. Grids provide a way of understanding other people; precisely; in their own terms.

- Remember constructive alternativism: alternative interpretations are always possible, and your job is to negotiate meaning with the other person until you understand **their** construction, not yours.

- Look at the constructs given as examples in Section 2.1.1 and in Figure 2.1.

- Every construct has two opposite ends, known as **poles**: the left-hand pole, and the right-hand pole. *If it's only got one pole, it isn't a construct.*

Your first exercise focuses on this property.

THINGS TO DO

Exercise 2.1 Specifying Constructs

(a) Take a sheet of paper and write down any five adjectives or brief phrases which describe your best friend or closest colleague.

(b) Now, next to each adjective, write down the opposite of that adjective, as it might apply to someone very different to the person you've described.

(c) Now check the result against the example given in Appendix 1.1.

Exercise 2.2 Understanding the Background

If you've been reading this chapter as I've suggested, first mastering the technical material, and then going on to the theory, you may have paid more attention to the non-indented comments and done the first exercise: excellent. Now read back over the chapter as a whole, paying particular attention to the indented material.

THINGS TO READ

If you really want to understand the theoretical background (and you should!), the most readable, user-friendly, short account is in the following.

- Burr, V. & Butt, T. (1992) *An Invitation to Personal Construct Psychology*. London: Whurr.

If you want to see an example of how the repertory grid as a technique in one field of application is embedded in its background theory (personal construct theory) but related to other theories which pertain to that field, a good example is in knowledge management:

- Gaines, B. & Shaw, M. (1993) 'Knowledge acquisition tools based on personal construct psychology'. *Knowledge Engineering Review* 8, 49–85.

This paper is useful, and more conveniently obtained on the Web as *http://ksi.cpsc.ucalgary.ca/articles/KBS/KER/*

If you're using this book to learn grid technique for a dissertation or project, you'll probably find yourself needing to refer to George Kelly's definitive book at some stage, so you may as well check to see whether it's available in the library and, if not, order it now through inter-library loan.

- Kelly, G.A. (1955) *The Psychology of Personal Constructs*. New York: Norton.

The original 1955 text, long out of print, is also available in a second edition, published by Routledge in 1991. It's the larger version of Kelly's theory, written from a strong clinical psychology perspective, but very useful for anyone who is interested in personal development and change.

If you're not particularly interested in clinical psychology, you may prefer to look at the shorter version Kelly wrote, as follows:

- Kelly, G.A. (1963) *A Theory of Personality: The Psychology of Personal Constructs*. London: Norton.

CHAPTER 3

ELICITING A REPERTORY GRID

The basic elicitation procedure is outlined in this chapter. You'll be asked to practise it. Next, I outline some variants, and the reasons for them, drawing on personal construct theory as a justification, and in order to provide you with guidelines for devising variants of your own.

3.1 GRID ELICITATION

This consists of a structured interview, best carried out on a single-person, face-to-face basis, although it is possible to elicit grids from several people at a time, working in a group setting.

3.1.1 The Interview: Setting and Style

Most people being interviewed for a repertory grid find themselves working quite hard. Your job is to put them to work in a user-friendly way, helping them to concentrate without pain or drudgery.

Since the procedure is, in one sense, repetitive, it's important to remember that you're involved in an interview, and that the interview is a social process. You're in a situation in which you need to draw on the substantial social and conversational skills which you possess, in order to arrive at a good understanding of the meaning the interviewee wishes to convey. The procedure outlined below consists of some rather dry, and bare, bones. It will be your responsibility to flesh them out.

This means, firstly, that the usual rules in interviewing apply:

- a quiet room

- guaranteed freedom from disturbance for an hour or so

- the phone off the hook

- a relaxed atmosphere, perhaps fuelled by a cup of tea or coffee

- most usefully, a table for you both to sit at, side by side or at the corner of one end, with good elbow room available for both of you.

Secondly, there is the issue of organisational and personal 'entry'. This guide treats grid technique in isolation. But in most situations you'll be doing a grid interview for some reason, as part of a research project perhaps, or maybe as a component in a training course, organisation development (OD) intervention, and the like, and your interviewees will come to you with expectations about their reason for being there, and of your role in a wider process.

Basically, the usual rules of research/intervention procedure, etiquette, and, indeed, ethics apply. Among these, perhaps the most important are as follows.

- Explain why you're both there.

- Check that this reason is understood by the interviewee.

- Provide a thumbnail description of the grid in the following terms.

  - It's a structured interview (the idea of being interviewed is familiar to everyone).

  - You're trying to understand the interviewee in his or her own terms, and *not* to collect 'right answers' (which expresses the most important part of the whole social encounter).

  - The way you go about it makes for great precision, but the interviewee can choose how much detail to go into (which provides reassurance).

  - You'll be asking the interviewee to make a series of systematic comparisons (which provides the lead-in and helps to get you started).

- State the conditions of confidentiality (and, where applicable, anonymity) which apply, explaining how, exactly, you intend to preserve both.

- Check that these are acceptable to the interviewee.

Prepare a blank grid sheet, like the one shown as Figure 3.1. You will be filling in the details, as you're told them by the interviewee during the course of the interview. You will write:

- the topic into the top left corner
- the elements along the diagonal lines at the top
- the left pole and right pole of each construct on either side of the grid, working downwards row by row
- the ratings inside the grid, also row by row, construct by construct.

Show the sheet now and again to the interviewee if you wish: there's nothing there that isn't his/hers! You might like to have a set of 5" × 3" (127×76 mm) file cards to hand.

3.1.2 The Basic Procedure Is in 10 Steps

(1) **Agree a topic** with your respondent and write it onto the sheet.

(2) **Agree a set of elements**, and write these along the diagonals at the top of the grid sheet.

(3) **Explain that you wish to find out how s/he thinks about the elements**, and that you'll do this by asking him or her to compare them systematically.

(4) **Taking three elements** (numbers 1, 3, and 5), **ask your respondent, 'Which two of these are** *the same* **in some way, and** *different* **from the third?'** Provide assurance that you're not looking for a 'correct' answer, just how s/he sees the elements.

(5) **Ask your respondent why: 'What do the two have in common, as opposed to the third?'** Write down the thing the two have in common, in the first row on the left side of the grid sheet; and the converse of this (the reason the third element is different) in the same row on the right of the grid sheet, making sure that you've obtained a truly bipolar expression – a pair of words or phrases which express a contrast. This is the person's construct.

(6) **Check that you understand what contrast is being expressed;** use the interviewee's words as much as possible, but do feel free to discuss what s/he means, and to negotiate a form of words that makes sense to you both.

(7) **Present the construct as a rating scale**, with the phrase on the left standing for the '1' end of the scale, and the phrase on the right standing for the '5'

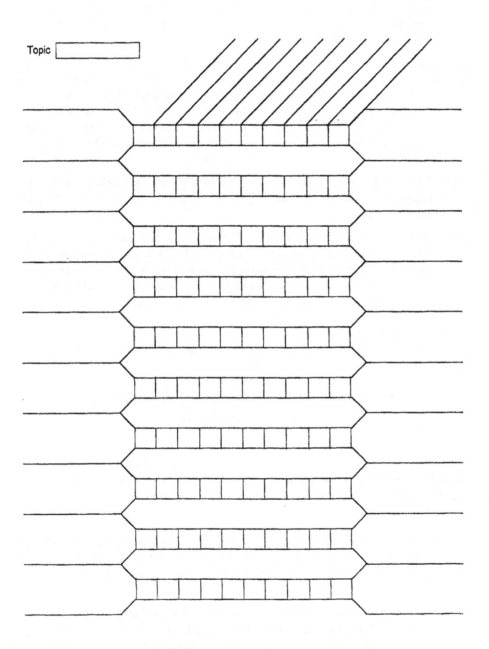

Figure 3.1 A basic grid sheet

end of the scale. A form of words like this: **'Now, the words I've written down on the left: imagine they define the "1" end of a 5-point scale. And that the words I've written down on the right define the "5" end of a 5-point scale.'**

(8) **Ask your respondent to rate each of the three elements on this scale**, writing the ratings into the grid as s/he states them: **'I'd like you to rate each of the three elements on this scale; give each of them one of the numbers, 1, 2, 3, 4, or 5, to say which end of the scale they're nearest to'**, or words to that effect. Occasionally, check that the directionality of the scaling is preserved, that is, that your respondent shouldn't be using a '1' when s/he is offering a '5' and vice versa.

(9) **Now ask the respondent to rate each of the remaining elements on this construct**. S/he's only rated three elements so far; now to complete rating the rest.

(10) **Your task is to elicit as many different constructs as the person might hold about the topic. So, repeat steps 4 to 8, asking for a fresh construct each time, until your respondent can't offer any new ones**; use a different triad of three elements each time: numbers 2, 4, and 6; then 1, 2, and 10, and so on. Aim to obtain 8 to 12 constructs in all.

You'll need to practise this procedure before progressing through this book. Skim-read the rest of this chapter if you like, but as soon as you can:

Please carry out Exercise 3.1 before reading the
next section in detail.

'Is that it, then? Er . . . a bit of a rigmarole to end up with these constructs and numbers? A whole book about this?' Yes and no! The value of a grid lies in two things:

(a) Getting an accurate picture of the way in which the other person sees the world (or part of it at least). Accuracy demands that you go about things in a particular way, but, to be sure, there's nothing especially difficult about doing it.

(b) The description and analysis of the particular topic being dealt with. Some subject matter is fascinating in its own right: imagine doing a grid on 'my policies' with the prime minister. And some subject matter depends on its context: the duke of Windsor, or Wallis Simpson, just before and just after the duke's abdication.

Like any other interview technique, in other words, its use has to be *designed* in accordance with the purpose of your investigation. The technique, in itself, is straightforward enough.

3.2 THE BACKGROUND TO THE STANDARD PROCEDURE

For something that claims to be a structured interview, the grid procedure is, nevertheless, a strange and somewhat peculiar way of asking questions. But if you've followed the argument in Chapter 2, and, particularly, if you've read the theoretical background, you'll recognise the reasons behind each of the 10 steps.

- Constructs represent meaning, and meaning is conveyed in terms of similarities and contrasts: that's the reason for steps 4 and 5.

- Words encode the meaning which exists in a construct, but the words themselves aren't the meaning. Other words could encode the same meaning more effectively (where the purpose is for the interviewee to share his or her meaning with you, and not for you to impose your own meaning!): that's the reason for step 6.

- The way in which a person construes (understands) the elements is indicated by the way in which they are arranged between the two extremes represented by the two opposing poles: that's the reason for steps 7, 8, and 9.

If you haven't already done so, go back over the indented material (the comments on theory) in Chapter 2 and read it thoroughly.

By now, it should be apparent that, though there are several points of simple procedure which should be followed exactly to use the technique properly, the advantage of a grid lies in its flexibility. The same procedure can be used for many different purposes, with an enormous variety of topics, with various kinds of elements to suit.

And quite apart from the basic technique, there are also some guidelines which are worth addressing when designing a grid for a particular purpose. (At this point, you might like to refer again to Table 2.1.)

3.2.1 Choosing the Topic

That's up to you. You decide what the grid is to be about, since this relates to some purpose you have for doing a grid in the first place.

Oh dear! That would be to throw away a wonderful opportunity to engage in collaborative research with your interviewee. Kelly (1955/1991) reminds us that we are all scientists, in the sense that we try to construe our experience based on what happened in the past; we draw on this to forecast what will happen in the future; and we are prepared to alter our construing in the light of what actually takes place. It seems such a shame to put yourself in the privileged role of 'investigator' (a particular, and privileged, sort of scientist), and see your interviewee merely as a passive provider of their personal constructs. Wouldn't it be best to see yourself and the interviewee as jointly exploring the interviewee's construing?

And, of course, collaborative research is by definition research in which there is a joint agreement on the subject matter to be investigated (Brown & Kaplan, 1981). Let's start by collaborating on the name of the topic!

Oh come on! That depends on the circumstances! In many situations, the investigator will know the potential of the grid technique and the interviewee won't, so the investigator's voice will inevitably carry more weight in specifying the topic.

Two Rules of Thumb

It's best to choose the topic yourself:

- while you are still learning grid technique. The rationale here is that it's easier to sort out, and learn from, procedural errors when one person makes them – you! – than when two do.

- when you are in a situation in which key participants expect you to take charge. This would apply to all research projects done for an academic qualification in which your supervisor is uncomfortable with participative research and expects you to take the lead. It would not apply in the case of collaborative research – which implies that you'd have to explain the basis of repertory grid techniques to your collaborators.

Qualifying Phrases

Once you have determined the topic for the grid, ask yourself why you're interested in this topic. Get as clear as you can about what point of view your interviewee is to be answering from. Then devise a qualifying phrase which sums it up. For example, in a grid about 'my friends', is the purpose to understand how the friendship was formed, or is it to help your interviewee decide which of them to go on holiday with this summer? A suitable qualifying phrase in the first instance might be 'friendship . . .

- ... in terms of how the relationship with them was formed'; and in the second

- ... 'in terms of what they might be like to spend a lot of time with'.

Another example. If this is a grid on what makes a manager effective in handling employees, suitable qualifying phrases might be 'effectiveness ...

- ... in terms of the social skills the manager uses'; or

- ... 'in terms of what managers actually, visibly, *do* to be effective'; or even

- ... 'in terms of the way managers handle their budget'.

The qualifying phrase will help to sharpen your own thinking about the topic, and why you're doing the grid. It is also immensely valuable at step 4 in the basic procedure outlined earlier. We'll return to this issue shortly, in Section 3.2.3. Bear with me!

3.2.2 Choosing Elements

Next, your job is to choose terms which sample or represent that topic. The best set of elements is one that covers the whole field of the topic evenly. Imagine you're drawing a map of (a part of) your interviewee's mind: a mental cartographer indeed! Cartographers work by surveying the physical terrain from a series of triangulation points spread evenly over the landscape, and you should usually try to do the same.

Anything can be an element: people, places, institutions, job responsibilities, teaching skills, policies, business strategies – the list is endless, provided it doesn't include constructs. Try to avoid words and phrases which have clear opposites, or words which represent qualities rather than actions or things.

Elements which are nouns are easier to handle than those which are verbs. Concrete nouns are easier than abstract ones. Names, people, textbook titles, job roles, occupations, products, brand images – all of these are nouns or can be expressed as such.

Where you're using verbs, try to express them as activities, each ending in '-ing', since this is easier to handle when you present each triad. Thus, 'deciding', 'delegating', and 'chairing' are a more user-friendly trio to offer than 'to make a decision', 'the delegation of job responsibilities', and 'chairmanship skills'.

A usable set of elements has an obvious 'neatness' about it in representing the topic. The set should be 'all of a kind'. If you can, try not to mix abstract nouns with concrete nouns, activities, and complicated verbal forms. How would you construe 'the Olympic ideal', 'mountain bikes', and 'Saturday afternoons spent acting as a sports coach'? It's possible, but rather messy to handle for you and the interviewee.

The set should certainly consist of mutually exclusive items – in other words, one element mustn't include another. It would prove impossible to work with an element set which included 'cats'; 'dogs'; 'Siamese'; 'budgerigars'; and 'Airedale terriers'.

A good set of elements will evoke a feeling of ownership on the part of the interviewee, and here you have four feasible alternatives in deciding how far to involve the interviewee in the choice of elements.

Elements Chosen by Investigator

You choose the elements based on your background knowledge and reason for conducting the grid interview. And, particularly if you decided on the topic, you should know how best to represent it by means of elements. By definition, though, you don't know how the topic appears to the interviewee, and this runs the risk of omitting elements which are important to him or her.

Elements Chosen by Interviewee

You let the interviewee choose the elements. This will ensure that the topic is represented from his or her point of view. But it may omit elements, and hence issues, that *you're* interested in.

Elements Chosen by Negotiation Between Investigator and Interviewee

You share the reasons for your investigation of the topic with your interviewee, and identify a set of elements jointly, by discussion and negotiation. One particular variant is for you to agree to add one or two key elements to the set which the interviewee has proposed: elements which encourage the interviewee to focus on himself or herself, as one of the elements – 'self elements', in fact. You'll find a description of the rationale for this in Section 4.2.8.

Elicited Elements

The 10-step procedure described in Section 3.1.2 elicits constructs, as you know. You can also elicit *elements*, as a first step before beginning to compare elements in order to elicit constructs. This is done by providing general

Table 3.1 Examples of elicited element categories

If the topic was...	...categories for eliciting elements might be
'My degree'	A course that you liked A course that you disliked The most difficult course you studied The course most relevant to getting you a job after graduation Etc.
'My friends'	My best friend My oldest friend My closest friend, emotionally Someone I like who avoids me Etc.
'Employee effectiveness'	A reliable employee A well-trained employee An employee with promotion potential An ineffective employee Etc.
'A job analysis for a telephone receptionist's job'	An important task A time-consuming task A difficult task A task requiring special training Etc.
'Potential sources of counselling help'	A clergyman A counsellor A parent A physician A lecturer A psychiatrist A psychologist A departmental secretary Another student

This procedure is useful when you are carrying out a set of grid interviews with several interviewees. It results in elements which are *unique* to each individual interviewee, using categories which are *shared by* all of them. This proves useful when you come to analyse the grids as a complete set (see the introduction to Chapter 7).

categories, which cover the range of the topic, that the interviewee responds to specifically.

For example, if your topic deals with 'people I know', you might ask your interviewee to name 'someone who I get on well with', 'someone I respect', 'someone I dislike', 'someone good at their job', and so on, covering a range of possibilities, each one of which becomes a particular named element, known to the interviewee, to be used in the grid. Table 3.1 provides you with further examples.

This has the advantage of allowing you to offer the same categories of elements to a sample of interviewees, knowing that, though they will each be thinking of different named instances, the existence of common categories can help you when you come to analysing the grids as a set. By choosing appropriate categories, you can test a hunch, or hypothesis, you may have about the way in which the whole sample construes the topic. There is more on this in Section 7.2.1.

It does, however, carry the possible disadvantage of suggesting the kinds of constructs you are looking for, in a way which may constrain the sorts of constructs you will be offered. Thus, the elements for the job-analysis grid shown in Table 3.1 may cause the interviewee to get stuck on the more obvious constructs which reflect management priorities to do with the importance, duration, difficulty, and training requirements of tasks that comprise the job, while omitting to mention more complex and revealing personal constructs such as:

I like it – I dislike it

When you do the task is up to you – The task has to be done regularly

You can get away with slipshod work – Mistakes are easily spotted

Only our receptionists do this job – This task is done by all receptionists

Done this one all of my life – This job was new to me

Generally speaking, if you choose to provide elements by elicitation, it's useful if you have a strong rationale, perhaps based on some previous work on the issue, for choosing the particular categories you use.

And if you are using grids as part of a research study, your literature review, or the research question which you are addressing, may suggest 'obvious' categories to you. I once did a piece of research on counsellor outreach programmes (Kaczmarek & Jankowicz, 1991) in which the research question was whether students at the end of a Masters course in counselling and guidance used more sophisticated constructs about the role of a 'helper' than first-year psychology students. (Yes, they did, when 'sophisticated' was defined as 'the way the professional counsellor thinks'.) The obvious categories to be used in this instance were the ones shown as the last example in Table 3.1 – since this set represents roles found to be important in the literature on counsellor approachability.

The elicited-element form is a generalised variant of Kelly's original Role Construct Repertory Test (Kelly, 1955/1991: 221), in which 24 standard categories that he found useful in his clinical work were used.

Once you've decided on a suitable set of elements, you might consider writing each one of them on a separate card, and offering the appropriate cards three at a time as you elicit each construct from the interviewee. Many people find that it helps them to think about and clarify their constructs if they have something physical to move around on the table.

3.2.3 Specifying Constructs

The investigator doesn't choose the constructs. They are elicited from the interviewee, and are, in that sense, the interviewee's. However, there's a lot you can do to ensure that the constructs represent what the interviewee wants to tell you, while being informative and useful to yourself.

In that sense, a 'good' construct is one which expresses your interviewee's meaning fully and precisely, and this is a matter of three things:

(a) a clear contrast

(b) appropriate detail

(c) a clear relationship to the topic in question.

As we saw in Section 2.1.1, it should have two *clearly contrasted poles*. These would rarely be logical opposites, such as 'happy versus not happy', but would contain a pole which says, somewhat more specifically, 'in what way "*not* happy"', in order to illuminate 'in what way "happy"'. To know that someone is 'happy as opposed to sad' is to know something rather different about his or her state of mind than that he is 'happy as opposed to furious'.

A 'good' construct is also one which is *appropriately detailed.* This means that the interviewee has had to think, often quite hard, about what s/he really means when using a particular label – prompted by yourself, as the investigator, making what is at times a somewhat intrusive judgement that the interviewee isn't really doing himself or herself justice.

For example, if your topic is 'effective management' and your elements are various people known to your interviewee who are more effective, and less effective, as managers, alarm bells would go off if you started to elicit constructs such as

Leads the team	–	Not a team player
On the ball	–	Takes his eyes off the ball
Charismatic	–	Lacks charisma
Good at the job	–	Bad at the job
Sticks to the knitting	–	Vague and woolly

and that self-serving hypocrisy of our times,

On-message   –   Off-message

Cliché, motherhood, and apple pie, anything which sounds like Eduspeak, Suitspeak, or Politspeak, as it were, needs to be handled with benevolent suspicion.

At this point, your own empathy, sensitivity, and sheer gut feelings have a part to play, and help to inform a judgement which you must make. These constructs may be provided by someone who has never thought about the issue before. Consequently, they could be clichés which reflect insufficient consideration and don't represent the interviewee's actual views. Alternatively, they might indeed represent his or her views precisely! You need to check out which it is.

Your judgement involves two rather distinct issues.

(a) From what you know of this interviewee (his or her age, educational background, experience, job title, role, vocabulary, status, and manner during the interview), is s/he likely to have more thoughtful and detailed constructs to put in place instead of each of these? And, assuming the answer to this question is 'yes', then

(b) bearing in mind the use to which your information is likely to be put, are the constructs being expressed in a sufficiently operational way? In other words, can the interviewee say in more useful detail what personal, behavioural expectations each of these constructs represents?

Handling constructs like these is very straightforward, and the same technique is used, regardless of whether the issue is (a) or (b).

Laddering Down

You ask the simple question, 'How do you mean; in what way?' *and use the answer as the construct to be noted in the grid sheet, rather than the one which was first offered.* This question can be asked in a variety of ways: you have plenty of options!

● 'What sort of thing do you have in mind when you say a person is, or isn't, a team player?'

● 'How do you mean, "on the ball"?'

● 'Charisma, now. What do people who are charismatic *do*, that's different from those who lack charisma?'

● 'Can you suggest a particular and important way of being good at the job?'

- 'I know what you mean! But suppose I was a Martian just landed in order to study good management: what would I observe when I saw someone "sticking to the knitting"?' or, quite simply,

- 'Can you give me an example of the one and the other?'

There is more on this procedure, which is known as 'laddering down', in Section 4.4.1.

> Before we go on. Some authors (Fransella et al., 2004, in particular) prefer to reserve the term 'laddering' for a procedure, also known as 'pyramiding', which turns *each* of the poles of the initially vague construct into a new, more specific construct, with two poles. We'll say a bit more about this issue in Section 4.4, and outline both techniques. Here, we're simply concerned with getting a clear, operationally defined, non-clichéd construct, and are using the term 'laddering down' for that activity.

Qualifying Phrases as a Focus

Finally, the interviewee should be clear that the constructs s/he offers are *relevant to the topic*, in two ways: that s/he considers them relevant, and that you do. You'll remember (see Section 3.2.1 above) that you've spent some time in thinking of a few qualifying phrases which help to clarify the topic. Well, you can use them now to help your interviewee to focus on the precise issues you have decided to investigate.

You do this quite simply by reminding the interviewee of the topic each time you offer a triad of elements. At step 4 of the basic procedure outlined in Section 3.1.2, add a brief qualifying phrase beginning with '...in terms of...' or '...from the point of view of...' the topic. For example, in a grid about managers' social skills, the qualifying phrase might be 'Which two are the same, and which one is different, in terms of how they handle people?' If the emphasis was less on abstract skills and more on day-to-day behaviour, the qualifying statement might be '...in terms of what you can see them *do*, that makes them effective?' (See Section 3.2.1 above.)

Suppose the topic was about classroom effectiveness, in which the elements are named teachers; the phrase to use at step 4 might be '(Here's another three of your teachers). Which two of them are *the same* in some way, and *different* from the third, in terms of what they do in the classroom that makes them effective, or otherwise?'

Further examples are given in Table 3.2. It takes a little forethought, and at times, ingenuity, to prepare an appropriate qualifying phrase, but you'll find that using one consistently helps to 'sharpen up' the constructs you elicit.

Table 3.2 Examples of qualifying statements for different topics

Topic	Elements	'In what way are two of them the same, and one different, **in terms of**...'
Learning during teaching practice	The 8 most important things that happened to you on teaching practice	'...what led to you learning, or otherwise, during your teaching practice?'
Key competencies in the analysis of any job	2 effective, 4 average, and 2 ineffective employees doing that job	'...what he or she does that makes them particularly competent at their job?'
Key competencies in the analysis of any job	The 8 most important tasks in the job	'...what you particularly need to know in order to be good at the job?'
Choosing an occupation	8 occupations being considered	'...what you're looking for from your first job?'
A person's understanding of personal change	8 events in your life from which you really, really learnt	'...what happened that helped you, or hindered you, in learning?'

You need to remind the interviewee occasionally about the negative possibilities: hence '...what led to you learning, *or otherwise*...?'

The use of an qualifying statement will occasionally lead to awkward sentence structures, but you don't have to use it obsessively with each triad of elements; just remind your interviewee now and again.

You'll have noticed, in the job analysis example, that two different kinds of element are feasible and, in fact, frequently used: existing job-holders; and key tasks involved in the job. Critical incidents (Flanagan, 1954) are also commonly used.

3.2.4 Obtaining Ratings

You should decide the range of your rating scale in advance. All of my examples use a 5-point scale, but there's no reason why you shouldn't use a 4-, 6-, or 7-point scale. To use a wider range is probably spurious, since you'd be asking people to make finer discriminations than they can accurately express in a consistent way across the whole grid.

You could always emulate Kelly, who generally used a 2-point scale. (In other words, he asked interviewees to allocate each element either to one pole of the construct, or to the other, with no in-betweens.) This throws the whole focus of the grid, and how you use the information obtained, onto the constructs and their meaning rather than on the numbers, which was, very broadly speaking, his intention at the time. However, it does limit the information potentially available from an analysis, and current practice is normally to use a 5- or 7-point scale.

You should also be careful to record the ratings for a particular construct on your grid sheet before going on to elicit a new one.

It may happen that your interviewee can't give you a rating for one of the elements on a particular construct, stating that the construct doesn't apply. There are several reasons why this might be so, and some of them are dealt with in Section 4.1.3. But, for the moment, the best thing to do in these circumstances is to check whether the construct applies naturally and comfortably to the other elements and, if so, to leave the rating for the 'problematic' element blank – just don't rate it.

It's time to put some of this information to work. Exercise 3.2 asks you to elicit another grid, to practise some of the techniques which I've mentioned.

Please carry out Exercise 3.2 before going on.

3.3 THINKING ABOUT YOURSELF

As a way of pulling all of this together, and giving you some more practice in elicitation, why not do a grid on yourself? The most fascinating topic in the world, of course.

Take a look at Exercise 3.3.

THINGS TO DO

Exercise 3.1 A First Practice Grid

(a) Make up a grid sheet like Figure 3.1.

(b) Find a friend with whom you both feel comfortable in having a gossip about people you both know. The topic is 'friends', that is, your mutual acquaintances.

(c) Ask your interviewee to list seven people, some who are known well by the interviewee; others less so; some with whom the interviewee is more friendly, and others less so. Enter their names along the diagonal element lines.

(d) In element line number 8, ask your interviewee to enter the word 'myself'; make it clear that this refers to your interviewee's picture of him or herself, and *not* to you! Using a 'myself' element can be interesting, but, if your interviewee is a little shy, you can drop this step if you prefer.

(e) Tell the interviewee that s/he can use initials, rather than names; if so, write the initials along the diagonal element lines. In this case, of course, you won't be able to discuss the elements in detail with your interviewee!

(f) Now follow the basic 10-step procedure for eliciting as many constructs as you can.

In doing this exercise, enjoy the gossip, but pace the whole session so that you complete the grid (aiming at 10 constructs) in under an hour.

At the end, jot down any procedural questions that occur to you, and then read Section 3.2 in detail. If, when you've done so, you still aren't sure, don't worry. Some common questions and problems are dealt with in the next chapter.

Exercise 3.2 Designing a Grid

Read over Section 3.2 before proceeding.

(a) Choose a subject you'd be interested in exploring with a colleague. Tell him or her why you're doing it, and negotiate a mutually acceptable form of words for the topic.

(b) Make a decision yourself on how you're to arrive at a set of elements:

- your choice

- interviewee choice

- mutually negotiated, or

- elicited; if you decide to elicit elements, decide on the categories you'll be using.

(c) Prepare a grid sheet with the relevant number of columns for elements, and mark in the triads you'll use. Prepare a set of cards, and write in the elements on each card once the elements have been determined.

(d) Decide on a suitable form of words for the qualifying phrase.

(e) Now follow the basic procedure, with the qualifying phrase added at step 4, aiming to arrive at between 8 and 10 constructs.

At the end, spend a little while in discussing what you might have done differently to achieve a better understanding of his or her views. Note the relevant points, and any others that may occur to you, especially any questions you might have about the details of the technique. Consider the suggestions for additional reading set out below.

Exercise 3.3 A Self-Grid

If you feel you need some further practice, especially in

• devising the wording for qualifying phrases

• trying out the laddering down procedure,

then I suggest you do a grid on yourself. Choose a topic (films I have seen? books I have read? bosses I have worked for? people with whom I've been in love during my life?) and go through the 10-point procedure, looking at the difference made by using slightly different qualifying statements. Try 'in terms of how effective they were in achieving their objectives'; in terms of why I liked or disliked them'; 'from the point of view of how I felt about them'. Practise laddering down to see what a more precise expression of a construct feels like.

THINGS TO READ

There is a brief account of grid elicitation and analysis in the following. You might like to read it as an overview, and to locate the grid as a research technique if you're using grids for a dissertation.

• Jankowicz, A.D. (2000a) *Business Research Projects*. 3rd edn. London: Thomson.

It's a useful procedural guide to the completion of a degree project or dissertation in support of undergraduate, postgraduate, and post-experience courses, aimed at business and management students working at a level below PhD.

If you want a flavour of how grid and related techniques that draw on a Kellian, constructivist perspective are used in human resource management and organisation development work, the following is informative and very readable.

- Jones, H. (1998) 'Bringing two worlds together: personal and management development in the NHS'. *Human Resource Development International* 1, 341–356.

Helen Jones used a variety of approaches to encourage UK National Health Service (NHS) consultants and managers to express their rather different ways of construing as they collaborated in running their particular part of the NHS, as part of a long-term personal development and team-building programme.

CHAPTER 4

QUESTIONS ABOUT GRID WORK

This chapter is closely linked to the previous one, which dealt with the bare bones of grid elicitation. Here, we build on your learning by addressing a number of questions which may have occurred to you when you were eliciting your first grid, or possibly, when you discussed the process with your interviewee. I hope you wrote them down as suggested.

Next comes flexibility. I outline some common variants of the elicitation procedure. This raises a question. Do we actually *need* the repertory grids to understand a person's constructs? Can people be understood in other ways? These issues are briefly considered in the third section of this chapter.

Finally, two further techniques are outlined, using which you can increase the precision and detail of the constructs obtained during a basic grid interview. These form an introduction to the idea that in eliciting a grid, you're not simply obtaining a description of how a person thinks about an issue per se but, rather, you're opening a window on their entire mental world. A grid is just a small part of a more complex data and meaning structure. The thought is developed later in this guide, and particularly in Chapter 8.

You are invited to complete two more exercises. The first is particularly important if you're a beginner, learning about grids for the first time. It gives you a feeling for the grids which you elicited in the previous chapter, allowing you to assess your own experience, in the light of an interview transcript of a grid interview done by an experienced user. The second exercise gives you an opportunity to practise further elicitation techniques.

4.1 SIMPLE PROCEDURAL ISSUES: QUESTIONS AND ANSWERS

4.1.1 Questions About the Elements

(1) When I did Exercise 3.2, I was a bit pushed for time and used only four elements. It seemed to work out okay. But your Figure 3.1 has space for 10 elements. Should I always use 10 elements or can I use more; or fewer?

You can use as many elements as you wish in order to cover the topic well, and to encourage your interviewee to provide as many constructs as possible. Just make up a grid sheet like Figure 3.1 for your own use, with as many element columns as you need.

For most uses, five elements is probably too few, and more than 12, too many; but I have seen grids with as many as 20 elements included. There's more on this in Section 4.2 below.

(2) Is there any rhyme or reason for the particular combinations of three elements at a time used in eliciting constructs?

Yes. The idea is to help the interviewee to arrive at a completely different construct each time, and this is helped by offering a different combination of elements. Think about it: a triad consisting of elements 1, 2, and 3, followed by a triad consisting of elements 1, 2 and 4, 1, 2, and 5, etc., might result in an interviewee 'stuck' on the same construct or constructs. Use triads whose element combinations don't repeat, as far as possible.

When you make up the grid sheet, mark the particular triads you're going to offer for each construct, onto the blank grid sheet itself, in advance.

4.1.2 Questions About the Constructs

(3) The interviewee took a long time to get the idea that I wasn't looking for 'right answers', either saying so directly, or making comments about 'oh, I wonder what you'll think of me for saying this, but . . .' Does this matter?

Only if it gets in the way of the constructs. These should, indeed, be the person's own, uncontaminated with socially or organisationally desirable ways of viewing the topic.

In this age of psychometric testing, pub quizzes, and selection interviews, where 'the right answer' matters, I suppose it's natural for people to wonder about this.

You need to check that your reasons for conducting the interview are understood (see Section 3.1.1), and to stress that your purpose is to discover what the interviewee thinks *for its own sake, regardless of whether people might agree or disagree.*

Point out that, in the topic you're exploring, there *are* no right or wrong answers and that, while there may (or may not) be preferred ways of looking at things, the only reason you're doing it this way is to 'avoid all that: otherwise, I'd have used a standard questionnaire or a different kind of interview', or words to that effect.

Emphasise the confidentiality and anonymity arrangements which have been made, and reiterate point 4 in the basic procedure (Section 3.1.2).

(4) The interviewee got stuck and couldn't offer any construct for a particular triad of elements at step 10. What to do?

No worries. Drop that triad and offer another one. Or try one of the alternative elicitation techniques listed in Section 4.2.

(5) The interviewee got stuck on the very first construct. Help!

Try each of these, in order until you find one that works.

Acknowledge that, 'Okay, that particular comparison doesn't suggest anything to you; here's another one', and offer another triad.

or

Illustrate the procedure by offering a construct of your own if the nature of the elements makes it feasible. (If they're names of people known only to your interviewee, it won't work.)

For example, if the topic is 'politicians' and the elements are the names of politicians, you might say something like, 'Well, if you were to look at Churchill, Hitler, and Stalin, one sort of contrast that occurs to me is, "Two of them were rather unpleasant, Hitler and Stalin; but, in contrast, Churchill, for all his faults, didn't rule through terror and fear." Do you see what I mean by looking for something that two of them have in common which the third one doesn't share? Now, ignore *me*, and tell me what contrast occurs to *you*', or words to that effect.

At this point, *it's essential* for you to emphasise that that was just one of *your* constructs; that you're interested in his/hers; to discard your own; and to invite the interviewee to consider the triad and find one of his or her own. The example you offer shouldn't be factual ('Churchill and Stalin died a natural death while Hitler committed suicide') because, while illustrating the idea of contrast very clearly, this may confuse the interviewee: you are not, after all, looking for correct answers. A straightforward but uncontentious opinion would seem to fit the bill here.

or

Consider some of the alternative ways of eliciting constructs (see Section 4.2 below).

(6) It was a real struggle to obtain more than four different constructs! Am I doing something wrong?

No, not at all. It's remarkable how few, genuinely different constructs a person has on any one topic! (Alter the topic, of course, and you realise that we have many more constructs than the ones previously offered; but that's not the point, since a grid is always done on a single topic.)

The following are usually helpful in eliciting further constructs. Firstly, you might share this observation with your interviewee, and reassure him or her on this point. Secondly, provide a short break, and have a brief chat about something else for a minute or two. Particularly, try one of the alternative construct-elicitation methods (see Section 4.2).

It all depends, of course, on the individual and the topic involved. In my own work with managers on occupational questions, I find that I usually get between 7 and 12 constructs during a 1-hour session with each manager.

On very rare occasions (one grid in a hundred or thereabouts), I've met someone who blocks completely. This wasn't their fault, and they weren't being dim! For them, the grid is a very contrived and artificial way of looking at things. They simply don't see that more than one or two constructs are relevant to the topic, and are rather uncomfortable with the notion that I'm obviously expecting more. In that situation, *abandon the grid*. It's useless for your purpose of understanding the other person in his or her terms. Find some other way.

> If you think about Kelly's idea of 'constructive alternativism', you'll recognise this is bound to happen at some stage! Personal construct theory asserts that we have our own personal theories – ways of making sense of experience – and that these may well differ from person to person. This is not said lightly. It's a fundamental epistemological position, and *his* whole theory depends on it. It follows that personal construct theory and approaches based on it may themselves be found useful by some people, but not by others – in this respect, there is no difference between a personal theory and an 'official' theory; between a theory held by a 'scientist' and one held by an ordinary Joe or Jane.
>
> Some of these other people (who find constructivist theories implausible) are called **positivists**. Their epistemological position is that there is a truth 'out there' which exists independently of the people who search for it, and therefore one *should* feel uncomfortable if someone doesn't see things the same way as a group of scientists who have spent years of dedicated effort discovering what's 'really' going on. There's an article by Rom Harré which puts this, and the constructivist alternatives, very well; see Harré (1981).

Whatever the reason for it, if your own interviewee doesn't see things your way, as a constructivist you have to treat this with respect. Drop the grid and seek some other way of understanding the person.

(7) Halfway through eliciting a construct, it emerges that the interviewee is being repetitive, offering a construct which we've already elicited and rated earlier; what do I do?

Share this impression with the interviewee, ask him or her if your impression is correct – drop the construct and move on to a new one if it is, but continue if s/he says that it isn't.

Listen to what s/he says, and be particularly alert to the possibility that it *isn't* quite the same. In any case, the ratings will show whether the construct is identical or not; if it's the same, the ratings will be the same. If in doubt, include it.

(8) Earlier on, you said that I should aim to get around 7–10 constructs, ensuring that each one represented a clearly different *way of construing the topic. But the interviewee mentioned so many slightly different things that I could easily have written down 20 or 30 constructs! You know: we were talking about a friend being 'trustworthy' as opposed to 'unreliable', and the interviewee said that this involved being able to keep a secret, and never lying to you, and supporting you when people unjustly criticised you, and, and, and…' Should I turn each of these into a construct and then rate each element on these different constructs? How do you decide when a construct is* clearly different*?*

It depends on your purpose. If the idea is to understand the interviewee in an overall sense, or to see how s/he understands the topic as a whole, you'd be inclined to aim for fewer, very distinct constructs. If, on the other hand, your purpose is to obtain a detailed view (for example, if you're studying a person's special expertise, in depth, as part of an attempt to capture their tacit knowledge in a knowledge-capture application), you'd aim at more, and live with any potential overlaps. Think of the first situation as one in which you're using a map of the whole country, where you're interested in the main rivers and mountain chains; and the latter as one in which you're looking at a region in much greater detail. Both kinds of map are useful, depending on your purpose.

One way of deciding in any one instance is to ask whether the ratings of elements on the various slightly different constructs are likely to be the same, or very different. You'd certainly include the different aspects if they lead to very different ratings, since the interviewee is clearly offering you different meanings!

If in doubt, ask the interviewee: 'Is this a different way of looking at things; how important to you is it that I should include it?'

As always, if in doubt, ask. Kelly would say: 'If you want to know what the other fellow thinks, why not ask them? They might just tell you.' (What Kelly actually said was, 'If you do not know what is wrong with a person, ask him; he may tell you'; Kelly, 1955/ 1991: 322). You should know that George Kelly was a clinical psychologist, concerned to understand his patients' distress *in their own terms.* This proved to be a very useful idea when dealing with other people in general, not just when they're ill, or in distress, which, of course, is why you're reading this book!

(9) What happens if a construct being offered seems strange, unlikely, or plain factually wrong?

For someone used to other forms of interviewing, or to psychological testing even more so, the idea of accepting the interviewee's own terms may seem a little peculiar at first. Some of the constructs may seem very idiosyncratic to you, weird and strange. The implications s/he's drawing may seem muddled, wrong-headed, or indeed, factually incorrect. *Never mind; accept them.*

> This idea of **credulous listening** (e.g., Jones, 1998: 346) is central to grid technique. There may be situations in which (if you're using the grid as part of a counselling, guidance, personal development, or team-building programme) you might want to come back to the matter later, to discuss and perhaps challenge the reasoning involved.

> But this is not the place for it. During a grid, accept what the interviewee tells you. Any debate or negotiation should be about clarifying what the individual means, regardless of whether or not you agree with it.

(10) Okay, but what if some of the constructs are a bit trivial, even when taken with respect to the interviewee's position? For instance, in the practice grid, which was about constructs to do with friends, my interviewee half-heartedly offered 'male as opposed to female' among a large set of fairly detailed constructs about what they're like as people; should I accept it?

It depends on three things:

(a) the purpose of the grid

(b) the context set by the other constructs

(c) whether the interviewee *feels* that it's trivial.

There will be situations in which you'll both agree that a person's sex is probably irrelevant and uninformative – for example, topic: job activities; elements: named employees. So ignore it and move on to another construct.

There will be situations in which you'll both agree that it's to do with gender role as well as sex, and so the person's sex, as a construct, is relevant and informative with respect to that other construct, gender! – for example, topic: attitudes to housework; elements: married friends known to me.

And there will be situations in which sex is socially and politically very relevant indeed – for example, topic: how a boss construes the work of employees in the department, carried out in the context of an appraisal for promotion purposes.

There's more on this in Section 5.3.3, under the heading of 'Propositional Versus Constellatory Constructs'.

So, ask the interviewee! Certainly, if you both feel the construct is a bit clichéd, remember to use a qualifying phrase (Section 3.2.1): ask 'in what way?' Seeking a more operationally defined expression for a construct is an excellent way of going beyond cliché.

4.1.3 Questions About the Rating Procedure

(11) Does it matter if I combine steps 8 and 9 of the basic procedure? In other words, should I always get the ratings of the elements in the triad first, before getting the ratings of the remaining elements, on a particular construct? Wouldn't it be simpler just to run along the row each time, from the first element to the last element, rating as I go?

If that feels more comfortable, fine. I do find that, for the first few constructs, until the interviewee gets used to the procedure, it helps to record the ratings of the particular triad first, before completing the rest. It seems more logical to the interviewee. And it makes it easier for you to check that the interviewee hasn't reversed the ratings unintentionally.

Let's do a deal. Until you get used to grids, always do step 8 before step 9 for the first two constructs you elicit. Then for the remainder, try it both ways and see how it feels, before deciding for yourself which suits you better.

(12) I got a bit tangled up with the ratings. Do you insist on doing step 5 that way round? What I mean is, should I always put the thing the two elements have in common on the left of the scale, and the opposite, which characterises the odd one out, on the right?

When my interviewee says, 'John and Mary go together because they're both nervous, while Alan is the opposite: he's very self-confident', it seems natural to put 'nervous' down on the left and 'self-confident' on the right – fair enough.

But if he were then to say, 'John is a bit rigid in his thinking; in contrast, Mary and Alan are alike because they're very liberal', it's more natural to put 'rigid' on the left, where it gets a rating of '1', and 'liberal' on the right, where it gets a '5'. Shouldn't the rule be, 'give the higher rating, "5" not "1", to the end of the construct which is "better", or "positive, more valuable" ', d'you see what I mean? It was certainly more natural for the interviewee!

That may feel right when a construct has a clear *positively* evaluated, and a clear *negatively* evaluated, end: 'nasty versus nice', 'evil versus good'. But not all constructs do. For example, if you were to characterise a person as 'socially skilled' and another, in contrast, as 'technically skilled', then, other things being equal, which is better? Neither, surely. It all depends.

Then there will be times when one end of a construct is slightly better, but only a little, and vice versa; and this, believe me, can lead to enormous confusion when you start to analyse constructs, and the way in which they relate to each other.

And so, trust me! I'm a psychologist! Write down the end of the construct which describes the 'two that go together' on the left; and the contrasting end of the construct, which describes the 'odd one out', on the right.

Always.

Regardless of 'which way round is positively evaluated'.

By the way, for future reference, the end of the construct which describes the two elements that are alike is called the 'emergent pole' of the construct; and the end of the construct that describes the odd one out is called the 'implicit pole' of the construct. So the rule is 'emergent on the left, and implicit on the right'.

(13) Earlier on, you talked about 'credulous listening'. But what happens if you suspect that the interviewee has made a genuine mistake in trying to express him- or herself? In doing the practice grid, I had a situation in which, bearing in mind everything else that the interviewee had said, I was sure she'd got the ratings the wrong way round, saying '5' when she really intended to say '1'. Do you really mean I've got to accept this, 'credulously', as you put it?

No, not at all. There's credulity, and there's carelessness.

As step 8 of the procedure tells you, if you suspect this is the case, just check what's intended. Point out that the ratings on this construct seem to be 'the wrong way round'. In the vast number of cases, your interviewee will recognise that they're not communicating their intention. Take their word for it either way!

Just to drive the point home. If the elements in a grid on politicians included 'Churchill, Hitler, and Stalin' and the construct was

1		5
'Used indisputably evil means of dealing with opposition'	–	'May have dealt with opposition robustly, but not by evil means'

and you were offered ratings of Churchill: '1', Hitler: '5', and Stalin '4', you'd usually have grounds for checking that the interviewee hadn't reversed the directionality of the rating scale, intending to say Churchill: '5', Hitler: '1', Stalin: '2'. All the more so if the construct was

1		5
Took the initiative in 1939 by invading Poland	–	Reacted to others' initiatives in 1939

and the ratings are Churchill: '1', Hitler: '5', and Stalin '4', where the factual incorrectness, rather than attitudinal idiosyncrasy, of the response alerts you to the possibility of an error of intention.

But if, after checking, the interviewee replied that the ratings *were* correct as s/he originally stated them, you'd have to accept them, as we said earlier.

> As Kelly puts it, 'People differ from each other in their construction of events', and that may include matters which we usually think of as 'facts'. To be an effective grid user, it's best to accept *all* facts as beliefs about nature, and to see accuracy as solely to do with a faithful recording of the interviewee's beliefs. For example, should an interviewee choose to deny the Holocaust, asserting it to be a historical fiction, it is your professional obligation to grit your teeth and accept this as an accurate statement of the way *s/he* expresses a construction of events. You can always explore the intention later. This lies at the heart of any constructivist technique.

(14) What happens when a construct applies to some of the elements but not to the others? Working with the grid you suggested as Exercise 3.1, my interviewee said that although the construct, 'their family always welcomes me – their family's a bit distant with me', was suggested by a particular triad of elements (friends), that construct doesn't actually apply to one of the other elements. He said that one of his friends lives by himself, the parents being deceased – so how his parents get on with the interviewee isn't in question. What do I do? I need to have numbers to be able to analyse the grid later on! So should I provide a rating or not?

No, don't insist on a rating. Your task is to express your interviewee's meaning as precisely as possible, and you'd be distorting the intended meaning by having a rating here. Leave it blank.

If you really, really, really have to have a rating in each cell of the grid (this may be the case with some analysis software you plan to use, though good software will be able to cope with missing ratings), then the least damage would be to put in a 'neutral', mid-point rating ('3' on a 5-point scale, or '4' on a 7-point scale).

In that example, there was an obvious indication that the construct didn't apply: one of the friend's parents was no longer alive! But it isn't always so clear-cut.

Sometimes you can encourage the interviewee to *reword* the construct in a way which applies to all the elements while expressing the idea s/he has in mind. For example, you could ask whether the construct

> Raised in a sociable and   –   Raised in a family which was
>   welcoming family   cautious with outsiders

might be a satisfactory substitute for the construct, 'their family always welcomes me – their family's a bit distant with me'. It would certainly allow the interviewee to provide a rating for all the elements! But it mightn't be what s/he wishes to say at that point. *Always ask.*

Finally, when there's no *obvious* indication that the construct doesn't apply, it might be that your interviewee is struggling to express a complex idea which should really be split up into two constructs. Check that your interviewee's construct expresses the contrast s/he has in mind, rather than, in fact, being made up of two separate contrasts. For example, the construct

Their family always welcomes me   –   Their family's a bit distant

could, actually, stand for two distinct things your interviewee wants to tell you, needing to be decomposed into

Their family always welcomes me   –   Their family is a bit distant with me

and

> Their family is very sociable and   –   Their family's a bit distant (with
>   welcoming   other people)

for the interviewee's meaning to be captured completely. Someone who was seen by your interviewee as having parents who were unwelcoming to the interviewee though they were very sociable towards other people would be difficult to rate on the construct as it was first offered, but could easily receive a rating on each of the two component constructs.

So you'd check with your interviewee whether the original construct needed to be decomposed into two and, if so, you'd write both into the grid, *instead of* the original, and rate all the elements on each construct.

> Underlying this bit of practical advice there are two fairly deep theoretical issues. The first has to do with the structure of a person's construct system, and the relative centrality of the particular constructs being offered. As we'll see in Chapter 8, people's constructs are hierarchically organised: some are central, and super-ordinate to others; other constructs are subordinate to others. Now, constructs which are central tend to be applicable to a wide range of elements, and when decomposed into more detailed aspects, their relevance may be more specific. More on this later, in Section 8.1.
>
> The second issue has to do with how clearly and precisely a person is helped to express the distinctions and contrasts they have in mind, when choosing the wording of a construct. This particular issue was explored in some detail in a famous exchange between Mantz Yorke and Jack Adams-Webber (Adams-Webber, 1989; Yorke, 1989),

and you should read their articles once you have mastered the basics of grid technique.

4.1.4 And, Overall...

It all seems a bit, well, simple and 'just so' to me. Not very 'high-powered'. After all that effort for a whole hour, both of us got this feeling of 'So what?' Where are the blinding revelations? How do I know that these constructs are the right ones? The ones which are really important to the interviewee? How do I know that I haven't missed any? If I were to repeat the same exercise tomorrow, what guarantee is there that I'd get the same constructs from the same interviewee?

All good questions, each of them with good answers which I'll provide in subsequent sections. For the time being, though, consider...

Firstly, if you get a 'so-what' feeling, it may be yoooou...! It may be that you need a little more practice to give your interviewee a chance to express themselves. Perhaps you might learn some advanced techniques, to get at the really exciting material that's there. There's a lot more to come, on how to identify a person's core constructs, personal values, and belief system. Take your time. These are only your first two grids. Once you're up to speed, you'll surprise yourself.

Secondly, it's useful to remember that, in some applications, straightforward descriptions may be a little dull, but nevertheless, very helpful, because they represent stuff we didn't know before. For example, the evaluative scales (constructs!) that people use when they think about the cheese they buy may not be self-evident and, on closer examination using grid techniques, these may seem a little, how shall we put it, unspectacular? But then, you're not a market researcher (most of you, anyway).

'Sharp – smooth', 'runny – hard' may be obvious to you, but 'sweet aftertaste – bitter aftertaste'; 'moist – dry', 'tastes foreign – tastes like a proper cheese'; 'tastes of itself – tastes of the herbs and other flavourings they put in it' may not have occurred to you when you first thought about cheese – or to anyone else either. This sort of basic information, clunky and banal to you, could be worth its weight in gold to the market researcher who's advising a cheese producer. (A true story, actually. Read all about it in O'Cinneide, 1986: the Cheesecraft case.)

Thirdly, the value in a set of basic, descriptive constructs may come from what's *not* there. Stewart & Stewart (1982) give an example which lists the characteristics of an effective merchant banker, as construed by a group of merchant bankers, and these constructs seem a bit, well – as you'd expect: 'good planner' (as opposed to someone who spends no time in planning ahead), 'strategic thinker', etc., etc. What's the point of a grid which shows you what you'd expect to see? But what is *not* listed is a set of characteristics which could, without the benefit of the grid investigation, have been equally plausible but which, in fact, don't pertain and are indeed irrelevant to and misleading for the particular job in question.

'Effective negotiator versus poor at negotiating', 'sporty and sociable versus shy and withdrawn', could conceivably be relevant when trying to decide what attributes a merchant banker should have, but it so happens that they're not, full stop. Job descriptions, appraisals, and selection procedures based on them would be seriously misleading.

Grids are very useful in dissecting conventional wisdoms. They distinguish between the plausible stereotype and the humdrum actuality, where accuracy, rather than excitement, is what matters.

If you're happy with the answers to the preceding questions in Sections 4.1.1–4.1.3, you've learnt a lot! So bear with me awhile on this last one. (And, in the meanwhile, if you still have a niggling little question that hasn't been covered above, try one or other of the websites mentioned in the 'Things to Read' section of Chapter 9.)

For the moment, though, be assured that the grid is a powerful but straightforward technique for providing you with descriptions of the main constructs which an interviewee uses to make sense of a given topic.

And now, please complete Exercise 4.1 at the
end of this chapter.
When you're done, come back to Section 4.2.

4.2 CAPTURING MEANING BY USING A GRID

We're doing all this in order to understand the other person in their own terms. We want to capture the significance which their experience has for them. We seek to capture their meaning, and a construct is our basic unit of analysis. It's the basic unit of meaning which expresses the implicit contrasts with which the individual understands his or her world.

In one sense, so long as we identify the other person's constructs accurately, as s/he understands them, and are sure of it since we've checked with the interviewee, it doesn't really matter how we do so. But four things are important and should pertain whenever you depart from the standard 10-point procedure outlined in Section 3.1.2:

- You should know exactly why you're doing so.

- You should encourage depth of detail whatever else you're doing.

- You should be encouraging clarity and specificity, as well as depth.

- You should continue to treat the interviewee as the ultimate authority about him- or herself.

The 10-point procedure outlined in Section 3.1.2 is simply one way of achieving all this. It's economic and effective and, like any technique, it has to be done properly. But there are other techniques and, so long as these four attributes are present, anything goes when eliciting constructs!

In doing a grid, you will find the following variants useful, and as your experience with grids grows, you will find yourself moving between them, as the flow of conversation between yourself and the interviewee demands.

4.2.1 Triadic Elicitation

This is the usual technique in which three elements are offered and a contrast is sought between two and one, as described in Section 3.1.2.

4.2.2 The Full Context Form

You present *all* the elements to your interviewee, and ask him/her to identify two elements which are most similar and why (specifying the attribute they have in common); then the element which is the most different on that attribute, identifying the contrasting pole.

If you're using file cards, with element names written on them, you can simply fan out all of the cards in front of your interviewee and ask him/her to choose three cards, put the rest to one side, and group the chosen three into a pair and a singleton.

4.2.3 Dyadic Elicitation

Two elements are presented and the interviewee is asked to indicate an important way in which they differ, or an important way in which they are alike. This approach works well where the basic triadic procedure is too difficult for the interviewee, as in working with children (Salmon, 1976).

However, if you *can* use the triadic form, it's best to do so. There are suggestions that the dyadic procedure leads to grids which don't reflect the full complexity and variety of constructs potentially available if dyadic elicitation is used as the sole elicitation technique (Caputi & Reddi, 1999).

4.2.4 Elaboration

Elaboration is sometimes called 'differentiation'. If you can see that the ratings of any two elements on all the constructs obtained so far are very similar, you can ask the interviewee if s/he can think of a new construct on which the two elements would receive very different ratings. This invites the interviewee to use what may be a new, or infrequently used, construct.

4.2.5 The 'Catch-All' Question

You will have seen this used at the end of the transcript in Appendix 2. Draw the interviewee's attention to all of the constructs and ask whether s/he has some new, different construct which has not yet been expressed but which clearly applies to the full set of elements. I often use this as a way of finishing my own grid interviews.

4.2.6 Alternatives to Rating

However they're arrived at, the constructs in a grid tell you something about *how* the interviewee thinks about a topic. The ratings tell you *what* s/he thinks about individual elements.

So far, all our examples have used ratings to indicate what the person thinks. However – as long as the interviewee indicates where, with respect to a construct, a given element is positioned – anything will do for this purpose!

Grouping the Elements

Kelly's original grids were very simple, the elements being divided into two groups: those described by the emergent (left-hand) pole of the construct, and those described by the implicit (right-hand) pole of the construct. If you think about it a moment, you'll see that this is simply a 2-point rating scale, with ratings of 1 and 2 defining the scale from emergent to implicit pole.

Hitherto, we have been using a 5-point scale to position elements on constructs and thereby identify the 'what's of the situation. You may wonder about the alternatives.

A scale with an odd number of points allows for the indication of a 'middle' position, which may convey 'neutrality' depending on the construct in question and the topic of the grid. A scale with an even number of points enforces a preference, no matter how slight, for one pole of the construct rather than the other.

This may be useful with topics in which the constructs have poles which stand for preferred and non-preferred characteristics. Assessments and evaluations of various kinds spring to mind (employee and managerial performance appraisals, teaching practice appraisals, and training course evaluations); indeed, any situation in which it may be tempting or politic to make a 'neutral-point' rating, or in which a 'drift towards the middle' occurs even where more extreme ratings are warranted.

However, as we saw in Section 3.2.4, the use of more than 8 or 9 points in the scale is excessive. To group elements into so many different categories along a construct is to assert that people can make very fine judgements, consistently for all the elements, regardless of the construct in question, and this is not the case. It is spurious precision.

Ranking the Elements

And that is the rationale used by people who avoid ratings and use ranks. In fact, they're a bit suspicious of the apparent precision claimed for *any* rating system: when a person rates any three elements on a construct as follows,

	1	John	Mary	Alan	5
	Predictable	3	1	5	Unpredictable

do they really mean that Mary is more predictable than John, exactly to the same degree as Alan is less predictable than John? Probably not, yet that's what the use of ratings implies. Three minus 1 equals 5 minus 3. This, they feel, is a misleading use of numbers. (Anyone who has done a course in statistics will recognise the issue. We're talking about the properties of interval, as opposed to ordinal, data here.)

Why not simply rank the elements along the construct to reflect their relative positions, without making claims about the distances between the elements? Exactly the same meaning would be conveyed about the elements, but without the spurious precision, by:

smaller/higher	John	Mary	Alan	**larger/lower**
ranks				**ranks**
Predictable	2	1	3	Unpredictable

Ranking systems *are* sometimes used with repertory grids; it's worth doing if you are concerned to obtain, and eventually analyse, a single grid, or several grids with the same number of elements.

There is a problem, though. It becomes very awkward to compare grids in which there are different numbers of elements (ranks would run between 1 and 3 for 3 elements, but 1 and 10 for 10 elements: so a given rank, '3', say, cannot be easily compared between the two grids). You would use the conventional ratings, rather than rankings, in such circumstances.

4.2.7 Supplied Constructs

You'll notice that the 10-step procedure, and many of the details in section 3.2.3, assume that you're eliciting the interviewee's own constructs. That's the fundamental definition of a repertory grid. It tells you what the interviewee's own constructs are. However, your purpose in using a grid is to understand how the other person construes, and, when you come to analyse the grid, that objective can be achieved to some degree by seeing how the interviewee uses constructs which *you* have suggested and supplied.

For example, some kinds of content analysis (see Section 7.3) require you to obtain the interviewee's 'overall summary' of the elements, by asking him or her to rate all the elements on a construct which summarises his or her overall view. A topic of 'good (and poor) lecturers I have known' would have the construct, 'overall, more effective as a lecturer – overall, less effective as a lecturer', supplied by the interviewer for the interviewee to use, if that construct hadn't yet been elicited spontaneously. A topic of 'the people in my life I find approachable when I need help' might have the supplied construct, 'overall, more helpful – overall, less helpful', and so on.

Or you may be doing a piece of work in which you want to see how the interviewee's constructs relate to some other construct which may not be in the interviewee's repertoire but which is nevertheless important to you. (You might be interested to know how the interviewee views the management style of his colleagues. You supply the construct, 'authoritarian – participative', and, in the analysis, look to see which of the interviewee's constructs are being used in a similar way: see step 6 of Section 6.1.2.)

> It's important to remember that the grid is now a mixture of constructs from the interviewee's repertoire, and constructs from your own. This is legitimate – indeed, in some kinds of research, grids have been used which consist entirely of supplied constructs, since this simplifies the analysis of whole sets of grids. Each interviewee works with identical constructs. However, you have to remember that something rather different is being measured in these circumstances.

> People are drawing on their own experience and judgement to express similarities and differences; so they are, indeed, construing the topic in question. To the extent that they provide different ratings from each other, you can say that their differing, personal construct systems are being tapped, and that you're learning something of the different ways in which each of them construes.

> However, left to their own devices, they may never have chosen to use constructs of the kind supplied. You'd have discovered much more about each individual person if

you worked only with the constructs you have elicited from that particular person – with his or her *personal* constructs!

This matter of elicited versus supplied constructs has had substantial research attention in its own right. You won't be surprised to learn that people find their own constructs more useful (Landfield, 1968) and meaningful (Cromwell & Caldwell, 1962) than supplied constructs, though there is some debate about the extent to which the richness and complexity of individual interviewees' thinking is, or is not, characterised better by allowing them to use their own constructs (Collett, 1979).

Think of this issue as follows:

- If you want to discover what the interviewee's own constructs are, and how s/he uses them, don't supply any of your own.

- If you want to check a personal belief about the interviewee's own constructs and how s/he uses them, supply a construct related to that belief and see how it compares with the interviewee's own. Section 6.1.2 tells you how to do so.

- If you want a reflection of the different ways in which a sample of people construes an issue, but you don't need to capture the respondents' own personal constructs, then don't elicit any constructs at all. Supply your own for all of them to use.

4.2.8 Supplied Elements

You'll recall, from Section 3.2.2, that there are several alternative ways of arriving at a set of elements. One approach (a variant of those described in Section 3.2.2) is to work with the elements provided by the interviewee, but for you to supply an additional one or two, to test out a belief of your own about the interviewee's construct system. This allows you to compare the ways in which the interviewee construes these key elements and the elements s/he has provided.

The most common use of a key element of this kind is the **self element**. Literally that: 'myself'. By asking the interviewee to rate him- or herself on the constructs, you find out what place his/her personal image or aspirations have among the other elements being construed. It can be fascinating, as well as useful to your purposes in eliciting a grid on 'people I admire' or 'the other students in my class', to see how the interviewee construes 'myself' as one of the elements in comparison to the others!

You give the interviewee an excellent opportunity to express his or her aspirations and thoughts about the future when you provide *two* self elements, the self and the **ideal self**. For example, 'myself as I am now' and 'myself as I would wish to be'.

These self elements needn't pertain to the individual person's actual self, current or ideal. If you're counselling someone who's seeking a new job, a grid in which the elements are possible companies to apply to could usefully include 'my own job here and now' and 'my ideal job'. A manager choosing between different strategies as elements could have 'my department now' and 'my department in a year's time' as elements.

The 'ideal' element is helpful in any situation in which the grid is being used to help the interviewee make a choice. A set of possible outcomes would be used to elicit constructs, and ratings of the elements on these constructs obtained. These would then be compared with ratings of the supplied 'ideal' element on the same constructs, with a view to discovering which element came closest to the ideal. Section 6.1.1 describes the procedure, and Jankowicz (2001) provides a simple example of the use of the ideal element in a decision procedure.

There is little contention over the use of supplied elements. Their use doesn't raise the same problems for analysis as those we discussed above in dealing with supplied constructs.

4.3 CAPTURING MEANING WITHOUT USING A GRID

So long as we follow the four criteria for meaning capture outlined at the start of Section 4.2 (an explicit model; depth of detail; clarity and specificity; feedback from the interviewee treated authoritatively), do we need to use a grid at all? No. A number of alternatives exist. In each case, combining one of the procedures outlined in Sections 4.3.1, 4.3.2 or 4.3.3 with a grid can round out the picture (though all of these procedures are valuable in their own right, of course).

4.3.1 Being a Good Observer

The usual, day-to-day alternative to the repertory grid! Of course, you can identify the way in which people construe events and circumstances from their general behaviour, as you interact with them. You look at what they do, and the way they do it. From this, you try to see how they understand the situation you're both in; the *distinctions* and *similarities* they recognise as events unfold. What do they consider to be 'the same', and therefore unremarkable? What, for them, stands out and grabs their attention?

The more you care about your interaction with other people, the more likely it is that you will try to see things from their point of view in order to interact more effectively with them.

Kelly felt that this was so important that he built it into his theory as a formal statement. For a list of these see Appendix 6. His Sociality Corollary states: 'To the extent that one person construes the construction process of another, he may play a role in a social process involving the other person.' Role relationships, he's saying (such as the relationship between a learner and a teacher; an employee and the owner of the firm; a person and his or her partner), depend for their success on the extent to which each person can see events of mutual importance through the other person's eyes.

This may seem obvious – until you realise what Kelly is *not* saying. Successful role relationships do *not* necessarily depend on people seeing the world (construing the meaning of events) *in the same way*. We don't have to have the same constructs as other people to relate to them effectively. All that's required is that we learn a little about their constructs, especially those which result in them seeing the *same* events *differently* to ourselves.

There's one exception. In those close situations in which the other person's constructs matter to us because they help to confirm how we think about ourselves (as in friendship formation, therapy, and marriage), having some shared constructs helps (Duck, 1973; Neimeyer & Neimeyer, 1985; Leitner & Pfenninger, 1994).

That apart, we can relate effectively even though our constructs differ (so long as we know this), and to the extent that we know what the other person's constructs are.

There are several ways in which you can use a grid to check your own attempts at sociality through observation, and the main procedure is described in Section 9.2.3.

People vary in how well they can put themselves in other people's shoes. Sometimes, the very pressure of events prevents you from getting a good 'fix' on the other person. A good way of creating the space in which to understand the other person's constructs, without going to the formal extent of a repertory grid, is by asking them to tell you a story about themselves (Mair, 1989, 1990).

4.3.2 Storytelling

Self-Characterisation

Self-characterisation technique requires the interviewee to write about him- or herself. The interviewee provides a character sketch, usually written in the third person as if s/he were describing someone else. The interviewee is encouraged to be explicit, but also to regard the task as a pleasant one rather than a clinical dissection, by being asked to write 'just as if he were the principal character in a play...as it might be written by a friend who knew him very intimately and very sympathetically, perhaps better than anyone ever really could know him' Kelly (1955/1991: 323).

The character sketch, which should be longer than just a few sentences, is then analysed, preferably in collaboration with the interviewee, to identify the themes, traits, and personal characteristics which the interviewee has attributed to him- or herself; the constructs, in other words, which s/he has about him- or herself. The picture you obtain can then be triangulated with a conventional grid for a more comprehensive account of the individual in the context of a given topic.

Characterising Others

It is also possible to provide characterisations of other people. The 'child characterisation sketch' relies on tape recordings rather than requiring a written account, and invites one person (in this case, a child's parent) to talk genuinely and thoughtfully about another person (the child). The elicitation starts by asking the parent to describe the personality of the child as completely as possible. The people who developed it (Davis et al., 1989) suggest that the interviewer should start the interview somewhat conventionally before introducing the technique to the interviewee. In Section 3.1.1, you'll recall that I emphasised the importance of a variety of process issues, including making the interviewee feel at ease. However you do it, using a grid or not, construct elicitation involves procedures which are unfamiliar to most interviewees, who need help in being eased into them.

The developers also suggest that, with this kind of topic, interruptions to clarify what is meant or to provide greater precision are by and large unnecessary! Analysis involves listing the different kinds of constructs which emerge from the description of the child, classifying them according to their emergent poles. Implicit poles can be identified in subsequent discussion (and here the authors and I part company: I would argue that they *have* to be, and preferably during elicitation) and ratings provided. However, useful information can be obtained without rating the elements on the constructs.

Notice what's happening. The most common way of eliciting constructs is by means of the triadic procedure. ('In what way do two of these differ from the third?') And you've seen that it's possible to use just two elements (the dyadic procedure) in certain circumstances. You can think of the child character-isation sketch, and indeed self-characterisation technique, as ways of identifying constructs using just one element! 'Monadic' procedures, in fact.

Other Monadic Procedures

If you want to find out about a person's central values, and the constructs s/he feels are particularly important, you can ask the interviewee to tell you about him-/herself using just one, vivid and dramatic, situation as the element: the monadic statement.

For example, if you had a choice about it, what would you like to see written on your tombstone? And can you think of a statement which is the opposite of that one? The answer to these two questions would be a construct which said something, possibly profound, about your own views of yourself!

Tombstone inscription		Its opposite
'I died with my boots on'	–	(I'd given up on life a while ago)
'Aw, just when I was beginning to get the hang of things'	–	(I was staggeringly competent from the age of 12)
'I burnt my candle at both ends, to cast a brighter light'	–	(My annals are short, simple, mute, and inglorious)

Other possible monadic statements listed by Epting et al. (1993) in describing some of the work of Leitner (who invented this technique) are as follows:

(a) Please describe your conception of God.

(b) Please list your earliest memories.

(c) What have been your most significant (life-turning) events?

(d) Do you have dreams which deal in the same theme? What is it?

Epting's article is worth looking at in detail if you're seeking further ways of identifying constructs, both grid and non-grid based.

4.3.3 Non-Verbal Techniques?

The grid itself, and the other techniques for eliciting constructs described above, all depend on words. In that sense, they require a reasonably articulate interviewee. But do you remember the definition of a construct given in Section 2.1.1?: 'Constructs are contrasts we devise when dealing with the world, in order to understand it.'

And, while they're commonly communicated in words – and we've got used to thinking of constructs as spoken or written pairs of single words, or phrases – it's the actual distinctions a person recognises and makes that are the constructs, and not the words in which these distinctions are expressed. Constructs in themselves are non-verbal.

Try me out. Do constructs exist before the words in which they're expressed?

Ask your interviewee to provide a set of objects (the real thing where practical; otherwise, a photograph of them) to act as elements. Next, ask the interviewee to group them (into two that are the same and one that is different, or place them into subgroups, or simply to arrange them) in such a way as to signal what s/he thinks of them – what s/he wishes to 'say' about the objects, non-verbally, as clearly as possible.

For example, the objects may be photographs of paintings a person has seen. (Or pictures on cards, or samples of textured material. You might care to look up Neimeyer, 1981, if you want to try out the following example for real!) The photographs might be lined up in order of preference, a smile and a grimace providing information about which end of the construct applies to which end of the line of photographs.

(smile)		**(grimace)**
I like these	–	I'm not so keen on these

And there you have it, in front of your very eyes and with nothing up my sleeve. You saw that the cards were arranged into a line according to that construct without words, and before your interviewee changed his or her facial expression. So, it's possible to have constructs without words, *or any other sort* of symbolic expression.

Ah! But is it possible to *communicate* constructs without some form of symbolic expression? Well, no: notice the function of the smile and the grimace in hinting at what the construct might be, and for indicating which pole was preferred.

That's fair enough: you can't *communicate* without symbols. But before we go on, let's examine that assumption about the need for symbolisation. Before the act of communication, *is* it possible to have constructs without relying on some form of symbol? Opinions differ on this. Some people point out that to construe is to differentiate ('in what way are two the same and one different?'), and that differentiation involves choice, some of it deliberate and explicit, but some of it less so and without any symbols being involved. They argue that choice is defined as a selection between alternatives, and that selections can be made without awareness. The pupil of your eye dilates more when you see an attractive person than an unattractive one, for example, and this is an act of construing as much as if it were consciously and deliberately made. In linguistics, Saussure (1915/1983) provides an early, systematic exposition of the argument that it is simple contrast (between a sign and all the signs not being used to express the thing being signified), bereft of deliberation, which lies at the heart of meaning.

Others would suggest, in contrast, that symbolisation *has* to exist before awareness. It is essential in order to engage in the organisation and reorganisation, called 'information processing', required for the processes of memorisation, storage, and recall.

Something which represents an attractive face as distinct from an unattractive face has to be processed, or stored in memory, and what is that something other than a symbol? It certainly isn't the face itself.

Both viewpoints would concede that, regardless of all this, attractiveness lies in the eye of the beholder and that all beholders differ in their experience! In other words, that what matters just as much in a representation is the background, history, and personality of the person making the distinction.

And both parties would certainly agree that the medium in which symbols are expressed need not be verbal. We've all encountered algebra; and those who are familiar with mathematical logic will be aware of other non-verbal symbol systems in which deduction, reasoning, and hence the recognition of similarities and contrasts, are possible. What's being said, then, is that it's certainly possible to have non-verbal constructs, but that the existence of some form of symbol system, verbal or otherwise, is essential for any work to be done.

Thank you! Now, to summarise all of that in practical terms. There's no doubt that verbal symbolisation is particularly efficient. Also, non-verbal construing, as in the case of the photographs above, is only possible because the people doing the construing are old enough to have developed language already. This enables them to represent, or encode, the distinctions and similarities which make up a construct more effectively than if they'd never learnt a language.

Yes, that's plausible. Kelly talked about pre-verbal construing in this exact sense. It is construing, it does occur, but it's inchoate. It's not expressed in consistent verbal symbols and is thereby 'primitive' in nature (Kelly, 1955/1991: 465).

Okay. Now, let's go back to communication. In order to be sure about what the construct is, even if the interviewee has been proceeding without words, *you* have to question your interviewee. Suppose, for example, the photographs were arranged into two heaps which grouped the paintings as follows:

Those in which colour, composition, and form are used to convey the essence of a concept, mood, or idea	–	Those in which colour, composition, and form are used to show what people, places, events, and things look like

You'd then have a fair notion that the construct in question is

Abstract art   –   Representational art

– but you'd need to ask, to be sure of it.

Any inferences about construing which you draw from your interviewee's non-verbal behaviour (smiles, pauses, or looks of puzzlement or contentment, the significant twitches of the social process in which you're engaged) need to be noted and checked. You'll find more about the importance of process in analysis in Section 5.3.1, by the way.

And so we're back to our point of departure at the start of this section. It doesn't matter how we do it, so long as we know the reason for doing it, and identify the other person's constructs accurately, as s/he understands them, being sure of it after checking with the interviewee.

4.4 INCREASING DETAIL AND VARIETY

There are two further procedures for obtaining an accurate understanding of the interviewee's constructs. Constructs, being contrasts, can be stated in more or less detail – in rather global terms, or in very precise terms which relate to details rather than generalities. Your interviewee might say, in general terms, that s/he's comfortable with some people and uncomfortable with others. Or, alternatively, the contrast may be stated in greater detail, in terms of whether those people could be trusted to help in a crisis, or could not be trusted in this way. Your interviewee might, indeed, go to greater detail still, contrasting people in terms of whether they could be asked for a loan of money if the crisis were a financial one, or otherwise. There are two different ways in which this greater detail can be identified.

4.4.1 Laddering Down – Asking 'How, in What Way?'

You've encountered the first way briefly, already, towards the end of Section 3.2.3. The focus here is on the detail with which a single construct is expressed when it's first elicited.

Glance again at Section 3.1.2, the 10-step basic grid procedure. Step 5 elicits a first approximation of the construct, and step 6 provides an opportunity to express the construct in sufficient additional detail so that you understand the intended meaning as precisely as possible. You do this by encouraging the interviewee to express each pole of the original construct in greater detail, being more explicit about the operational, behavioural or affective content involved. In the language of Section 4.3.3, your concern is with the precision of the symbols your interviewee uses in communicating the construct to you. Take a look at the upper half of Figure 4.1. The questions you ask, (a) to (e), result in a more precise and detailed expression,

I could get a loan from this person – I wouldn't even dream of asking them!

of the original construct,

    I can be comfortable with this – I'm never really at ease with this
    person   person

It's assumed that there is a particular level of detail which you and the interviewee will find the most effective in understanding the way in which the interviewee construes. The level depends very much on the topic, and why you're both doing a grid. Attention to ensure this kind of specificity is particularly important

- if your topic is one about which people have 'motherhoods' and think in clichéd terms

- if you are doing the grid interview as the qualitative phase of a market research study

- if you're trying to identify faults in manufacturing or service provision in a quality-control context and discover, in detail, why a sample is or is not of acceptable quality.

At step 5, then, you always have a choice: whether to accept the construct as first offered, or whether to take and repeat step 6, looking for more detail. The procedure by which you do so is quite simple, and if you look again at the 10-point procedure, or glance again at Exercise 4.1, you'll see that what you're doing, in effect, is adding an additional substep (call it step 6b) to step 6 of the procedure.

6b Put a *'how'* question to the interviewee.

'How can I tell?' or 'in what particular way?' or 'can you give me an example of the kind of thing you mean?' **about the emergent pole of the original construct**. (When the elements are people, 'what kind of person is like that?' is a useful form of words.)

Write the answer down below the emergent pole of the original construct.

Put a 'how' question to the interviewee about the implicit pole of the original construct.

Write down the answer below the implicit pole of the original construct.

Stop at that point, or repeat the *'how'* question in more detail still, about the construct you've just written down.

Apply the remaining steps of the basic grid procedure to the final construct you arrive at using step 6b, and not to the original one you obtained in step 5.

The result, if you were to write each step down before writing the final one into the grid, looks a little like a ladder – the contrasts provide us with the 'rungs', and the superordinate–subordinate relationships at each successive step constitute the 'uprights' of the ladder. See Figure 4.1. Hence the term, 'laddering down'.

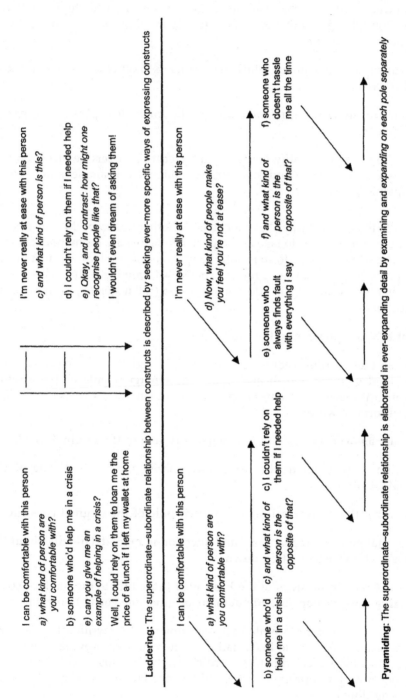

Figure 4.1 Laddering and pyramiding

Rating the Laddered Construct in the Grid

At step 6 of the basic procedure, you would write down just the lowest construct you got to, on the grid sheet. You would then obtain the ratings of all the elements on this final version of the construct, following steps 7 to 9.

Since you have carried out Exercise 4.1 before getting to this point – you did do the exercise, didn't you? – you'll remember that three examples of laddering down occur: see pages 258, 261, 266 of Appendix 2, and refer to Appendix 1.2.

4.4.2 Pyramiding Technique

'Hold on!' you might argue. 'When you're laddering down, there is surely more than one way in which a person can answer that *'how'* question!'

A person can feel comfortable with someone because the other would help in a crisis, or because the other never ever challenges things that the person says, or because the other person's reaction to events always includes the funny side of those events – or, indeed, for a great variety of reasons. Why pick on a particular one to write down as *the* construct at step 6 of the procedure?

As with so much of grid technique, the answer is: it depends what you're wanting to do! Why, in particular, are you interviewing the other person? The answer may relate to the topic of the grid, or to the circumstances in which the topic is being investigated. There are times when you'd want to identify constructs at a detailed level from a particular point of view, using the qualifying phrase technique described in Section 3.2.3. Here, you'd be content with a simple laddering procedure which expresses the construct most *precisely* from that point of view.

There are other times when you want to investigate the *variety* of a person's construing – the range of a person's points of view, if you like. For example, the grid may be about feelings towards people, and whether the interviewee feels comfortable with other people is just one thing you wish to learn about. Or the grid may be about what an interviewee understands by the idea of trusting other people – trust may be the topic – and you seek as many different aspects of that superordinate concept as possible. In this case, where you want to understand the range of a person's construing, there is an alternative to laddering, called 'pyramiding'.

The procedure is a little more involved than in laddering. (Refer to the lower half of Figure 4.1). Now add the following substep to step 6 of the basic 10-point grid-elicitation procedure.

6b As before, put a _'how'_ question to the interviewee.

'How can I tell?'; 'in what way?'; 'can you give me an example of the kind of thing you mean?'; 'what kind of X is like that?' about the emergent pole of the construct.

Write the answer down below the emergent pole of the original construct.

Ask what is the opposite or contrasting pole of the construct you wrote down above, and write _it_ down.

Go back to the implicit pole of the original construct and ask a 'how' question to the interviewee about it.

Write the answer down below the implicit pole of the original construct.

Ask what is the opposite or contrasting pole of the construct you wrote down above, and write _it_ down.

Stop at that point, or repeat the 'how' question in more detail still, about the constructs you've just written down, noting the emergent poles, and asking in each case what their opposite is.

Apply the remaining steps of the basic grid procedure to _all_ of the constructs you arrive at.

As you can see, the shape of the data structure you're creating is rather like a pyramid: hence the name given to this procedure by Landfield, who first developed it (Landfield, 1971: Ch. 8).

Rating the Pyramided Constructs in the Grid

Since your aim in using pyramiding is variety, you rate all of the constructs this procedure has provided (as opposed to the _single_ construct which is the end of the laddering-down procedure described earlier). Write each construct which results from the pyramiding procedure on the grid sheet, and ask your interviewee to provide ratings of all the elements on each.

Pyramiding is something you do for a reason, often one relating to the overall design of the investigation in which grids are to be used. So the way in which the ratings of pyramided constructs are recorded and analysed will, in fact, be determined by that design.

Please carry out Exercise 4.2 before going on.

In conclusion, if you're reading this guidebook in conjunction with Fransella et al. (2004), please note that those authors make no distinction between laddering down and pyramiding. They use the two terms as synonyms for the procedure I have just described in Section 4.4.1, 'pyramiding'. There is, however, a distinction between the two, both procedurally (see Kelly, 1963: 57–58) and with respect to the theory of self-reference (see Jankowicz, 2000b), and I have retained it here as one which I believe to be useful, particularly when you're coming to grips with construct elicitation for the first time.

THINGS TO DO

Exercise 4.1 Handling the Interview

By way of feedback on your use of basic grid technique and to provide you with a self-check on how much of the above you have found helpful, please read Appendix 2. This is part of a transcript of a grid interview, which starts as the first construct is being elicited. *Please don't look at Appendix 1.2 for the feedback yet.*

Go through the transcript and see how many of the procedural issues dealt with by the questions in Sections 4.1.1–4.1.3 arise in the transcript. Take a sheet of paper and, working through the pages of Appendix 2, write down:

(a) the page number in Appendix 2

(b) whether one of the procedural issues occurs on that page

(c) which one it is. (You'll notice that each procedural issue in Sections 4.1.1– 4.1.3 has been numbered for just this purpose. No expense has been spared.)

(d) how the issue was handled, refreshing your memory about the principles involved, in Sections 4.1.1–4.1.3.

When you've finished, check your answers in
Appendix 1.2.

Exercise 4.2 Practising Pyramiding

Read over Section 4.4.2 before you begin.

(a) Go back to the grid you did in Exercise 3.2.

(b) Ask which construct your interviewee feels is the most important to him or her. This should be one which, your interviewee feels, 'stands for a lot of things'. Call this construct X.

(c) Then ask your interviewee which is the least important, one which is 'just so', without standing for a lot of other things that need expressing. Call this construct Y.

(d) Now carry out the pyramiding technique on construct X. How many different subordinate constructs come to mind? Try for at least four.

(e) Now do this with construct Y. Aim for at least two subordinate constructs. Are there more?

Consider two questions.

Was it, in fact, easier to pyramid lots of constructs for a construct that is important to your interviewee, and fewer for a construct that isn't particularly important?

Looking at the two sets of constructs, how would you characterise them? I'm asking you not to consult with your interviewee, but to make a judgement yourself. Are they of any particular kind? Do they differ systematically between construct X and construct Y?

Now check Appendix 1.3.

THINGS TO READ

At this point, you might want to go over either of Kelly's two books. The most useful at this point is his summary of basic personal construct theory:

- Kelly, G.A. (1963) *A Theory of Personality: The Psychology of Personal Constructs*. London: Norton.

Alternatively, if you're not ready for Kellian theory but want to know a little about the use of the grid as a simple decision-making procedure, and gain some insights into the use of grids for making tacit knowledge explicit, why not glance at

- Jankowicz, A.D. (2001) 'Why does subjectivity makes us nervous? Making the tacit explicit'. *Journal of Intellectual Capital* 2, 61–73.

But that's scarcely essential, and at this stage, if it's a question of a choice between exercises or reading, I'd much rather you completed Exercises 4.1 and 4.2.

CHAPTER 5

DESCRIPTIVE ANALYSIS OF A SINGLE REPERTORY GRID

In this chapter, I outline the basic approach to the analysis of single grids, and the kinds of information which can be derived from a grid once it has been completed. The examination of relationships in single grids is dealt with in Chapter 6, and the analysis of multiple grids is described in Chapter 7. As with the other sections of this introductory guide, I can't be comprehensive. The material is a straightforward foundation, and you would be wise to look elsewhere, as indicated, for more advanced and detailed procedures.

5.1 AN OVERVIEW

There are many analysis procedures. Given the nature of the repertory grid and its underlying theory, both qualitative and quantitative approaches are available to you. If you believe that quantification matters, there are certainly numerate procedures; but if you happen to be uncomfortable with numbers, there are procedures that don't depend on them.

> Hold on a moment. I happen to believe that 'qualitative' and 'quantitative' are misleading terms. They're certainly not mutually exclusive. The most quantitative technique involves an element of subjective judgement about the nature of things – naming the factors in a factor analysis, for example. The most qualitative technique involves some concern for the extent to which the behaviour or narrative being examined is typical or

idiosyncratic; or how important the features and trends discovered might be – both matters of *degree*, and hence quantity. And there's no doubt that, to understand what someone is saying in a grid, a blend of both approaches is required.

To make a distinction between the words in which the constructs are expressed, for example, and the ratings used to record the relationship between elements and constructs, calling the former 'qualitative' and the latter 'quantitative' would be somewhat misleading.

Some people identify the *content* of what is being said with the words that have been used to label the constructs, and the *structure* of how it's been said with the matrix of ratings provided. While that's a little more useful, it's still a bit oversimplified.

Meaning is what has been captured in a grid, and, if you think back to what the grid interview involved, you can see that meaning is expressed by *both* the words *and* the numbers. You need the words to express and communicate a construct – a dimension through which meaning can be expressed. And you need the numbers to characterise the elements with respect to that dimension – that is, to express the position of the elements on that dimension – in other words, to ascribe the meaning attached to the elements by their positions on the various constructs in the grid.

Agreed. What you're concerned with when you analyse a grid is a blend of both. My job is to outline the procedures in a way which does not frighten off either the verbally or the numerically inarticulate reader. I stop at the point at which my own inarticulacy prevents me from going any further, and hand you over to other authors.

In a grid analysis, the job is twofold: firstly, to identify the interviewee's meanings, and, secondly, to draw whatever implications seem to be appropriate to you. This is best thought of in terms of achieving one or more of the following goals. The various techniques I deal with are listed under each heading.

Describing the Basic Grid

The first step in any analysis is description. You outline what's there, to gain an understanding of what the interviewee is trying to tell you, in detail, staying close to his or her intentions. You know whether you've been successful because s/he will recognise the result: there's a sense of ownership on the part of the interviewee. The following techniques are outlined below:

- process analysis

- eyeball analysis

- construct characterisation.

These are dealt with in this chapter.

Describing the Structure in the Grid

One possible next step, after the basic description, is to investigate the relationships between elements, and between constructs, in the grid. These may not be immediately obvious to your interviewee, but are usually recognisable, on reflection, when you have pointed them out. The sense of ownership is still there. Four techniques will be outlined, the first two requiring less computation than the last two:

- simple relationships between elements
- simple relationships between constructs
- cluster analysis
- principal component analysis.

These are dealt with in the next chapter.

Index Analyses of the Grid

Another possible next step, which may, depending on your purpose, replace describing the structure in the grid, is to summarise the way in which the interviewee construes, by means of one or more of several indices. They won't be obvious to your interviewee, who is unlikely to have any sense of ownership, but they can be helpful to *you*. They depend on the structure within the ratings of the grid, and say something about the interviewee's style of thinking in this one grid. A comparison with other people is implied.

There are many such indices, each summarising some structural characteristic of an individual grid. They can be broadly classified as follows:

- cognitive complexity: the number of constructs about a topic; the number of constructs being differently used (functionally independent construction: see Landfield & Cannell, 1988); the number of distinct construct clusters (articulation). Burleson et al. (1997) provide a review of measures and an interesting example.

- extremity scores of various kinds, such as ordination, integration, and constriction, which examine the proportion of extreme as distinct from mid-point ratings.

These measures are used in counselling and therapy, where they are likely to be just one of many information sources which the interviewer has about the interviewee. I don't cover them herein. That's because I'm wary of making statements about an interviewee ('he has a cognitively complex way of thinking about this issue; she construes in a differentiated way') on the basis of just one grid elicited from that person, with no other information or personal history in support. My guess is that you'll be doing single grids with individuals without necessarily getting to know them deeply, using other, supporting, sources of information. Should this change, you'll be able to find out more in the references I listed above. For further particulars, look in Fransella et al. (2004, Chapter 5) in the first instance.

Before any of this, though, a word about some basic assumptions.

5.2 A STANCE TOWARDS ANALYSIS

You'll notice that the techniques have been grouped and ordered, according to the extent to which the interviewee can recognise the implications of the analysis. As soon as you move away from the grid interview as a social encounter, and come back to the reasons for which you're conducting the interview, the investigatory or research design which you're following, and the kinds of analysis you're going to make of the interviewee's grid material, then issues of stance, expertise, and communication are raised. Without making a song and dance about them, we need to consider them briefly, since they're rather important.

You'll recall doing Exercise 4.2 after you'd read the previous chapter. (Assuming you did the exercise. I hope so. Life is pointless otherwise.) The purpose was unremarkable. I wanted you to practise pyramiding, the technique I'd just described. In doing so, though, I asked you to do two things.

Firstly, I asked you to take on a reason in inspecting the grid which would not necessarily be anticipated by the interviewee. Here, you were addressing a research question (whether there is a relationship between the importance of a construct and the ease with which subordinate constructs can be identified) that your interviewee may not have shared. You had objectives different to those of your interviewee. Secondly, you were asked to express a personal opinion about the constructs: to characterise them.

All analysis has those two properties. The objectives of the person doing the analysis may differ from those of the person who provided the material, and the person doing the analysis is involved in making judgements about that material.

Doesn't this negate, you might wonder, all the assumptions outlined earlier about the interviewee being the definitive authority about his or her own constructs? Moreover, if we were right about constructive alternativism (that there's always more than one way of making sense of anything), how on earth can we claim to an *authoritative* analysis? Who am I to decide what sort of constructs a person has? What kind they are? They're not mine, so whence the privileged view? More generally, how much of myself do I put into any study as a result of the analysis that I do?

The simple answer is that you have as much right to make your sense of the world as your interviewee has. The judgements and interpretations you make of the material you analyse are as much part of your own view of the world as the material you're analysing is part of the interviewee's. If interviewees believe that constructs are found under gooseberry bushes, that is their right. They are the final authority in managing the interpretations they make of their own worlds. But, by the same token, you have your own understandings, and these include your interpretations of the other person. You are the final authority in managing any interpretation of *your* interpretations. You may have good reason, based on your own experience, for believing that gooseberry bushes don't come into it and that one should look elsewhere for constructs.

But what if the interviewee doesn't agree with your analysis and conclusions? That's a bit more complicated, isn't it? I understand the reason for being a faithful recorder and taking the interviewee at their word in eliciting the constructs themselves, as we discussed in Section 4.1. 'Credulous listening' is all very well, but 'credulous analysis' is a flabby way of resolving a disagreement of interpretation, I'd have thought.

Okay, let's look at it step by step.

Firstly, there is the question of representation. Given that you have jointly negotiated the interviewee's meanings, and that you initiated the encounter in the first place, it does mean that you're responsible if you misrepresent the information the interviewee provides, just as the interviewee must live with the consequences of his or her own way of construing. Before you do your analysis, you have to get the basic information down accurately, even if you believe that information to be 'erroneous' in some way.

Next. You have access to a body of knowledge and technique (personal construct theory and repertory grid technique) which the interviewee has not.

The purpose of all analysis, investigation, and research is to come to understandings which are useful – which seem to lead to accurate predictions about what will happen next. This is true whether we're talking about the investigation that is being carried out by the interviewee trying to understand his or her experience, or the one being carried out by you as you try to make sense of your interviewee as part of your own investigatory or research purpose.

Now, your own activities are informed by a body of knowledge, personal construct psychology, to which a lot of people subscribe; a lot of work has been done on it. It's a consensus that has emerged because it made sense in the past to those who seek to understand other people, and it *may* (I do *not* say will) lead to predictions which work better than your interviewee's. And, provided you have used the techniques as they are intended, you are likely to come to conclusions which those other people would also have come to, given the same information.

So if, after all that, you and the interviewee still disagree, then, ultimately, all you can do is agree to differ, and see whose predictions turn out to be more accurate.

Either of you could be unsuccessful in those predictions. The interviewee because s/he's stopped checking some part of his or her beliefs, perhaps. And you, because no technique or procedure is perfectly reliable, or because you've made a misjudgement in making inferences in the analysis, or because you and the collegial consensus have yet to realise that the interviewee's understanding is indeed more effective than their own since the appropriate evidence is not yet in, or is unrealised by them to be relevant to the issue in question. In the meantime, you're both trying to get by in understanding the bit of the world that's engaging you at that time.

I can't be sure if this line of reasoning works with people who are in spectacular, bizarre, and distressed disagreement with others – I'm thinking of some of the clinical patients with whom the repertory grid can be used as part of diagnosis and treatment. I rather think that it does, but it's not my field.

Now, take this line of reasoning one step further. In talking about a body of knowledge to which many people subscribe, I'm saying that knowledge is socially defined. (This argument is best outlined in Berger & Luckmann, 1976.) Personal understandings may have to relate to a constituency. Indeed, to more than one constituency (you will probably have heard of role conflict, for example?), and the people in those constitu-encies may vary in what they expect and understand when they, in turn, seek their own meaning in existence. Whatever you discover by means of your analysis will also be given sense and meaning by other people; they will construe your construing of your interviewee's construing! This needs thinking about, and carries implications for your choice of analysis technique.

In fact, your choice of analysis technique depends on three factors:

(a) how well it summarises your interviewee's meanings

(b) how well it allows you to draw inferences and conclusions from them

(c) how well it communicates this to your own constituency.

If you're a student reading this book to help prepare a term report, bear your lecturer's expectations and knowledge of grid technique in mind. This is particularly important in the case of doctoral students and their supervisors: what kinds of analysis does your supervisor expect, and what is s/he comfortable with given the subject matter of your dissertation? Repertory grids are not a widely known technique. How much explanation of what you're doing will you have to provide them? How important is it to them that you take an approach that comes over as quantitatively inspired? And how will you explain it all to them?

If you're a manager or professional with an occupational application in mind, the issue of communication with a constituency is the same, but the question is slightly different. When you write the report and executive summary of your grid-based job analysis/development review/OD intervention, how can you best summarise the results of your analysis without all the technical jargon?

Finally, if you're neither a student nor a manager – simply someone who's interested in understanding other people – you also have a constituency, and that's the interviewee him- or herself. How well can you explain the basis of your analysis if s/he asks you about the ways in which you have come to your understanding of his/her understanding?

5.3 DESCRIBING THE BASIC GRID

This is a straightforward account of *what* the interviewee thinks, and *how* s/he thinks. The immediately obvious relationships within the grid are examined.

5.3.1 Process Analysis

This examination should best be done in context. You can glean a lot about your interviewee and his/her stance towards the topic by ignoring the grid results for a moment, and simply thinking back to the interview itself.

The grid interview is not a psychometric test. It has no norms, to be sure; but, less obviously perhaps, it does not have to have 'results' to be useful. The *process* by which the information is obtained is informative in itself, and understanding this will provide you with a background for the other analyses you'll be doing – the ones in which you 'look at the results'.

In point of fact, when counsellors use the repertory grid for counselling and guidance purposes, they frequently give greater priority to what goes on *during* the elicitation, and far less to what's in the grid when the elicitation process has been completed. The grid becomes a specialised form of counselling dialogue – a technique for directing attention during a social encounter – rather than a procedure which has to be completed to be enlightening (Jankowicz & Cooper, 1982). You may not be engaged in anything remotely resembling counselling, but you do want to understand your interviewee, don't you?

And so, you should always carry out a process analysis if you were the person who conducted the grid interview. It's your basic first step whatever other analysis you do later. If someone else conducted the interview, it may be possible to talk to the interviewer about any process issues which s/he noted or can recall. If the grid was a self-grid, try to think about how it went, following and amending the questions shown below, as appropriate.

Run through them, jotting down anything which occurs to you. Keep the notes as a refresher when you use any of the other analysis techniques.

The Topic

How did the interviewee react to your introduction of the reasons for doing the grid; how did s/he handle his or her side of the negotiation over the topic? Indeed, who initiated the contact which led to the grid: did the interviewee approach you, did you approach the interviewee, or was it through a third party? What was the implied contract? Is any of that remarkable or significant?

The Elements

How did the interviewee respond to the elements you proposed? If they were proposed by the interviewee, did you use them all? Which ones didn't you use, and why not? – does this tell you anything about the way the interviewee views the topic?

If you used eliciting statements to choose elements, which elements were offered under which characteristic? In a grid which evaluated a training programme, for example, suppose you agreed on the element set proposed by the interviewee in response to a request to think of two training sessions that were 'very good', two that were 'poor', and two in between. You could glean some useful information simply by seeing *which* actual training sessions were proposed in each category, and how readily the interviewee proposed them, even before you see how they were construed in the grid itself.

If you're conducting a classroom exercise in which you want to discover and discuss how pupils construe the eight most important social developments of the twentieth century, and you ask each pupil to nominate their eight as elements, then a simple examination and classroom discussion of all their elements is surely *de rigueur* if you wish to understand their perspective on recent social history before you start eliciting their constructs!

The Constructs

The qualifying phrase helps the interviewee to address constructs which are especially relevant to the topic. How did the interviewee respond when you introduced it? Hopefully, s/he received it as a useful but otherwise unremarkable part of your technique.

How useful did s/he find it during elicitation? Was it followed or avoided? For example, if the qualifying statement was 'from the point of view of how you feel about them', and at the end, *none* of the constructs related to feelings, and your steering in that direction was ignored, it could be very informative!

More generally, which constructs required more thought than others? Constructs don't just sit there in a heap inside the interviewee's skull. Some are available at the top of their repertoire, as it were, and are readily articulated, while others represent distinctions that the person may not have found it necessary to make before, in making sense of what life was presenting. S/he may struggle to express the distinctions in words. Where are the hesitations and why?

And now, the constructs themselves! What are they, what are they saying, what are they like? You may have formed an impression of the kinds of constructs being offered during the process of elicitation, and feel there's something significant there. Let's leave that issue over for more detailed consideration in Section 5.3.3.

The Ratings

How straightforward was the procedure as a whole? Was it sufficiently sensible to the interviewee for the results to be credible, or was it like pulling teeth – clearly meaningless as an interviewing technique? Though the time may vary a little depending on the circumstances and the reasons for doing a grid in the first place, in most cases it'll usually take between 30 and 60 minutes to elicit and rate between 6 and 12 constructs. Most interviewees find it an appreciable task, since it requires some concentration. After 60 minutes, both of you might feel a wee bit tired if all went well, and drained if it was meaningless.

> Don't use the results, drop all further analysis, if you recall that the task wasn't very meaningful to the interviewee. (An hour to arrive at two constructs? Why on earth didn't you abandon the grid and do something that made more sense to the interviewee?) A grid is not a test, that is, a procedure which must be completed to be meaningful. You've already discovered what it means to this interviewee – zero, nada, zilch!

As you worked through the grid, did you find that there were particular elements which fell outside the range of convenience (see Section 2.1.1) of some of the constructs? Did your interviewee comment on this, talking about the way in which some constructs are generally applicable, while others refer only to particular elements? If you were able to encourage the interviewee to ruminate in this way, are there, in retrospect, any particular comments s/he made that were worth noting?

Was it emotionally involving? Were there moments of upset; pauses for deep thought soon after a construct was elicited, rather than during its elicitation? The former may point to an emotional experience, while the latter may be affectively neutral, simply a pause for thought as the best words are found in which to express the construct. Remember the constructs in question and look at them particularly carefully during any other analyses that you carry out on them.

What kinds of emotion? Anger? Sadness? Regret? Impatience? Elation? What sort of thing gave your interviewee a good giggle when s/he recalled it? And so on.

What kinds of comments did the interviewee make during the procedure, about the procedure? What were his or her own assessments of the process as a whole, or of anything specific that happened during the elicitation?

Did you have to depart from your usual procedure for any reason? In fact, overall, was this one of your more personally satisfying grid interviews, or, er, perhaps not one of your best? How good were *you*?

Pause for a moment and do Exercise 5.1.

5.3.2 Eyeball Analysis

Regardless of what other analyses you may have planned, your next step is to read the grid as a whole, and familiarise yourself with what's there. If the grid is one which you have elicited yourself, and you're familiar with it already, you need to step back from the detailed elicitation procedure and provide yourself with an overview. This is a simple description of what the grid presents, before your very eyes and with nothing up your sleeve. An eyeball analysis was what I drew on in Section 2.2, when I described the grid which appeared in that section as Figure 2.1.

You should always carry out an eyeball analysis before doing anything else, especially if:

• The grid is the result of an interview by another interviewer.

• It is the outcome of a self-interview.

• The grid was elicited by a semi-automated software package. (See the comments on software in the introduction to Chapter 6.)

For the moment, it's best to assume that you are focusing attention on this single grid and this particular topic, and that you're not intending to make inferences about how your interviewee thinks in general.

Use the following six-step procedure.

(1) What is the interviewee thinking about? Note the topic of the grid; if there is any information available on any qualifying phrases which were used during elicitation, note that, too.

(2) How has the interviewee represented the topic? Note the elements. If there is any information available about the way the elements were agreed, note it.

(3) How does s/he think? Constructs! How many constructs were obtained, given the length of the interview? As suggested in the account of process analysis above, the number of constructs you get is related to the meaningfulness of the procedure; by and large, you'll get more constructs about a topic

- which interests the interviewee

- in which the interviewee has special expertise

- which the interviewee has to confront frequently in his or her work

- which the interviewee has thought about before.

The obvious question: what are the constructs; that is, what constructs does the interviewee use in making sense of the topic? Read *both poles* of all the constructs and note the particular distinctions being made. Bear in mind that these are constructions *from a given point of view*, so remind yourself of the qualifying statement.

(4) What does s/he think? Element Ratings! Note the scaling interval used (a 5-point scale, a 7-point scale, or whatever). Look at the ratings. Is there anything obvious about the whole matrix of ratings? Probably not, but check. Are they mainly 1s and 5s (or 7s) with no finer shading? Are there lots of missing ratings because certain constructs didn't apply to certain elements? Lots of 3s (4s, in a 7-point scale), which could mean the same thing?

Column by column (element by element) find out what is being said about that element. How has it been rated on all of the constructs? What picture of that element is being conveyed? Note, particularly, whether that element receives a lot of 1s and 5s (or 7s), and on which constructs. Repeat for all the elements.

(5) Look at the supplied elements and constructs and ratings. Familiarise yourself with the ratings given to each of the elements on any constructs which have been supplied. Similarly, familiarise yourself with the ratings given, on all the constructs, to any self elements, or ideal self elements, which have been used. What, in this context, is being said about the Self? How does the interviewee characterise his or her ideal? How do ratings on the supplied construct compare with the others?

(6) Draw your conclusions. Summarise the main points of what you have gleaned. Where you find yourself making interpretations of your own, you should do so in the light of the process analysis you have already conducted. If you're working collaboratively with your interviewee, the process issues should be discussed, as well as the substantive information derived from the grid. And, in a collaborative analysis, the *interpretation* is, by definition, collaborative: you both propose your viewpoint on what the significance might be, and what it all means, and you both assess that viewpoint, as critically as you decide it deserves. You negotiate a common understanding, according to the stance I have outlined in the previous section.

And that's all there is to the basic, first-step analysis procedure. If, at the end of this procedure, your reaction is 'so what?', there may be something wrong. Most people have at least something interesting about their construing! A reaction of this kind may occur:

- because you're tired and jaded, having looked at a lot of grids at the same time. No problem: take a break.

- Because you're working with a sample of interviewees. You're working with several sets of grid results, and it's the type of investigation in which the big hits will emerge only after you have completed the analysis of the whole set. Be patient!

- Because you don't quite know how you'll continue the analysis of the grid, but you're sure you'll think of something soon. That *is* a problem.

In the latter two cases, look at the material in Section 7.1.2 on design. But usually all will be well. Onward.

Go straight to Exercise 5.2!

5.3.3 Characterising Constructs

Your eyeball analysis will have informed you about what the constructs are. You will know their content; in other words, you will have identified the actual terms of reference which the interviewee finds relevant in thinking about, and working with, the issues involved in the particular topic you have chosen. As you do this analysis, it may occur to you that some, or all, of the constructs are of a particular kind, and this may be significant in itself.

As with process and eyeball analyses, so with construct characterisation: make it a standard part of your analysis routine, regardless of what other kinds of analysis you intend to carry out.

What is the proportion of the following types of construct, and is this significant given your aims, and the topic of this particular grid?

Core Versus Peripheral Constructs

Some constructs are obviously ones which have a deep and personal significance to the interviewee, and others are fairly humdrum.

> 'Core constructs' remind the person of who s/he is; what really, really matters to them, and what they value in existence; 'peripheral constructs' summarise their feelings, understandings, and knowledge concerning cheese, and cabbages, and kings. In other words, core constructs are central, while the peripheral ones, though they reflect the core constructs, deal in the small change of existence. And then there are those which lie somewhere in the middle, neither core nor peripheral: those which encapsulate meanings about friends, spouses, jobs, and the like.
>
> From this you can infer that the closer to the core a construct is, the more it concerns matters which touch on the selfhood of the individual. Core constructs are those which 'govern the individual's maintenance processes and which are central to his or her identity' (Winter, 1992: 11).

Myself as I am now   –   Myself as I would wish to be

Being in control of one's life   –   Being a hostage to fortune

Justice and fairness to people   –   Arbitrary and unfair to people

are all examples of constructs about people which appear to touch on some fundamental personal issues in existence and, depending on context, could be regarded as core constructs.

There's a lot more about core constructs in Chapter 8, where the structure of the construct system is discussed in the context of personal value measurement. For the time being, let's just say that it is important, in describing the constructs the interviewee uses, to do the following.

1. Identify Core Constructs

These are constructs that particularly matter to your interviewee. How can you tell which ones they are? Look at the content of the construct, and from your memory or notes of how the process proceeded when you were eliciting it. If in doubt, ask your interviewee! (There is also the technique of systematic **laddering upwards** and an approach called **resistance to change technique**, both used in the identification of core constructs and personal values. These are outlined in Sections 8.1.1 and 8.2, respectively.)

2. Assess the Proportions Which Are Core

Of the full set of constructs, how many sound as though they're personally fundamental to the interviewee, or could lead directly to matters of personal values if explored further? How many are 'just so', and peripheral in this sense? (They could easily all be peripheral! It partly depends on the topic of the grid.) Context matters, so –

3. Ascribe Significance to This in Context

Given the topic of the grid and the circumstances in which the interview is carried out, is the appearance of core constructs, or their absence, remarkable or unremarkable? For example, in a grid on the topic of death and bereavement, with elements which include 'my father', 'my mother', and 'myself', it would surely be surprising if all the constructs dealt solely with the trivia of death certification and choice of undertaker services.

Conversely, a grid devised for market research purposes which had brands of coffee for its elements would be unlikely to deal in the eternal verities, and the absence of core constructs would be unremarkable.

4. Assess Relationships. How do core constructs relate to other constructs; do any of the other constructs appear to receive the same ratings as the core constructs?

As you'll see when we analyse relationships within grids in Chapter 6, you can obtain a good insight into your interviewee's personal understanding of the topic by examining the ways in which a grid is structured and, in particular, how sets of constructs hang together. If the ratings on the two constructs

Doesn't have office favourites   –   Encourages flatterers

Reluctant to apportion blame   –   Seeks scapegoats

were very similar to each other and to the core construct

Justice and fairness to people   –   Arbitrary and unfair to people

there's a sense in which the two constructs help you to understand what the interviewee means by 'justice' as distinct from 'unfairness' – they serve to exemplify in somewhat more specific terms what the core construct means to the interviewee.

There again, you need to be careful: the centrality of a particular construct may not be obvious from its wording, and you will want to refer back to your process notes. A grid done by a manager on the performance of his/her sales team may contain issues that sound trivial, but may matter a lot to the manager if these have a bearing on the manager's own job security. The construct 'met the annual sales target – didn't meet the annual sales target' may sound like a rather peripheral, behavioural construct summarising operational matters, but it could lie very close to some personal core constructs relating to personal security and the stability of one's professional existence, if the manager's own performance was under review when the grid interview took place!

Propositional Versus Constellatory Constructs

Propositional constructs are those, often peripheral, constructs that offer simple descriptions of basic and, at first glance, superficial element characteristics. A grid with the topic of 'people' might have 'male – female'; or 'right-handed – left-handed' as constructs. Sometimes dealing with basic physical characteristics and easily recognisable attributes, propositional constructs may have a very narrow and overspecific range of convenience.

One consequence of their specificity is that they offer no basis for making inferences on other constructs. If you know that a car is red as opposed to white, for example, you can't readily characterise it in terms of its reliability, its performance, and so on.

Constellatory constructs, on the other hand, are those which imply the position of an element on other constructs very strongly indeed. The construct 'family saloon – sports car' is fairly constellatory for many people – there's a lot wrapped up in that distinction. Construe a car as more of a 'family' car, and you're prepared to construe it on other constructs such as 'safe – unsafe', 'steady – exciting', 'slow to accelerate to 60 – fast to accelerate to 60', and so on; construe a car as more of a sports car, and the chances are that you'd also be prepared to construe it along those dimensions (at the other end of each!). Consequently, cars of either kind merit different marketing strategies, and different forms of advertising based on the relevant associations to each, as a result. In contrast, whether a car is red or white is likely to carry few such associations. (This is an empirical issue, though, and much market research consists in seeing what kinds of associations people might have for constructs which at first glance appear to be merely propositional.)

Also, it's worth noting that a construct is constellatory or propositional *depending on the topic*. 'Red as opposed to white' may not be constellatory for cars, but, for some interviewees at least, it is when it's applied to people – in terms of whether they're a redhead or a blond(e).

Which reminds me: constellatory constructs are often characteristic of stereotyped thinking.

As with all construct characterisation, your analysis procedure is fourfold:

(1) Identification – though this isn't necessarily clear-cut. Just keep the propositional–constellatory distinction in mind as you look at the constructs, thinking back to the interview process and remembering whether you agreed to exclude some propositional constructs because you both felt they were irrelevant.

(2) Assess proportion. Are there a lot of constructs which are clearly propositional or clearly constellatory?

(3) Ascribe significance in context. If you decide that there are *a lot* of either propositional *or* constellatory constructs, it may lead you to decide that the grid as a whole never got beyond the superficial. Perhaps there are a lot of propositional constructs because the interviewee wasn't encouraged to express any of the deeper, original, or more thoughtful constructs in his or her repertoire. On the other hand, maybe the interviewee's thinking on this particular topic is indeed clichéd, and there aren't many deeper, original or thoughtful constructs in the repertoire, and all that's available are constellatory constructs.

The former is unlikely to happen after you've gained experience in grid technique, and know how to relax the interviewee and encourage appropriate rumination. The latter is a finding in itself. (And *of* itself. Don't assume a person who's clichéd on one topic is clichéd on others.)

(4) Assess relationships of any propositional constructs used. It is common to agree with the interviewee that a particular propositional construct *will* be used, because it will be particularly informative when you analyse the constructs in detail. In effect, you're using the propositional construct as you would a supplied construct, to check out a hypothesis you have about the relationships within the grid.

Suppose, for example, you both decided to use the propositional construct, 'male – female'. Looking at the grid row by row, what other constructs have ratings which are similar to the construct 'male – female'? This would be useful in gender studies. Constructs being used the same way as a 'male – female' construct may suggest what masculinity and femininity mean to the interviewee: what other attributes the interviewee associates with a person's sex. There's more on this in Section 6.1.2 below.

Key propositional constructs which relate to the topic of the grid, or which encapsulate a hypothesis in a research study based on repertory grid technique, can be very useful in analysing grid material. (You may be doing a study of the way in which left- and right-handed people are construed, for example.)

Finally, there is one important field of application for grid techniques which works almost exclusively with propositional constructs. Grids are used in quality-control studies in the case of products or processes in which quality is not readily specified in physical terms, but can be determined by the subjective judgements of a very experienced employee. For example, it can be difficult to determine what constitutes 'good finish' as distinct from 'poor finish' in the case of a garment; or 'mature taste' as distinct from 'immature taste' in the case of a cheese. One can't tell, from these particular constructs, what the other constructs are: in a sense, the constructs aren't constellatory enough!

Experienced employees would be encouraged to provide as many distinct constructs, relating to physical and measurable attributes, as they could think of. Further analysis would show which attributes do, and which don't, match – with the notion of 'good finish – poor finish' in the case of the garment example. Once they were explicitly identified, they could be highlighted in the training of new quality controllers, or production employees could be trained to recognise them during the manufacturing process as part of a zero-defects initiative. (And, once they're explicitly known, it may be possible to develop physical measures for some of the attributes. For example, it turns out that acidity is a measure of maturity in some kinds of cheese, and the acidity of cheese can be measured more reliably in a test tube than by popping a piece into your mouth!)

Pre-emptive Constructs

Propositional constructs are those in which the relationships to other constructs aren't obvious. In contrast, **pre-emptive** constructs have no useful relationship, or, rather, their relationship to the others is fixed in such a way as to make the other constructs redundant so far as the interviewee is concerned. They predetermine the rating of elements on the other constructs to the extent that those other constructs could, to all intents and purposes, be ignored.

For example, if the construct 'domineering – easy-going' was used pre-emptively, one would, in effect, be saying, 'If a person is "domineering as opposed to easy-going", s/he can't *possibly* be anything else (for example, a "nurturing as distinct from careless" parent; "an empathetic as opposed to insensitive person", and so on). So the rating I might give on the other constructs doesn't matter.'

Where 'domineering – easy-going' is used in a pre-emptive way, a domineering person is seen as *nothing but* domineering, and an easy-going one is *nothing but* easy-going.

(1) Identification. Identification of a construct as 'pre-emptive' depends on the way in which it is used, rather than on being an attribute of the construct itself. Thinking back to the process analysis, were there constructs which, once elicited, seemed to foreclose the possibility of others being mentioned, or to predetermine, with a feeling of inevitability, the ratings the others received?

(2) Assess proportion. There may not be many!

(3) Ascribe significance in context. Granted that a construct is being used pre-emptively, how does it relate to the topic, and how does it influence the way in which the topic is seen by the interviewee?

(4) Relationships: glance at the structure. What do the ratings of any other constructs look like? Are they similar to those for the construct which you feel is being used pre-emptively?

Other Types of Construct

You may find it helpful to ask the same questions about the relative frequency and significance in context of the following kinds of construct. You would identify them quite simply from their content and/or by asking the interviewee about them.

- **affective:** those expressing a feeling or emotion

- **behavioural:** those which describe what the elements do, or the part they play in some process to which they belong

- **evaluative:** those through which an opinion or assessment is offered

- **attributional:** those which incorporate perceived reasons for behaviour

- **unremarkable:** those which are just so, *sui generis*, without any great implications to be drawn from them. I include these as a reminder that grids may not be dramatic or inferentially rich – they may consist of simple straightforward descriptions of how and what the interviewee sees.

Don't overinterpret the constructs in a grid.

Some examples of all of these are given in Table 5.1.

Now try Exercise 5.3 to see what your feel for different constructs is like.

Standard Classification Schemes

Finally, in this context, I should mention that the categorisation of constructs provides the most important technique for analysing more than one grid, being used to indicate how a group, or sample, of people construe some topic of common interest and, by implication, to say something about how individual members of the group compare with each other.

There is more on this in Section 7.2.3, where the use of pre-existing standard classification schemes is outlined. The discussion also covers the development

Table 5.1 Characterising constructs

Construct		Type
Would require careful planning of application form, reading up on things	– I could start without any special preparation	Behavioural
Requires dedication, commitment, heart	– Requires a cool head	Unremarkable?
Not a bandwagon or a fashion: could really make a difference to other people who need me	– Just the current fashion, may sound good but not really genuine	Core construct
Men rarely do this	– Men as likely to do this as women	Propositional. Might be useful in a counselling setting
Has its stresses; am a bit nervous of it	– Any problems encountered wouldn't be stressful	Affective
My learning would be through people who want to help me	– My learning would be through people just doing their own thing	Attributional
Best for me in the long run	– Won't do quite so much for me	Evaluative

The topic was 'How I might spend the next year', by a mature student with a general degree in psychology currently finishing a postgraduate diploma in education. He was particularly interested in what would be the best choice so far as his personal development was concerned. The elements were
- a year's voluntary work
- a job in a secondary school
- register for an MPhil/PhD
- register for an MA in educational psychology
- look after their baby while his wife supported the family
  and, given the developmental flavour to the grid, two self elements:
- me as I am now
- me as I intend to be.

of your own classification scheme as part of a technique called **content analysis**, described in detail in Section 7.2.

THINGS TO DO

Exercise 5.1 Practising Process Analysis

Look at the grid which you elicited when you did Exercise 3.2. Go through the process issues, under the headings of 'topic', 'elements', 'constructs', and 'ratings' described in Section 5.3.1, and try to remember anything which happened under these headings when you conducted that interview.

- How many of these involved procedural mistakes on your part? Don't worry if there were a lot of those. You improve with practice!

- How many issues can you remember? Probably not many, particularly if your first grid was some time ago.

- If you can, talk to the colleague from whom you elicited that grid. Can s/he help you to remember anything else that's worth noting about the process?

Remember: process analysis needs doing soon after the grid was elicited. If you don't plan to do any further analysis for a while (perhaps because you're doing a series of grid interviews), it's useful to make notes of your impressions of the process shortly after the interview took place. And, unless there is some special reason why you can't, always consider discussing your process impressions with the interviewee.

Now return to Section 5.3.2 and carry on reading.

Exercise 5.2 Practising Eyeball Analysis and Construct Categorisation

Working with the grid in Appendix 2 (the one you used for Exercise 4.1), carry out an eyeball analysis; in other words, answer the following questions:

(a) What the interviewee is thinking about:
   - How did the interviewer negotiate the topic with the interviewee?
   - What was the qualifying statement?

(b) How the interviewee represented the topic:
   - What were the elements?
   - How were they agreed?

(c) *How* does the interviewee think?
   - What are the constructs?

(d) *What* does the interviewee think?
   - What kind of scale is used, and how would you characterise the ratings?

(e) Look at the supplied elements and constructs
   - At an initial glance, which element seems as though it received the most similar ratings to the supplied element?

- Similarly, form a quick impression of which construct seems to have received the most similar ratings to the supplied construct.

(f) Draw your conclusions
- What are the main points, bearing in mind any process analysis you have already conducted?

Now check your answers and reasoning in
Appendix 1.4.

Exercise 5.3 Characterising Constructs

Glance again at the grid produced in Appendix 2. How would you characterise the constructs? Which would you want to explore in more detail with the interviewee because they appear to be

(a) core

(b) propositional

(c) affective

(d) evaluative

(e) attributional?

Now check your impressions in Appendix 1.5.

THINGS TO READ

Now that you have a good feel for the repertory grid, how it's elicited, and how to appreciate, in some depth, the meanings it conveys, it might be a good point to take in a little more theory. I suggest that the most valuable activity at this stage would be to go outside the field of personal construct psychology, and read what some other people of a constructivist inclination have to say about how people construe and, in particular, how they come to share constructions of their experience.

- Berger, P.L. & Luckmann, T. (1976) *The Social Nature of Reality*. Harmondsworth: Penguin.

One field in which process analysis is important is personal counselling and guidance. The following is directly relevant as an example of professional practice.

• Jankowicz, A.D. & Cooper, K. (1982) 'The use of focused repertory grids in counselling'. *British Journal of Guidance and Counselling*, 10, 136–150.

It would also serve to show how approaches from personal construct psychology are relevant to the process work done by OD consultants and anyone taking an action learning approach to organisation development.

CHAPTER 6

ANALYSING RELATIONSHIPS WITHIN A SINGLE GRID

In this chapter, we concentrate on the relationships within a grid, and assess them systematically. It's the longest chapter in this guidebook, but the procedures it describes are very straightforward, depending mostly on simple addition and subtraction. Simplifying analysis in this way makes for a longer account, as I explain it all, but once you've gone through this chapter, you'll simply fly through the procedures. Ferrets, drainpipes, and doses of salts spring to mind.

Chapter 5 dealt mainly with the analysis of *content*; there wasn't a lot there about structure. In contrast, Chapter 6 deals with *structure*, and this requires us to look at the relationships among the elements and the constructs in a person's grid.

We'll be sitting back from the immediacy of grid elicitation, and dealing with things which aren't obvious at first glance. Along the way, we'll be returning to the informal impressions about a person's construct structure that will have occurred to you during the grid interview, and examining them systematically. You have at your disposal:

• simple relationships between elements

• simple relationships between constructs

- cluster analysis

- principal components analysis.

In the first two of these, once the relationships and links you identify have been pointed out to the interviewee, s/he will recognise them as a fairly direct outcome of what s/he had in mind when s/he was providing the ratings; or, at least, as implied, fairly directly, by those ratings. There is a sense of *ownership*.

In the last two, that sense of ownership may not be there, unless your interviewee understands the statistical manipulations involved in cluster and principal components analysis, or can follow the explanations which you provide. You'll need to draw on your own understanding of these procedures to discuss how the links you have identified necessarily follow. My objective in the relevant section is, in part, to provide that understanding painlessly, and without involving you in particularly deep statistical reasoning.

As I mentioned in Chapter 1, I try to appeal to your intuition as much as to any great degree of developed numeracy (a quality which is, at times, rather over-rated). In these circumstances, people who are comfortable with numbers may find what follows to be rather basic and ploddy. Please bear with me, since I want to take all my readers with me on what is a fascinating journey. (And forgive any comments which strike you as gross oversimplifications.) There again, this approach also means that people who aren't naturally comfortable with statistical analysis will need to take some of what I say on trust.

I'll try to keep the latter to a minimum. In fact, there's really just the one thing I ask you to accept 'because I say so'.

In dealing with simple relationships, between elements or between constructs, you're dealing with the ratings directly, and your interpretation of the numbers is very straightforward, based on the notion that a rating of '1' defines the emergent pole and a rating of '5' (or '7', on a 7-point scale) defines the implicit pole. In these circumstances, there's no limit on the size of grid to work with. A grid with three elements and two constructs may not tell you a lot, but the same analytic procedures apply as with a grid of, say, 20 elements and 15 constructs, and your analysis is capable of making as much, or as little, sense of either.

With the other two kinds of analysis (cluster analysis and principal components analysis), you use procedures which depend on additional assumptions about the meanings attached to the numbers you're using, and, as a general rule, you shouldn't use them unless your grid has at least six elements and six constructs. (Some would argue that you shouldn't use principal components analysis at all unless you have 50 constructs; but I feel that that is an excessively stringent requirement.)

Finally, you'll notice that these last two procedures rely on a software package, about which I've relatively little to say, my concern being to help you to understand the output of any such package without wedding you to any particular one. There are many purpose-built repertory grid packages available, some reviewed in detail in Sewell et al. (1992), and others more briefly, but more recently and with good access information, in Scheer (2003). If you know your way round it, you can, of course, use any general-purpose statistical package for cluster and principal components analyses of repertory grids; Scheer (2003) provides you with a way of accessing some notes by Richard Bell on how to use SPSS for this purpose.

If you prefer to have some software available to you right now, as you work through Sections 6.2 and 6.3, you will find the following website very useful: *http://tiger.cpsc.ucalgary.ca:1500/* It's the location of WEBGRID, a platform-independent package which will

- elicit a grid

- allow you to enter the details of an existing grid for detailed analysis

- provide you with a cluster analysis (discussed in Section 6.2 below)

- provide you with a principal components analysis (discussed in Section 6.3 below). (Note that the package uses the term 'map' in place of the term 'principal components analysis', in case you're wondering where to find it.)

This package really is a remarkable achievement, since it does its job for you regardless of what type of computer you run, and regardless of where in the world you're located. You can save grid data on the server under perfectly secure conditions, accessible from anywhere; and it won't cost you a penny or a cent! Further particulars are also at *http://repgrid.com/*.

6.1 SIMPLE RELATIONSHIPS

By the time you have thought over the process by which the grid you're analysing was elicited, carried out an eyeball inspection of the grid, and developed a feeling for the kinds of construct being used, you will probably be noticing relationships within the grid. Some elements seem to have received rather similar ratings on the various constructs, while others were construed very differently. Perhaps there are constructs on which the ratings are practically identical across all the elements, as if the constructs were expressing similar meanings. You may have noticed that the presence of certain kinds of construct precludes others (pre-emptive), or appears to make others easier for the interviewee to offer (constellatory).

Let's take this in two stages. Firstly, using as an example an extract from a grid about training officers, let's examine relationships between elements. Secondly, let's examine relationships between constructs, illustrating the procedure with a grid showing the ways in which a department store manager views her sales staff.

6.1.1 Simple Relationships Between Elements

You would carry out analyses of element relationships if you:

• didn't have access to a computer for more detailed analyses

• didn't understand heavy statistics but are happy to do some simple counting

• wanted to continue the analysis in a collaborative style with your interviewee

• were using the grid as part of a counselling or personal development interview

• were using the grid as a simple decision-making device.

When you carried out your eyeball analysis (Section 5.3.2), you did an examination of the ratings of elements on constructs as a way of identifying *what* the interviewee thinks. It is a natural next step to ask whether the interviewee thinks of one element *in the same way* as s/he thinks of another.

How would you tell? Glance for a moment at Table 6.1. It summarises the ways in which a training officer thinks of other trainers he has known. Do an instant eyeball analysis to familiarise yourself with the content of this grid. Now, focusing on the elements, which two look as though they're construed in much the same way by the interviewee?

It looks like trainer 1 and trainer 3 (T1 and T3). Now, how did you arrive at that answer? Think about it: what did you actually *do*? Another way of putting it: if you had to tell someone else how to arrive at that answer, what is the procedure you would ask him or her to follow?

'What did I do? Well, I could see that the ratings for T1 and T3, reading down those two columns, were practically identical, which wasn't the case with the other elements. There was practically no difference between them.'

Exactly so: you focused on *differences*, and the procedure involved in simple element relationship analysis is straightforward. It's a matter of *summing differences* and comparing the outcomes, as follows.

(1) Calculate differences in ratings on the first pair of elements on the first construct. Take element 1 and element 2 (column 1 and column 2). Find the

Table 6.1 An extract from a grid interview with a young training officer on 'trainers I have known'

1	T1	T2	T3	T4	Self	5
Prepares thoroughly	5	2	5	3	2	Seat-of-pants speaker
Energetic, moves about	1	2	1	5	1	Just stands there stolidly
Intellectual	3	1	3	5	2	Pedestrian
Language articulate, precise, and concise	5	1	4	2	3	Language shambolic, appeals to intuition
Makes it seem so obvious and clear	3	1	2	5	3	You have to work to understand his point
Tells jokes	1	5	2	4	3	Takes it all very seriously
Overall, enjoyed his courses	1	3	2	5	2	Overall, didn't enjoy his courses

absolute difference between the two ratings on the first construct (that is, take the smaller rating from the larger regardless of *which* element has the larger, and which the smaller, rating).

(2) Summing down the page. Do the same on the second, and subsequent, constructs, systematically down the page, summing the differences as you go. Jot this total down when you've finished.

(3) Repeat for all pairs of elements. Now repeat for columns 1 and 3, 1 and 4...2 and 3, 2 and 4...etc., noting down the sums of differences as you go.

(4) Compare these sums of differences. The smallest difference, indicating the two elements which are construed most similarly, and the largest difference, indicating the two elements which are construed as most dissimilar, are particularly useful to examine.

Glance again at Table 6.1. Trainers 1 and 3 are construed the most similarly: both 'seat-of-pants' rather than careful preparers (5–5); both 'energetic' (1–1); both halfway between having an 'intellectual' rather than 'pedestrian' style (3–3); trainer 1 being 'shambolic' in his presentation, a little more so than trainer 3 (5–4); trainer 3 being slightly more, but not extremely, 'clear and obvious' compared with trainer 1 (2–3); both inclined to 'tell jokes' but T1 more than T3 (1–2); and both receiving similar ratings on the 'overall' supplied construct (1–2). These differences (and remember, we're taking the absolute value each time, subtracting the smaller from the larger) sum to 4.

Repeat this for all the other pairings, and you see that no other elements are as close to one another as those two. T3 and Self are the next most alike (a sum of differences of 7), while T1 and T4 are the least alike, with a sum of differences of 20.

Go on: check it for yourself by doing Exercise 6.1.

The next step is highly recommended if you're working collaboratively with the interviewee.

(5) Discuss these relationships with the interviewee. The grid used in this example was a very simple one. The interviewee would easily be able to see what s/he said as you fed it back, pointing to the two columns of the grid. If the relationship isn't obvious in a larger and more complicated grid, simply repeating the rationale *about finding the smallest sum of differences* to your interviewee, and running through an example as under step 4 above, should be sufficient.

At that point, your conversation with the interviewee will depend on your purpose in eliciting the grid, but will also depend on the extent to which the interviewee is interested, intrigued, and possibly surprised by the information about the relationships among the elements. It shouldn't come as an enormous surprise, by the way: at the most, an 'ooh yes' response, 'I hadn't noticed that before, but now that you point it out I can see that', or words to that effect. Much of the time you'll be confirming what's known already.

The interviewee should have a sense of ownership of what you're pointing out. And if s/he doesn't – if s/he doesn't recognise, or disowns, the relationship – then you may wish to explore the apparent disparity between your analysis and the interviewee's own view, in greater detail. (The chances are that you haven't yet elicited some fairly important constructs, on which the interviewee would rate the two elements very differently.) Next,

(6) Examine relationships with supplied elements, if any. These will most commonly be

- *relationships between any 'self' element and the other elements.* This helps to answer the question, 'Who do you see as most similar to yourself?'

- *relationships between any 'self' element and any 'ideal self' element.* How close is the interviewee to his or her ideal? This approach is often used when measuring change, or assisting the interviewee in clarifying his or her thoughts about some possible change. The applicability to counselling is obvious.

These are two much-researched fields, and if your work in construct elicitation has an advisory, guidance, or counselling element, you may want to familiarise yourself with some of this research. Probably the best place to start is Winter (1992). If you look at page 42, for example, you'll see nine different measures of self-construing listed, some of which require you to do more complex structural analyses (see Section 6.2 below). Others, however, like the Self–Other Score, the Death Threat Score, and the extent of polarised self-construing, can be derived by simple counting of the kind described earlier (see Winter, 1992: 42–43).

- *relationships between any 'ideal' element and the other elements.* This helps to answer the question, 'which element comes closest to your Ideal?', and is the basis on which grids are used in the choice situations which arise in many knowledge-management applications. The rationale here would be that, if the interviewee is helped to compare all the courses of action which s/he feels it is possible to undertake, with the way in which s/he views the 'Ideal course of action', the one which matches best with the Ideal should be the one to put into effect.

This isn't an exercise: real choices can be made in this way, particularly if some of the constructs summarise the results of empirical work done using other, more 'objective', techniques! However, the value of the grid as a decision-making device often lies in the stimulus it gives to a discussion about:

- the things the decision-maker is taking for granted

- his or her strategy in identifying alternatives

- choosing among them

- putting the chosen one into action

- revising his/her views in the light of the outcomes.

rather than in some total figure that you have calculated.

The simple rationale you mention above provides a useful procedure in situations in which the attributes expressed in the constructs carry *equal* weight for the inter-viewee. There will be times when more complex procedures are required, though. (See Humphreys & McFadden, 1980.) Also, there is a debate (see the short overview in Jankowicz, 1990) about the extent to which the outcomes of a grid interview, however rich in complexity, can be used to make decisions in an *automated* way. There again, some quite simple grid techniques based on the above procedure have been used in developing quite complex expert systems (Boose, 1985) by focusing on the ways in which experts make inferences.

Okay. Thank you for that. This would be a good point at which to practise doing a simple element-relationships analysis in a choice situation.

Enjoy Exercise 6.2 before continuing.

And, finally, one tiny last step:

(7) **Ensure comparability with other grids**. There may be occasions on which you want to compare the element-relationship scores across different grids. As your measure of the relationship depends on the sum of differences over all

Table 6.2 Sums of differences vary depending on the number of constructs

Interviewee 1	Boss X	Ideal	
He always gives clear job instructions	1	1	Sometimes unsure of what he wants
Has a sense of humour	1	1	Lacks the light touch
Approachable when I need help	2	1	Doesn't like it when I ask for help
Good at building a team	1	3	Treats us all as individuals
Sum of differences			
Boss X against	–	3	

Interviewee 2	Boss Y	Ideal	
He always gives clear job instructions	1	1	Sometimes unsure of what he wants
Has a sense of humour	1	1	Lacks the light touch
Approachable when I need help	2	1	Doesn't like it when I ask for help
Good at building a team	1	3	Treats us all as individuals
Can't delegate	2	5	Good at delegation
Handles stress well	3	1	Loses his cool
Sum of differences			
Boss Y against	–	8	

the constructs, comparison is only possible if each grid has the same number of constructs. You need to use a different form of relationship score where the grids being compared have different numbers of constructs! (Skip the next two paragraphs and Table 6.2 if this is obvious.)

For example, you may have interviewed five people in your firm's new product development department about how they feel about their team leader, asking them to construe the bosses for whom they've worked in their career so far, and have discovered, for each one, which of their bosses came closest to a personal ideal of what the manager of a technical development department should be.

Table 6.2 shows the comparison for just one element with the Ideal, in two different cases. Assume this is the most similar element to the Ideal in both cases. You can see that the element-relationship score is sensitive to the sheer number of constructs in the grid, rather than being a simple measure of the differences in the grid. (Of course: it's a sum of differences, and if you sum over more items – six constructs in the second grid, but only four constructs in the first – you're bound to get a different value anyway.)

I suppose you could take an average difference score, dividing each sum of differences by the number of constructs in each case. As it happens, the usual practice is to turn each of the sums of differences into a percentage. (In doing so, the opportunity is also taken to turn it into a % *similarity* score on the rationale that it's easier to think of the extent to which things are *the same* than the extent to which they're *different*.)

The procedure is the same as for any percentage calculation. You express the value you're interested in as a proportion of the largest possible value. A half is a half is a half regardless of the size of the total value. You then multiply the proportion by 100 to stretch the result onto a neat little 100-point scale. I'll repeat that, with an example. Five as a percentage of 10 is 5 divided by 10 (in other words, a proportion of five-tenths, or a half); the answer multiplied by 100 gives 50. Please bear with the triviality; but, in analysis, every step needs to be understood; otherwise, why bother?

The value you're working with is the sum of differences you calculated earlier. And what's that as a percentage? Let's take it step by step.

- The largest difference on any single construct is the *largest rating* that's possible on the scale (5 on a 5-point scale; 7 on a 7-point scale) minus 1. Call this (LR−1).
- This will happen as many *times* as you have constructs in the grid (the sum of differences accumulates as you add them up, down the grid). Call the number of constructs C. So the largest possible sum of differences in the whole grid is given by (LR−1) *times* C.
- Now take the value you're interested in, that is, the particular *sum* of differences you want to turn into a percentage. Call this SD.
- Divide SD by the largest sum of differences to get the proportion; then multiply the outcome by 100 to get the percentage. And that's it. In other words:

$$\frac{SD}{(LR - 1) \times C} \times 100$$

Or, if you prefer it all on one line, $\{SD/[(LR-1) \times C]\} \times 100$.

- Finally, turn this percentage sum of *differences* into a percentage *similarity* score by subtracting it from 100.

$$100 - \frac{SD}{(LR - 1) \times C} \times 100$$

On one line, that's $100 - (\{SD/[(LR-1) \times C]\} \times 100)$.

Now you can compare similarities across grids made up of differing numbers of constructs. This can be useful when your interviewees have each given you different numbers of constructs; or when you're interviewing the same person twice to see how his/her construing might have changed. (Chapter 9 provides you with alternative procedures for examining change, by the way. Changed construing may mean different ratings than before; but it can also mean that the person has added more constructs, or even dropped some, the second time round!)

And now that you know how % similarity is computed, let me save you the tedium of doing so! For a 5-point scale, at any rate. Take a look at Appendix 3. If you use a scale which isn't a 5-point scale, or if you're working with a different number of constructs, you'll need to do the calculation yourself.

Table 6.3 shows the grid on 'trainers I have known' which you worked with when you did Exercise 6.1. The sums of differences which you calculated (and checked for correctness against Appendix 1.6) have been replaced by % similarity scores. As you can see by comparing this table with your answers in Table 6.16 (or preferably with the correct answers given in Appendix 1.6!), the element % similarity scores are as you'd expect: trainer 1 and trainer 3 are seen

Table 6.3 An extract from a grid interview with a young training officer on 'trainers I have known', together with element % similarity scores

1	T1	T2	T3	T4	Self	5
Prepares thoroughly	5	2	5	3	2	Seat-of-pants speaker
Energetic, moves about	1	2	1	5	1	Just stands there stolidly
Intellectual	3	1	3	5	2	Pedestrian
Language articulate, precise, and concise	5	1	4	2	3	Language shambolic, appeals to intuition
Makes it seem so obvious and clear	3	1	2	5	3	You have to work to understand his point
Tells jokes	1	5	2	4	3	Takes it all very seriously
Overall, enjoyed his courses	1	3	2	5	2	Overall, didn't enjoy his courses

Simple Element Analysis	T1	T2	T3	T4	Self

% Similarity scores

	T1	T2	T3	T4	Self
T1 against	–	35.7	85.7	28.6	67.9
T2 against		–	50.0	42.9	67.9
T3 against			–	35.7	75.0
T4 against				–	46.4
Self against					–

as the most alike (a similarity of 85.7%), while trainer 1 and trainer 4 are seen as the least alike (a similarity of 28.6%).

A little practice in working out % similarity scores: do Exercise 6.3 right now!

6.1.2 Simple Relationships Between Constructs

When you examine the relationships between elements, you're addressing similarities in *what*'s being said about the elements. Similarly, it's possible to look at the relationships between constructs; but here, you're addressing similarities in *how* the interviewee talks about the elements.

Is s/he using the various constructs in similar ways? Do the constructs represent very different aspects of the interviewee's thinking, or do you get the impression that they're simply minor flavours of one rather obsessive theme which seems to underlie the way in which the interviewee thinks about that particular topic?

And that needs stressing. These are all questions dealing with a person's thinking about a particular topic; but, because they deal in '*hows*' rather than '*whats*', it's very tempting to feel that you're discovering something about the person him- or herself, rather than something more straightforward about the person's views on the topic. You may begin to overgeneralise, and start talking about the interviewee's style, or personality, both being rather more enduring characteristics.

Grids were developed as a way of describing individuals and the characteristic, and differing, ways in which they construe experience. In that sense, they have been understood by some psychologists as a form of personality assessment. I'd suggest that you don't think of what you're doing in this way, though. No doubt, if you were to elicit several grids on different topics from the same person, and found the same kinds of constructs, hanging together in the same way, you'd be inclined to feel that you were getting a good idea of the other person as a unique human being. Now, if you were to spend more time with them, talking in ways that are more spontaneous and natural than a grid, and possibly, if you had the appropriate training in using other techniques and making clinical judgements, you could certainly describe what you were doing as a form of personality assessment. And there's no doubt that the grid is an excellent technique for doing so.

But if you're simply interviewing a person on one topic, on one occasion, well, then, that's all you're doing. If you choose to see it as a personality assessment, that's your affair. I'd rather, though, that you were to think of what's going on in this way. In making their tacit knowledge explicit, *you're* construing *their* construing. Would other people agree with *you*? That includes the interviewee! Remind yourself of what was said in

Section 5.2, which provides a different slant on the same issue, and keep checking. I'll suggest ways of doing so below.

As with elements, so with constructs: a simple examination of relationships is an optional part of the analysis, and you might instead choose a more detailed structural analysis.

You'd choose to analyse simple construct relationships for the same sorts of reasons:

• because you didn't have access to a computer

• because you're uncomfortable with number-crunching any more involved than the calculation of simple similarity scores

• because you want to explore the relationships between constructs with this interviewee.

Your approach is very similar to the approach you adopted in looking at the elements. You make inferences from *differences* between ratings, but, this time, you're counting *along* the rows of the grid, rather than *down* the columns.

Take a look at Table 6.4. This is an attempt to make tacit knowledge explicit: to get inside a department store manager's head, encouraging her to be explicit about what it takes to be an effective sales clerk. Do a quick eyeball analysis to familiarise yourself with it. Particularly, look at the constructs, row by row. Do you notice anything about the ratings on the first construct, and the fourth one from the top? Both constructs are shown highlighted in boldface.

Practically identical! Element by element working from left to right, whatever rating is given to 'learns the new models quickly' is also given to 'awareness of sizes, colours, and availability' – with the exception of a difference of '1' in the case of the third element along from the left, Billie. Let's examine the two constructs in detail.

In the example shown in Table 6.5, the sum of the differences, construct 1 against construct 4, is just 1. This is recorded in a new section of the table, in the right-hand half of the table. (Read along the construct 1 row and find the intersection with the construct 4 column.)

Is the interviewee using these two constructs as equivalents? Are they linked in some way, or is it just a coincidence? These and other fascinating questions can be asked as you explore the interviewee's knowledge structure. First, though, let's run through the procedure. It's very similar to the one you used for elements, though it varies in one important point.

(1) Calculate difference in ratings of the first element on the first pair of constructs. Working with the full grid, as in Table 6.4, take construct 1 and

Table 6.4 Grid interview with the manager of the clothing section of a department store (an attempt to get at her tacit knowledge of effective sales performance as part of the development of a competency system)

1		Jane	Ann	Billie	Ian	Alma	May	5
Con 1	Learns the new models quickly	5	1	1	1	4	2	Takes a while to learn the features of new lines
Con 2	Too forward in pushing a sale: tends to put customers off	3	4	3	1	2	1	Good balance between active selling and just being helpful
Con 3	Could be more interested in after sales	1	5	4	4	1	3	After sales (alterations, other bespoke elements) well handled
Con 4	Awareness of sizes, colours, availability	5	1	2	1	4	2	Availability and choice knowledge poor
Con 5	Pleasant and easy-going	3	1	2	5	4	3	Takes it all very seriously
Con 6	Overall, an effective salesperson	5	1	2	4	4	2	Overall, a less effective salesperson

construct 2 (the top row and the next one down), and find the absolute difference between the two ratings on the first element.

(2) Sum across the page for the remaining elements. Do the same for the other elements, working systematically from left to right, cumulating as you go. Put this sum in the appropriate space at the right, on the intersection of the appropriate row and column.

(3a) Repeat for all pairs of constructs. In other words, for rows 1 and 3, 1 and 4...2 and 3, 2 and 4...etc., noting the sums on the right as you go.

Table 6.6 shows the results of these first three steps. The sum of differences for construct 1 against construct 2 is 10; for construct 1 against construct 3 is 18; for construct 1 against construct 4 is...(work it out for yourself: $5-5$ plus $1-1$ plus $2-1$ plus $1-1$ plus $4-4$ plus $2-2$ equals)...1. And so on.

And in among all these sums of differences, we see that the two constructs we identified by eyeball inspection earlier are indeed very highly matched for the manager: the sum of differences between construct 1 and construct 4 is just 1,

Table 6.5 Grid interview with the manager of the clothing section of a department store, examining the simple relationship between two constructs

	1	Jane	Ann	Billie	Ian	Alma	May	5	Simple construct analysis	
									Against Con 1	Against Con 4
Con 1	Learns the new models quickly	5	1	1	1	4	2	Takes a while to learn the features of new lines	–	1
Con 4	Awareness of sizes, colours, availability	5	1	2	1	4	2	Availability and choice knowledge poor	–	

Table 6.6 Grid interview with the manager of the clothing section of a department store, examining the simple relationship between constructs

| | | | | | | | | | | Simple construct analysis | | | | | |
	1	Jane	Ann	Billie	Ian	Alma	May	5	Against Con 1	Against Con 2	Against Con 3	Against Con 4	Against Con 5	Against Con 6
Con 1	Learns the new models quickly	5	1	1	1	4	2	Takes a while to learn the features of new lines	–	10	18	1	8	4
Con 2	Too forward in pushing a sale: tends to put customers off	3	4	3	1	2	1	Good balance between active selling and just being helpful		–	10	9	12	12
Con 3	Could be more interested in after sales	1	5	4	4	1	3	After sales (alterations, other bespoke elements) well handled			–	17	12	14
Con 4	Awareness of sizes, colours, availability	5	1	2	1	4	2	Availability and choice knowledge poor				–	7	3
Con 5	Pleasant and easy-going	3	1	2	5	4	3	Takes it all very seriously					–	4
Con 6	**Overall, an effective salesperson**	5	1	2	4	4	2	**Overall, a less effective salesperson**						–

and that's the lowest sum of differences in the grid. There certainly seems to be some shared meaning here.

Moreover, if we want a single indicator of how she construes 'effectiveness overall' (a construct which happens to have been supplied by the interviewer – construct 6), we can see that the construct which is being used most similarly is construct 4. (Look in the rightmost column at the right-hand side of the table, the column for construct 6; and glance downwards) 'awareness of sizes, colour, and availability versus availability and choice knowledge poor' has the lowest sum of differences of just 3. This supervisor appears to construe effective sales performance in terms of the extent to which the salesperson is informed about what's available. (There is more on this kind of analysis, against overall, summary constructs, in Section 7.3.2.)

> *I suggest you take a break now. You don't have to do an exercise at this point, but you do need to take some time out. Put the kettle on. Take the dog for a walk. Whatever appeals.*

Now let's consider a small additional step: a very important way in which the procedure for analysing construct relationships differs from the procedure, discussed earlier, for analysing element relationships.

(3b) Repeat step 3 for all pairs of constructs with one set of ratings reversed. Unlike an element, a construct is bipolar, and can express the same meaning with ratings which run from '1' to '5', *or* with ratings which run from '5' to '1', so long as the words at each pole of the construct are reversed from left to right. Your construct analysis needs to take this into account.

Confused? Let's put that in a different way: take a look at Table 6.7. Suppose you're doing a grid in which the elements are people known to the interviewee, 'my friends' being the topic. If you run through steps 1 to 3 for these two constructs $(2-2)+(5-1)$...and so on, you'll get a sum of differences of 10. Quite a large difference, really. There seems to be little relationship between these two constructs.

Table 6.7 Relationship between two constructs about six people

		E1	E2	E3	E4	E5	E6		Against Con A	Against Con B
	1						5			
		✓		✓	✓					
Con A	Friendly	2	5	4	1	3	4	Remote	–	10
			✓	✓	✓					
Con B	Shy	2	1	2	5	3	4	Outgoing		–

But do you remember the basic grid elicitation procedure (Section 3.1.2)? Whatever the two elements have in common is written down on the left, and the contrast to this, which characterises the odd one out, is written down on the right. For the first construct, the triad E1, E3, and E4 was offered, E1 and E4 were said to be similar in that they are both rather 'friendly', and so this emergent pole was written down on the left, defining the '1' end of the scale for the first construct.

Likewise, elements E2, E3, and E4 were offered for the second construct, E2 and E3 were reported as similar in that they are both 'shy', and these were written down on the left, defining the '1' end of the scale for the second construct.

Now, suppose that the triad offered in the case of the second construct had been E2, E4, and E6? (Remember, which triads are offered is arbitrary: all that matters is that they should present different combinations of elements each time, to encourage fresh constructs.) Well, if E4 and E6 are both construed as relatively outgoing (as indeed they are: see Table 6.7) as opposed to E2, then 'outgoing' would have been written down on the left, and would have defined the '1' end of the scale.

The meaning being conveyed by the second construct would then have been expressed by the ratings as shown in Table 6.8. Aha! They are, indeed, strongly related, with a sum of differences of just 4! *Nothing has changed. Both versions express the same meaning.*

An element that is rated '5' on a scale that runs from 'shy = 1' to 'outgoing = 5' *must* receive a rating of '1' if the scale runs from 'outgoing = 1' to 'shy = 5', if the same meaning is to be expressed. And so on, for all the other ratings.

But the first variant obscured the relationship that was there, for the entirely arbitrary reason of the particular triad that was presented when construct B was elicited.

Table 6.8 Relationship between two constructs about six people, showing a reversal

		E1	E2	E3	E4	E5	E6		Against Con A	Against Con B
		1						5		
			✓		✓	✓				
Con A	Friendly	2	5	4	1	3	4	Remote	–	4
			✓		✓		✓			
Con B	Outgoing	4	5	4	1	3	2	Shy		

And so, when calculating construct similarity, *you have to do it twice*, once with each construct as it stands; and once with the ratings of the first construct of the pair being the same, but the rating of the second construct of the pair being 'reversed'. On a 5-point scale, 1 reverses to 5, 2 to 4, 3 stays the same, and so on: whatever the rating is, just subtract it from 6 to reverse it. (If you happened to be using a 6-point scale, you'd subtract the rating from 7 to reverse it; on a 7-point scale subtract the rating from 8 to reverse it; etc.)

Now return to our main worked example, the grid about sales clerks' performance. Take a look at Table 6.9. This is the same as Table 6.6. The sums of differences for each construct compared with each construct, both being 'unreversed', are shown, as before, in the top-right corner of the right half of the table. However, the spare space in the right half of the table, below the diagonal indicated by the dashes, has been used to record the sums of differences for each construct 'unreversed' compared with each construct 'reversed'. The actual reversed ratings are shown in parentheses below the unreversed ratings in the left half of the table.

This may seem like a lot of calculations, but it isn't, really. You'd calculate the unreversed comparisons as normal. Then you'd reverse the ratings of construct 1 and work out sums of differences between those, and all the remaining constructs from construct 2 onwards. Then you'd reverse the ratings of construct 2 and work out the sums of differences between those, and all the remaining constructs from construct 3 onwards: it's quicker than you think. The result would be a table that looks like Table 6.9.

(4) Compare these sums of differences, the smallest sum of differences, and the largest sum of differences, unreversed and reversed. The smallest difference, indicating the two constructs which are being used most similarly, and the largest difference, indicating the two whose meanings are most dissimilar, are particularly useful to examine. Search for these, smallest and largest, in the whole of the right-hand side of the table, and note whether the relationship is an unreversed or a reversed one.

If the smallest sum of differences was from a reversed comparison, make sure you swap the two ends of the constructs round when you're reporting the two. In Table 6.9, for example, while the smallest difference, indicating the two most highly matched constructs, is, as we already know for constructs 1 and 4,

1. Learns the new models quickly   –   Takes a while to learn the features of new lines

4. Awareness of sizes, colours, etc.   –   Availability and choice knowledge poor

there are some quite small differences, indicating a strong relationship, between reversed constructs. Take a look at the sums of differences for

Table 6.9 Grid interview with the manager of the clothing section of a department store, examining the simple relationship between constructs, and showing reversals

	1	Jane	Ann	Billie	Ian	Alma	May	5		Against Con 1	Against Con 2	Against Con 3	Against Con 4	Against Con 5	Against Con 6
												UNREVERSED			
Con 1	Learns the new models quickly	5 (1)	1 (5)	1 (5)	1 (5)	4 (2)	2 (4)	Takes a while to learn the features of new lines	R	–	10	18	1	8	4
Con 2	Too forward in pushing a sale: tends to put customers off	3 (3)	4 (2)	3 (3)	1 (5)	2 (4)	1 (5)	Good balance between active selling and just being helpful	E V	12	–	10	9	12	12
Con 3	Could be more interested in after sales	1 (5)	5 (1)	4 (2)	4 (2)	1 (5)	3 (3)	After sales (alterations, other bespoke elements) well handled	E R	4	12	–	17	12	14
Con 4	Awareness of sizes, colours, availability	5 (1)	1 (5)	2 (4)	1 (5)	4 (2)	2 (4)	Availability and choice knowledge poor	S	19	11	3	–	7	3
Con 5	Pleasant and easy-going	3 (3)	1 (5)	2 (4)	5 (1)	4 (2)	3 (3)	Takes it all very seriously	E	12	4	6	11	–	4
Con 6	Overall, an effective salesperson	5	1	2	4	4	2	Overall, a less effective salesperson	D	16	8	4	15	14	–

Simple construct analysis

construct 3 and construct 4, for example. Unreversed, the sum of differences is 17, practically negligible, you would imagine. But if you reverse one of them,

3. Could be more interested in after   –   After sales (alterations, other
                        sales   bespoke elements) well handled

4. Reversed
Availability and choice knowledge   –   Awareness of sizes, colours,
                       poor   availability

you can see that the two constructs are highly related, with a sum of differences of just 3. Whenever the manager thinks of a sales clerk as 'lacking interest in after sales', she also tends to think of them as having relatively 'poor knowledge of availability and choice', and whenever she thinks of them as 'handling after sales well', she also construes them as 'aware of sizes, colours, and availability'.

(5) Discuss these relationships with the interviewee. And that would be the way to put things. 'Have you ever noticed that, whenever you say "x", you tend to say "y"?' Your interviewee may find this unremarkable, since it's as plain as a pikestaff to him/her and always has been. 'Of course!' Alternatively, the relationship may come as a surprise, since the knowledge involved is tacit but should, on reflection, make sense. After all, your analysis is based directly on the ratings you were given by the interviewee.

In other words, as with the elements, there should be some sense of ownership of the relationships you indicate. (If there isn't immediately, point to the ratings for the particular two constructs and go over them pair by pair.) This kind of analysis is particularly fruitful in counselling, guidance, personal development, and decision-making situations, as you explore the ramifications of the interviewee's thinking, and point to the implications of those particular ways of construing.

> If you think about it, this is an excellent technique to use in counselling, since you're pointing out the implicational connections of your interviewee's own construct system directly, rather than doing what usually happens; that is starting with your own construct system to identify implications in the interviewee's construct system! Jankowicz & Cooper (1982) is worth looking at in this respect.

There are three possibilities to examine. Glance at Table 6.9 again, where the two most highly matched constructs are, as we noted, construct 1 and construct 4 (unreversed). The fact that these two constructs are highly matched (a small sum of differences) may reveal:

(a) a belief about the causal influence of construct A on construct B. Thus, the manager believes that the sales assistant who learns the new models quickly is, *as a result*, aware of the different sizes and colours in the range.

(b) alternatively, a belief about a causal relationship which runs the other way round: construct B influences construct A. For example, the manager may be telling us that she believes that sales clerks' general trade knowledge about what kinds of sizes and colours are available at different times of year will help them to learn this year's new models quickly.

(c) that the high match is a sheer coincidence. The manager's ratings on both constructs may be unrelated. Other factors may influence the values they take. How quickly a sales assistant learns new lines may relate to their intelligence as perceived by the manager – how quick they are as learners – while the awareness of sizes, colours, and availability may reflect something very different; for example, how long the sales assistants have been working for this particular company.

And, as you will expect by now, the best way to examine the possibility of associations (and, just possibly, causal relationships of this kind) is to draw them to the interviewee's attention and ask which one might be the case!

Let's continue with our standard procedure for examining the simple relationships between constructs.

(6) Focus on relationships with supplied constructs, if any. As suggested in Section 4.2.7, these will most probably be of two kinds.

(a) Relationships with a supplied construct which summarises the topic of the grid: the 'overall summary' construct. A performance-appraisal grid for a PA job, for example, might have eight PAs as its elements, and the qualifying statement 'from the point of view of what it is that they *do* that makes them effective in their job'. After eliciting the interviewee's own questions, you would ask him/her to give an overall impression of each PA on the supplied construct, 'overall, more effective – overall, less effective'.

You would then look to see which constructs had ratings which were similar to this one. In a sense, *this is what the interviewee means* when s/he characterises someone as, overall, an effective, or less effective, employee – his or her implicit definition of effectiveness in that particular job. (Do this with 20 other interviewees and you have the makings of a usable performance-appraisal questionnaire: see Section 7.2.3.)

(b) Relationships with a supplied construct which summarises some *belief of your own* which you want to test about your interviewee's construction system.

This may be a relatively informal impression you've gained from the earlier constructs offered (e.g. 'she seems to think of people largely in terms of how fit and healthy they are; if I'm right and I supply her with a 'fit – unfit' construct, it should have similar ratings to the others').

Alternatively, it may be a more formal belief, identified before you ever met this, or other, interviewee, which you wish to test as part of a research project. For example, you may be interested in the tacit knowledge which bankers have about business lending. A reasonable way of researching this would be to ask, 'Which kind of constructs match closely with the supplied construct, "I would lend them money – I wouldn't lend them money", when bankers think about different examples of business loan applications?'

> Indeed, it's possible to identify the constructs which bank commercial lending officers on the one hand, and venture capitalists on the other hand, have in mind when they think of good prospects. It turns out that these are not simply the 'objective' factors to do with balance sheets, business plans, profit and loss accounts, etc. Of course, these 'objective' indicators play an important part: but only in getting the applicant through the banker's door, as it were. After that, the lending officer's knowledge, expressed in the form of intuitions, and judgements of more 'subjective' factors play a huge part. Moreover, bankers and venture capitalists differ in the constructs they associate with a good prospect as opposed to a poor prospect. If this interests you, have a look at Jankowicz (1987b) for bank lenders, and Hisrich & Jankowicz (1990) for venture capitalists.

As you may recall from Section 5.3.3, propositional constructs are often used in this way.

At this point, it would be useful to have a little practice at computing construct difference scores and handling reversal.

Please do Exercise 6.4 before continuing.

(7) Ensure comparability with other grids. Finally, you may need to turn your sums of differences into % similarity scores, just as you did for element comparisons, and for a similar reason; that is, you want to compare similarities in grids which have different numbers of elements. You may be talking to a trainer about the teaching aids she uses before attending an in-service continuing development course, and after attending it.

When you repeat the grid after she's attended the course, to see what, if any, impact the course has had, you may find she wants to talk about two new teaching aids she's played around with during the course, resulting in a grid which has two additional elements.

And so, because the sums of difference scores are based on a sum across a different number of elements, they can't be compared directly but must be turned into a % similarity score. The procedure is almost identical to the one you followed for element % similarity scores, as follows:

- The largest possible rating is $LR - 1$ as before, but this time multiplied by the number of *elements*, E. So the proportion of actual sum of differences to largest possible sum of differences is

$$\frac{SD}{(LR - 1) \times E}$$

- Now, remembering that constructs have two poles, you need some way of signalling that a reverse relationship may be involved. The conventional way to do this is to spread the range of possible percentages over a 200-point scale; this means that you multiply the proportion by 200, not 100.

$$\frac{SD}{(LR - 1) \times E} \times 200$$

or, if you prefer it all on one line, $\{SD/[(LR - 1) \times E]\} \times 200$.

- And so, when you turn this percentage sum of *differences* into a % *similarity* score by subtracting it from 100 (and not 200!), you achieve two things. You turn percentage difference into percentage similarity, and you scale the range of possible scores neatly between -100 and $+100$.

$$100 - \frac{SD}{(LR - 1) \times E} \times 200$$

or, all on one line, $100 - (\{SD/[(LR - 1) \times E]\} \times 200)$.

And there you have it. If you check back to Section 6.1.1, step 7, you'll see how similar it is to the procedure for calculating element % similarity scores. Now you can compare the extent to which pairs of constructs are matched, in grids which have differing numbers of elements.

As before, I've provided a ready reckoner to save you some time in doing the calculations which turn sums of differences into % similarity scores. It's in Appendix 4. If the grids you're working with are different, you'll need to calculate the % similarity scores yourself. Follow the bulleted procedure shown above, or just use the formula directly.

Table 6.10 shows the same grid as Table 6.9, with some of the sums of differences turned into % similarity scores. That sum of differences of 1 shown in Table 6.9, between

> Learns the new models quickly   –   Takes a while to learn the features of new lines

and

> Awareness of sizes, colours,   –   Availability and choice knowledge availability   poor

corresponds to a % similarity score of just under 92%, 91.67% to be absurdly precise, in the first row and the fourth column in the right-hand side of the table.

The very large difference of 18 between

> Learns the new models quickly   –   Takes a while to learn the features of new lines

and

> Could be more interested in   –   After sales (alterations, other after sales   bespoke elements) well handled

in Table 6.9 translates to a % similarity score of −50% in Table 6.10, which makes you suspect that reversing one of these two constructs may show a higher relationship. Indeed, you can see from Table 6.9, in the 'reversed' part of the table, that there is a sum of differences of 4 between

> Learns the new models quickly   –   Takes a while to learn the features of new lines

and

> After sales (alterations, other   –   Could be more interested in after bespoke elements) well handled   sales

which corresponds to a % similarity score of just under 67% in the 'reversed' part of Table 6.10. The relationship between these two constructs should indeed be read this way round, reversed.

Now do Exercise 6.5 and complete Table 6.10!

In doing the exercise, you may have noticed that the values of % similarity scores for reversed constructs aren't symmetrical about the zero value with respect to unreversed constructs. That's simply a consequence of the way in which the maximum possible difference is expressed in the formula, and doesn't matter. The thing to hold on to is that you always choose the higher of the two values – *the bigger and more positive, the better* – in expressing the relationship between any two constructs, regardless of whether they lie in the unreversed or the reversed side of the table. Then, if the value in question

Table 6.10 Grid interview with the manager of the clothing section of a department store, examining the simple relationship between constructs, and showing reversals (% similarity scores)

	1	Jane	Ann	Billie	Ian	Alma	May	5		Against Con 1	Against Con 2	Against Con 3	Against Con 4	Against Con 5	Against Con 6
												Simple construct analysis			
													UNREVERSED		
Con 1	Learns the new models quickly	5 (1)	1 (5)	1 (5)	1 (5)	4 (2)	2 (4)	Takes a while to learn the features of new lines	R	–	16.67	−50.00	91.67	33.33	66.67
Con 2	Too forward in pushing a sale: tends to put customers off	3 (3)	4 (2)	3 (3)	1 (5)	2 (4)	1 (5)	Good balance between active selling and just being helpful	E / V	0	–	16.67	25.00	0	
Con 3	Could be more interested in after sales	1 (5)	5 (1)	4 (2)	4 (2)	1 (5)	3 (3)	After sales (alterations, other bespoke elements) well handled	E	66.67	0	–			
Con 4	Awareness of sizes, colours, availability	5 (1)	1 (5)	2 (4)	1 (5)	4 (2)	2 (4)	Availability and choice knowledge poor	R / S	−58.33	8.33		–		
Con 5	Pleasant and easy-going	3 (3)	1 (5)	2 (4)	5 (1)	4 (2)	3 (3)	Takes it all very seriously	E	0	66.67			–	
Con 6	**Overall, an effective salesperson**	**5**	**1**	**2**	**4**	**4**	**2**	**Overall, a less effective salesperson**	**D**	−33.33					

comes from the reversed side of the table, you would report the relationship with the direction of one of the two constructs reversed.

6.1.3 Simple Relationships in Summary

That's all there is to the analysis of simple relationships. If you've followed the argument and practised all the exercises, I suppose you could be forgiven for thinking how tedious and pedantic all this computation is! But, actually, it's not really like that.

As you start using grids with interviewees, you'll soon get into the habit of spotting the relationships on the hoof, without having to do all of these calculations.

(a) Your process analysis will alert you to the particular elements and constructs whose relationship to others is worth paying particular attention to.

(b) Your eyeball analysis may confirm these initial impressions, and will lead you to examine the supplied elements and constructs in particular.

These will be the elements and constructs whose relationship to others you'll want to check by a simple relationships analysis, as described in these last two sections. *Ignore the remainder*. Spend time on the relationships that you're interested in, and no more.

Of course, if you're being very systematic (for example, if you're analysing a grid as part of a research project in which you have to be comprehensive), then you'll want to do the full analysis of 'everything compared with everything'; but the chances are that, in this situation, you'll be using a computer with appropriate software to do all these calculations for you.

In practice, then, it's rarely that you'll have to do all the work which you've done hitherto in this chapter. But, if needs be, you can! Furthermore, if you have plodded through all of the exercises above, you'll also be in a position to understand the way in which our next analysis technique works.

6.2 CLUSTER ANALYSIS

Cluster analysis is a technique for highlighting the relationships in a grid so that they become visible at a glance. You would normally use one of the many software packages accessed through the websites I've mentioned in the introduction to this chapter to do the hard work for you (though if you want to know how to do cluster analysis by hand, for those moments in life when the electricity supply fails, Jankowicz & Thomas (1982/1983) provide a detailed step-by-step manual procedure). My purpose in this section is to

(a) give you a simple rationale by which you can understand how cluster analysis works, without going into all the detail

(b) provide a procedure for interpreting a cluster-analysed printout.

6.2.1 Rationale for Cluster Analysis

The rationale is simple enough. If you remember Exercise 6.4, and the answers given in Appendix 1.9, you'll remember that there were several relationships between constructs to be noticed in the grid on choosing a computer:

Easy to set up   –   Difficult to set up

Good build quality   –   Flimsy build

Fast   –   Slow performer

with the last construct being reversed with respect to the second. It appears that there is a group of constructs which stands out as receiving somewhat different ratings from the others.

Exercise 6.2 had you working out the relationships between elements for this same grid, and if you look at the answers given in Appendix 1.7, you'll see that elements can group together in a similar way. The sums of differences between the iMac G4 and the Ideal, between the eMac and the Ideal, and between the iMac G4 and the eMac are all small, ranging between 4 and 10. They're rather distinct from some of the other sums of differences, and appear to stand out as a distinct cluster. Elements can cluster together as well as constructs.

Sometimes the relationships are obvious, as you carry out an eyeball inspection. Just look at the column of ratings in the iMac G4 column and the Ideal column! If it wasn't for the fact that the iMac G4 didn't have an enormous range of software available, these two columns would be very similar, and very different from the other columns of ratings.

It's asking a lot of your powers of observation to get you to look for such groupings directly. You go cross-eyed as you try to look at which columns are similar to which and different from others; and then, for the constructs, which rows form one pattern, with other rows forming other patterns. Wouldn't it be so much easier, and make the patterns more obvious, if you could shuffle the columns and rows around, so that the most similar values lay side by side?

Suppose you were to pick up the paper on which a grid is printed, take a pair of scissors, and cut the grid into strips, one strip for each vertical column. Then shuffle the columns about until the columns with the most similar ratings lie side by side. Just as I've done in Figure 6.1, in fact. That is, in effect, what a cluster analysis does, except that it repeats the procedure for the constructs as well, snipping the grid into rows while checking for reversals, and then shuffling the rows around until the constructs with the most similar ratings lie side by side. This whole procedure is illustrated in Figure 6.1.

Let me offer you an analogy for the whole procedure. It's as if you and your interviewee had been looking at the original grid through a camera which was slightly out of focus, so that the structure in what you were looking at wasn't entirely distinct; and then you adjusted the lens until the relationships you were viewing sprang into focus. Indeed, the particular statistical procedure developed by Laurie Thomas and Mildred Shaw for their grid software (Thomas and Shaw, 1976; Thomas, 1977; Shaw, 1980), and adapted for subsequent analysis packages, was first called 'Focus' for this very reason.

Cluster analysis starts by working out % similarity scores exactly as we did in Sections 6.1.1 and 6.1.2 when we looked at simple relationships. The remaining computations are too tedious to go into here. (Use a software package; most of them include a grid cluster analysis routine.) The results are fairly obviously

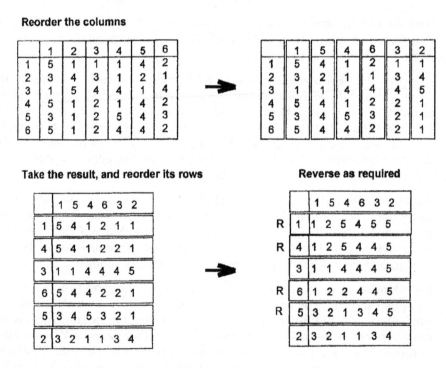

Figure 6.1 Cluster analysis – focusing the picture

related to the original grid and, especially valuable if you're working with someone in a client capacity, readily explained to the interviewee by pointing to the results on paper.

6.2.2 Procedure for Interpretation of a Cluster Analysis

As an example, take a look at Figure 6.2. It consists of the printout of an original grid (the one used in Tables 6.9 and 6.10, in which a supervisor assesses the job performance of her sales staff) in its original state, and after it has been focused by cluster analysis.

The ratings have been clustered and the grid printed accordingly, with the columns showing the most similar ratings being printed side by side. Ditto for the rows. (You'll notice the ratings are identical to those shown in Figure 6.1, by the way.)

You'll notice something else. Very conveniently, the % similarity scores for adjacent elements, and the % similarity scores for adjacent constructs, have also been provided, in the form of *dendrograms*, or tree structures. (Why are they called 'tree structures'? Well, take a look at the inset in Figure 6.2: a dendrogram on its side looks like a tree or bush, bare of its leaves, but with the structure readily visible, in the form of clusters of branches – and that bare structure of clusters of branches is helpful in quickly and efficiently interpreting the structure of a person's constructs.)

The procedure for analysing a cluster-analysed grid is straightforward, and would be followed after you had carried out a process analysis and the first three steps of an eyeball analysis (1. What is the interviewee thinking about?; 2. How has the interviewee represented the topic?; 3. How does s/he think?), as outlined in Section 5.3.2.

Yes. Let me reinforce that. In your rush to use the elegant and helpful computer software available for grid elicitation and analysis, don't forget to look at the words first! Remind yourself of the circumstances in which the grid interview was conducted; refresh your memory of what it is the interviewee was saying to you; and, only then, look at the numbers which summarise the relationships in your interviewee's thinking. Numbers by themselves mean nothing, and you need to put them together with everything else before you can understand the meaning being conveyed.

Here goes. Each of these steps is applied to the cluster-analysed grid in Figure 6.2, giving the result shown in Table 6.11: follow the procedure in both.

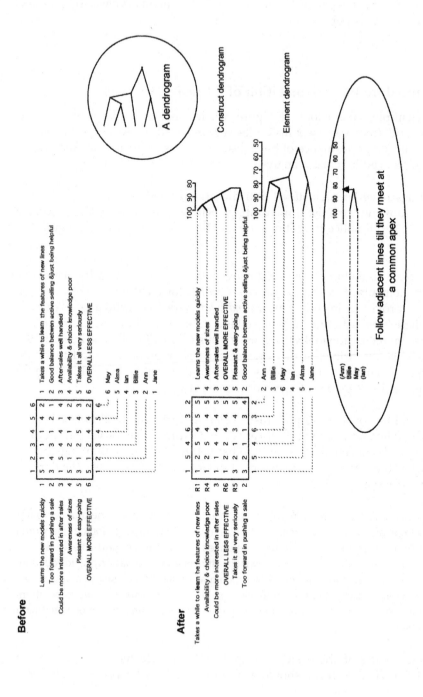

Figure 6.2 The store manager's grid, before and after cluster analysis

Table 6.11 Example of cluster analysis procedure for elements in Figure 6.2

1	Examine the elements	Alma and Jane, and Ian and May, have been reordered ...
2	Examine the shape of the element dendrogram	... resulting in two main structures, Alma + Jane versus the rest; among the rest, there's a subcluster of May + Billie then Ann, with Ian next.
3	Identify construct similarities and differences	Alma and Jane are similarly rated on all the constructs, with no more than one rating point difference between them, being largely at the left poles of all the constructs: tending to be Overall less effective. May and Billie are even more alike on three of the constructs (being aware of the range of sizes in stock, handling after sales well, and tending to be Overall more effective); differing little on the remainder; Ann tends to get similar scores to Billie. Ian's ratings are more similar to May's than to Alma's.
4	What does this mean?	A useful question to put to the interviewee at this point would be to ask whether Alma and Jane do indeed have more in common with each other than with any of the others; and whether Billie and May are, indeed, so different from Alma and Jane.
5	Find the highest % similarity score	Billie and May show the highest % similarity: follow the lines across until they meet at the common apex. Then erect a perpendicular to the % scale: about 83% similarity in their ratings. Ann and Billie are matched at 80%. (Note: their common apex, that is, where their lines come together, is at 80%, not at 83%. Imagine you're following tracks on the inside of the lines from Ann and Billie: the tracks come together at 80%.) Thus, Ann, Billie, and May form a cluster whose *lowest* similarity score is 80%. Ian matches 75% with May.
6	Examine the remaining scores.	Alma and Jane form a distinct cluster, being matched at 80%; their highest match with the other cluster is through Alma's 54% match with Ian.

Elements

(1) Examine the elements, and notice which elements have been reordered, and are now next to each other.

(2) Examine the shape of the element dendrogram. How many major branches does it have; in other words, how many distinct clusters of elements exist?

(3) Identify construct similarities and differences. For each cluster, follow the lines to the left and upwards to the relevant set of adjacent columns in the main grid. On which constructs do these elements receive similar ratings, and on which ones do they differ?

(4) What does this mean in terms of the way in which your interviewee is thinking? If the interviewee is with you, point out the similarities of element ratings within each cluster, and the differences between the clusters, and discuss with the interviewee what this might mean.

(5) Find the highest % similarity score. Look at the element dendrogram again. You'll see that there is a % scale above it, which allows you to read off the % similarity scores between any two *adjacent* elements. Each element has a line to its right which meets with its neighbour in a sideways V-shape. If you draw a perpendicular line from the apex of that V-shape to the % scale, you can read off the % similarity score between those two adjacent elements.

So, now: find the two adjacent elements which have the highest % similarity score and note its value. Next, find the next pair, note its % similarity score, and whether the pair forms a separate cluster from the first pair of elements you identified, or whether it belongs to that cluster.

(6) Examine the remaining scores. Continue this procedure, discussing the clusters and what they might mean with your interviewee.

Now turn to the constructs. The results of each step of the procedure are given in Table 6.12.

Constructs

(1) Examine the constructs: notice how they have been reordered.

(2) Look at the shape of the construct dendrogram, and what this might suggest about the similarities and differences in your interviewee's construing.

(3) Identify element similarities and differences. For each cluster, follow leftwards to the relevant rows of ratings. Which elements have received similar ratings on these constructs, and which received very different ones?

(4) What does this mean? Discuss the implications with your interviewee.

(5) Find the highest % similarity score. Working with the separate construct % similarity scale, find the two adjacent constructs which have the highest % similarity score, follow the lines to the right until they meet at an apex of the V-shape, and draw a perpendicular line to the % similarity scale to read off the value. Find the next pair, note their score, and see whether they are a distinct cluster or form part of the same cluster as the previous pair.

(6) Examine the remaining scores. Continue this procedure, discussing the clusters and what they might mean with your interviewee.

Table 6.12 Example of cluster analysis procedure for constructs in Figure 6.2

1	Examine the constructs	All of the constructs have been reordered, with the exception of 'learns the new models quickly', 'could be more interested in after sales' and 'takes it all very seriously'. Constructs 1, 4, 6, and 5 have been reversed.
2	Examine the shape of the construct dendrogram	There's one distinct branch comprising 'takes it all very seriously' plus 'too forward in pushing a sale', and another rather broad branch comprising the remaining constructs.
3	Identify element similarities and differences	The ratings of all the elements on both 'takes a while to learn new features' and 'availability and choice knowledge poor' are very similar (97%), differing in only a single scale point in total. Is there substantial shared meaning between these two constructs? On the other hand, there is at least one scale point difference on many of the elements on the constructs 'overall less effective' and 'takes it all very seriously'.
4	What does this mean?	The obvious question to put to the interviewee would be as follows. 'Has it ever struck you that, whenever you think of a salesperson as able to "learn the new models quickly", you also see them as having a "good awareness of sizes"; and whenever you see them as "being slow to learn", you also characterise them as having insufficient "knowledge of availability and choice"?'
5	Find the highest % similarity score	In fact, those two constructs are matched at 96%, and this would be something to point out to the interviewee as part of that previous question. Your own impression suggests that 'learning the new models quickly' *includes* learning about which sizes are in stock, but you'd want to check that with the interviewee.
6	Examine the remaining scores	With one exception, there isn't another obvious construct cluster to explore. The obvious one arises from the supplied effectiveness construct. The highest similarity score is with the extent to which a salesperson is good at after sales enquiries, and it would be useful to point this out. 'Your closest construct to overall effectiveness is whether an employee handles after sales well; in fact, your ratings are matched at 88% on these two constructs. Do you tend to assess sales effectiveness in terms of after sales in particular?' And so on.

If you have followed this procedure with Figure 6.2, the kinds of conclusions you would have arrived at are shown in Tables 6.11 and 6.12.

A few points are worth noting. Some of the findings from your cluster analysis are the same as those you made when doing the simple analyses of elements and constructs; thus, in following step 4 of the construct procedure in Section 6.1.2, you discovered that 'learns the new models quickly', versus 'takes a while to learn the features of new lines' has a very small sum of differences with 'aware of size' versus 'availability and choice knowledge poor'. This, of course, anticipated what step 4 in Table 6.12 has just told you in the cluster analysis. And so it should: the structure of meaning is the same regardless of whether a simple structure inspection or a cluster analysis is carried out.

In that sense, the two procedures are in practical terms identical. If you don't have a computer, the hand analysis involved in the simple analysis will give you almost as much information as a cluster analysis. However, there's one difference. It would have taken you a little while to identify the similarity between these two constructs without the cluster analysis, since the ratings on these two constructs, numbers 1 and 4, are cluttered up by the intervening ratings on constructs 2 and 3. You'd only have been sure of the high match if you'd systematically computed all the sums of differences.

And some of the similarities would have been almost invisible. There's a very high match, over 90%, between

> Availability and choice   –   Awareness of size
> knowledge poor

and

> Could be more interested in   –   After sales well handled
> after sales

as you can see immediately from the cluster-analysed grid; the same information was there in the original grid, but since the relationship was recorded as

> Could be more interested in   –   After sales well handled
> after sales

and

> Awareness of size   –   Availability and choice
> knowledge poor

it wasn't at all evident, requiring reversal to become obvious. It is this 'at-a-glance' obviousness of a cluster analysis which makes this particular analysis technique so useful.

However, this clarity is only possible with respect to *adjacent* elements in the elements analysis, and *adjacent* constructs in the construct analysis. If you know that two adjacent constructs in a cluster analysis are matched at 85%, all you know about the next construct which is *non-adjacent* to either is that its match with either must be less than 85%, but the dendrogram doesn't indicate how much less. (Remember the rationale given in Section 6.2.1, and Figure 6.1? You shuffle the elements/constructs around until the *most similar* lie side by side. So the single-line % similarity scale in a dendrogram can only show you the value for adjacent elements. Or adjacent constructs, as the case may be.)

Fortunately, all construct-analysis computations have to do what you did in Section 6.1 when you calculated simple relationships, and provided tables of sums of differences between elements, and between constructs, together with the corresponding tables of % similarity scores between elements, and between constructs. These tables are part of the cluster-analysis computation procedure. So any cluster-analysis software package will provide you with these tables, too, as part of its output, in addition to the focused grid and the dendrograms for adjacent items. So you can discover the % similarity score between *any* pair of elements or constructs, as required.

6.3 PRINCIPAL COMPONENTS ANALYSIS

As in the previous section, my purpose is to provide you with an intuitive rationale for the way in which principal components analysis works, just sufficient for you to use appropriate software packages safely and without over- or misinterpretation. I then suggest a procedure to follow when you do this interpretation.

6.3.1 Rationale for Principal Components Analysis

Glance at Table 6.13. Scan the columns from top to bottom, as if they were element ratings in a grid. Then run your eye along the rows from left to right, as if they were construct ratings. What do you notice about them?

Looking Downwards. Not a lot is going on here. The ratings don't change much going from top to bottom, except in the two rightmost columns: 4 and 4 followed by 2s and a 1; 5 and 5 followed by 1s and 2s. There's more variability in the numbers in these last two columns.

Table 6.13 Just some numbers

1	2	3	3	4	5
2	3	3	3	4	5
1	2	3	3	2	1
1	2	2	2	2	1
2	2	3	3	2	2
1	1	2	2	1	1

Looking Across. There's lots going on here.

- Firstly, can you see how the values increase from left to right in the first row and the second? Next, notice how the values increase, then decrease again, as you go from left to right, in the third, fourth, fifth, and sixth rows. The first two rows follow one kind of pattern, while the last four rows follow a different pattern.

- Something else to notice, too, is that the ratings are more varied in the first two rows (they take values ranging across the full width of our conventional 5-point scale in the first row, and vary from 2 to 5 in the second). In contrast, there's less variability in the last four rows, with ratings taking values of 1, 2, or 3 only.

There seem to be two *distinct patterns* of variability in this grid: two different ways in which the values of the ratings vary.

Principal components analysis works by looking at the variability (technically, the 'variance') in figures arranged in a table like Table 6.13. It identifies distinct patterns of variability, following procedures which

- work out the *extent* to which the ratings in each row of the table are similar to each other (using the correlation between each row and each other row), to identify each distinct pattern

- work in a way which attributes as much as possible of the total variability to each distinct pattern, using as few different patterns as possible.

The process is iterative. Firstly, the pattern which accounts for the largest amount of variability is identified, reported, and removed – think of it as being subtracted from the original table – set aside as it were. The next pattern is identified likewise, and so on, until all of the variability has been accounted for. These patterns of variability are called 'components'.

And there seem to be two of them in our example in Table 6.13. Let's call the first one, which accounts for the kind of variability we see in rows 1 and 2, 'component 1'; and the other, which accounts for most of the remaining variability, 'component 2'. (There are, in fact, two more components, but the amount of variability they account for is tiny, as you can see in Table 6.14. This was obtained by running Table 6.13 through a grid-analysis package.) Principal components analysis packages always provide a variance table like this one. This is useful, but the output which chiefly concerns us consists of information about these patterns of variability in the form of a series of graphs which plot the way in which the columns and rows (or, in our case, the elements and the constructs) are arranged with respect to the principal components. Figure 6.3 shows a graph of this kind.

Table 6.14 Percentage of variance accounted for by each component of Table 6.13

Component 1	Component 2	Component 3	Component 4
64.84	30.67	4.22	0.27

Two dotted lines *stand for* the first two components; by convention, the horizontal line represents the first component and the vertical line the second. They're vertical and horizontal, set at right angles to each other, because they represent maximally distinct patterns in the data. The constructs are plotted as straight lines whose angle with respect to each component reflects the extent to which the construct is *represented by* the component, and whose length reflects the amount of variance in the ratings on that construct.

In other words, each component is a statistical invention, whose purpose is to represent, or stand for, as straightforwardly as possible, one of the different patterns in the grid. The whole thing represents, in graphical terms, the intuitive feeling we had when we looked at Table 6.13 and thought we recognised two distinct patterns of variability – two sets of ratings with rather differing variances. And as you can see in Figure 6.3, there are indeed two groupings of lines representing constructs. Constructs A and B lie close to the horizontal component line, which represents the pattern of variance which we recognised in the first two rows of Table 6.13; constructs C, D, E, and F, lie very close to the vertical line reflecting the pattern of variance in the bottom four rows of Table 6.13.

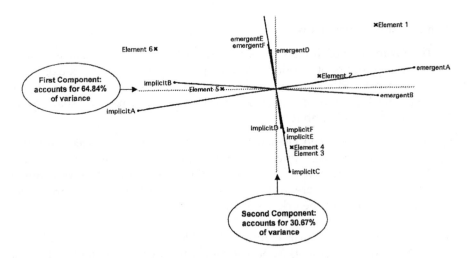

Figure 6.3 Principal components analysis graph for the data in Table 6.13

Because each component 'stands for' several constructs, the *elements* can be positioned along each component, in place of their original position along each construct; and there they are, plotted in Figure 6.3.

Now, because the resulting plot is a graphical representation, in which the lengths of lines and the positions of points reflect the original ratings – because the whole graph is a picture of patterns of similarity – *distances matter* and can be meaningfully interpreted.

Constructs and Components

(a) The angle between any two construct lines reflects the extent to which the ratings of elements on those constructs are correlated: the smaller the angle, the more similar the ratings.

(b) The angle between a group of construct lines and the lines representing the components reflects the extent to which the component can be taken to represent the grouping of constructs in question: the smaller the angle, the greater the extent.

In Figure 6.3, for example, the first (horizontal) component represents construct A and construct B very well; it represents the remaining constructs very poorly. The vertical component, on the other hand, stands for constructs C, D, E, and F very well (they form a tight 'fan' angled very closely to the vertical component).

Elements and Components

(a) The position of each element with respect to each component is exactly like the position of a point on a graph: so far along the x-axis (first component) and so far up or down the y-axis (second component). Of itself, this doesn't mean a lot; but what is enormously useful is that it gives us a way of talking about:

(b) Relationships between elements – that is, the distance between any two elements reflects the ratings each element received on all the constructs. Any two elements which are close together in the graph received similar ratings, any which are printed far apart would tend to show rather different ratings in the original grid.

Look at the third and fourth columns in Table 6.13. They received *identical ratings*. Now look at elements 3 and 4 in Figure 6.3: they are plotted in the *same position* on the graph (in fact, I had to move the 'element 3' label in preparing

Figure 6.3, since the computer printout from which this figure was prepared printed it directly on top of the 'element 4' label).

This property of a principal components analysis is particularly useful when the differences between elements carry special meaning for us; for example, when we want to compare how closely we construe 'myself as I am' and 'myself as I wish to be'; any element and an 'ideal' supplied element; and so on. We ask how far away from each other the two elements are, in the plot; we draw inferences from what might need to change if 'myself as I am' were to become more like 'myself as I wish to be'. Along which constructs would movement have to occur? That is, on which constructs would the ratings have to be different for 'myself as I am' to move towards 'myself as I wish to be'?

Finally, you need to know that a principal components analysis provides you with plots showing the relationship between *all* the components, not just the first two. You would examine these using the same approach as you used in addressing Figure 6.3. As a rule of thumb, you ought to examine the plots for all of the components that, between them, account for 80% of the variance. Remember that distances matter, so that the horizontal and vertical components within any graph are 'to scale', so far as variance goes.

Get a feeling for principal components by doing Exercise 6.6.

6.3.2 Procedure for Interpretation of Principal Components Analysis

The preceding rationale has been rather abstract. In Exercise 6.6, you were looking at patterns in numbers, without knowing just what those numbers stand for. No element names, just labels 1 to 6; no idea of what meanings the constructs carry, just the blank and austere construct labels, each end of constructs A to F. (Though, hopefully, things warmed up a little for you when you addressed the last question of the exercise.)

Brr! You, the reader, have my sympathy! And you also have my congratulations. What you've done is a necessary first step in understanding a principal components analysis plot, but it's the only step which is statistically faithful to the ratings provided by your interviewee.

As soon as you start interpreting the principal components analysis any further

• by looking at what the actual elements are and where they lie with respect to the principal components

- by looking at how the constructs are grouped and which components seem to underlie them,

(all of which are essential if you're to get the benefits of the analysis), you move away from the direct meaning offered to you by the interviewee, and into a realm in which your own interpretations condition, influence, and possibly distort the information in the original grid.

This becomes particularly important when you try to interpret the principal components in terms of the constructs. What sort of component 'underlies' the constructs? This sort of question is often resolved by trying to find a name for the component: a label which reflects the meaning in common between the constructs which lie closest to that component – as at step 3 in the procedure below. And that act of naming reflects your own judgement.

Like any complex analysis, such as the cluster analysis we examined in Section 6.2, principal components analysis requires you to make assumptions when you interpret the original grid. Unlike cluster analysis, though, these assumptions are less visible. They are less easily described to your interviewee in terms of comfortable analogies like 'cutting up the grid with a pair of scissors', and, unless the interviewee has some grounding in statistics, your interpretations take on the flavour of 'because I, the expert, say so'. When this happens, you have less scope for negotiating a meaning with your interviewee (and especially, for checking your understanding of the interviewee), and, accordingly, it's worth being rather cautious in the interpretations you make using this analysis procedure. Be careful how you name the components. Do so collaboratively if the interviewee understands the procedure. Don't play the guru.

Point taken. And the following procedural guide seeks to take these comments into account.

Let's do it by moving right away from abstraction and looking at a familiar grid. This is the one shown in Table 6.4, which we cluster-analysed in Section 6.2 with the results which appeared as Figure 6.2. We know a lot about it already, which will help us to make sense of it using the present analysis. The original grid is on the left, the table of variance accounted for on the right, and the plot of the first two principal components at the lower right.

As always, the procedure starts with a familiarisation with the original grid: a process analysis and the first three steps of an eyeball analysis. (1. What is the interviewee thinking about? 2. How has the interviewee represented the topic? and 3. How does s/he think?, as outlined in Section 5.3.2.)

Quite so. To avoid excessive overinterpretation, stick to the original grid as your bedrock; that means reminding yourself of what the interviewee actually said, and the circumstances in which s/he said it!

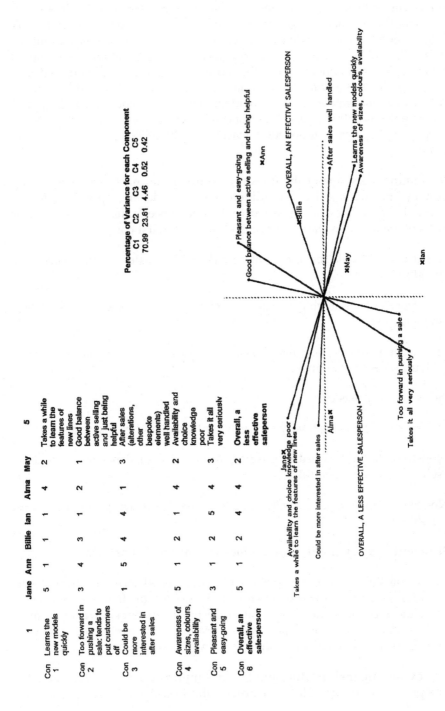

1		Jane	Ann	Billie	Ian	Alma	May	5
Con 1	Learns the new models quickly	5	1	1	1	4	2	Takes a while to learn the features of new lines
Con 2	Too forward in pushing a sale: tends to put customers off	3	4	3	1	2	1	Good balance between active selling and just being helpful
Con 3	Could be more interested in after sales	1	5	4	4	1	3	After sales (alterations, other bespoke elements) well handled
Con 4	Awareness of sizes, colours, availability	5	1	2	1	4	2	Availability and choice knowledge poor
Con 5	Pleasant and easy-going	3	1	2	5	4	3	Takes it all very seriously
Con 6	Overall, an effective salesperson	5	1	2	4	4	2	Overall, a less effective salesperson

Percentage of Variance for each Component

C1	C2	C3	C4	C5
70.99	23.61	4.46	0.52	0.42

Figure 6.4 Store manager's grid, variance accounted for, and plot of first two components

(1) Determine how many components you'll need to work with. How many components in the percentage variance table of Figure 6.4 do you need to look at, to cover 80% of the variance? Here, the first two components account for $70.99 + 23.62 = 94\%$ of the variance, so you can safely rely on just the one plot: that of the first component against the second. (If you'd decided you needed to look at the first three principal components, you'd need to work with the other plots which the software has provided: the plot of component 1 against component 2 as in this case, but also of component 1 against component 3, and component 2 against component 3, teasing out the relationships for each plot as follows.)

(2) Examine the shape of the lines representing the constructs: how tightly are they spread? Are they well differentiated, or do they spread evenly all round the plot like the spokes of a bicycle wheel? Here, the constructs differentiate into two sheaves or fans of lines. The first consists of

- construct 3, 'could be more interested in after sales – after sales well handled'

- construct 1, 'takes a while to learn the features of new lines – learns the new models quickly'

- construct 4, 'availability and choice knowledge poor – awareness of sizes, colours, and availability'.

The second consists of

- construct 5, 'takes it all very seriously – pleasant and easy-going'

- construct 2, 'too forward in pushing a sale – good balance between active selling and being helpful'.

(Notice how the supplied 'overall effectiveness' construct lies between these two sheaves.)

(3) Identify any similarities in the meaning of these constructs:

- **by inspection**: does there appear to be any shared meaning? You're very tentatively 'naming the components'. In Figure 6.4, the first grouping seems to relate to product knowledge and interest in using that knowledge to make a complete sale, while the second grouping appears to describe the salesperson's personal style while dealing with a customer.

- **by examining their relationship to any supplied construct** which might be helpful in this respect. Here, construct 6, the 'overall effectiveness' construct, aligns neither with the first grouping nor the second. No single construct or group of constructs is particularly associated with effectiveness in a well-defined way. In fact, you'd be tempted to argue, from the position of the 'overall effectiveness' construct, lying between the two groupings, that being an effective salesperson depends neither on product knowledge nor on personal style alone, but more or less equally on both.

(4) Note the position of any meaningful groupings with respect to the two principal components: the vertical axis and the horizontal axis. So far, we've almost ignored the components themselves, but they tell us something very important. You'll recall that components are derived sequentially, and in a way which seeks to maximise their independence. So any sheaves or groupings of constructs which lie near to one of the principal component axes can be interpreted as, *in some sense*, independent of sheaves or groupings which lie near to the other principal component axis. Can you find a meaning for the groups of constructs based on this characteristic of the analysis?

In our own case, the position of the 'product knowledge' grouping near to the first principal component, and the 'style with customers' grouping near to the second, suggests that these are indeed two independent sets of constructs.

The psychologist might label this a 'cognitive versus affective' distinction, while the trainer might think of this as indicative of two distinct sets of skills to be learnt. A job analyst might view it as a statement about the structure of the competency framework that pertains to this job, while someone interested in knowledge management would view it as a statement reflecting the interviewee's experience and expertise in running a fashion section of the department store.

It follows that you can't decide, on the information present in the grid, which of these is in any way definitive! That depends on your purpose, and the context in which the grid interview was conducted. If you're doing this grid analysis in a research context as part of a dissertation, your supervisor will be asking you about the analytic framework which underlies your use of the repertory grid as a research technique! (Remember constructive alternativism?!)

Finally, be careful about overinterpretation. The two groups don't sit squarely on top of their components; they're rotated through some 20 degrees clockwise. This suggests that whatever these components are, while they're statistically independent of each other (they're plotted at right angles), their meaning isn't completely separate. (There are further procedures in multivariate statistics which might possibly clarify this, but these lie beyond the scope of this guide.)

(5) Check your interpretations with the interviewee. *Resist the temptation to pronounce about them.* For, example, if you'd decided in Figure 6.4 that the first principal component is a 'product knowledge and interest' component and the second is a 'customer relations' component, do *not* tell the interviewee that that's what they are. All you've done is to construe the interviewee's construing, and until you check it out, it has the status of a useful fiction, regardless of the impressive statistical manipulations on which it's based. Instead, explore the links which you feel you've identified between the constructs by asking questions to check whether those links make sense *to the interviewee*.

> Exactly. You'll notice that we've both ganged up on you to reinforce the point. A repertory grid isn't a horoscope or a psychometric test, both of which depend on something resembling a priest-and-peasant relationship between expert interviewer and client. If your interview technique has been a good one, your interviewee will be hanging on your every word, you'll have noticed, and the temptation might be there! But remember that the whole point of the interview is to work *collaboratively*, and that's as important in the analysis as in the original construct elicitation.

Useful questions at this point might look like the following (with reference to Figure 6.4):

- 'D'you see those three lines labelled "availability and choice knowledge poor"; "takes a while to learn the features of new lines"; "could be more interested in after sales"? They hang together so they look like they have something in common. How do they differ from the other two ("takes it all very seriously" and "too forward in pushing a sale")? What is each set saying about sales staff?'

- 'Ann and Billie are overall the most effective; that's how you rated them originally. And d'you see where they lie along the line marked "overall a less effective salesperson" and "overall an effective salesperson"? Jane, on the other hand, is a long way away from them on the graph. What would need to change to move her along closer to Billie and Ann?'

This would be to encourage the interviewee to recognise that the position along each of the lines representing constructs is related to the original ratings, and that 'movement along' each of the lines is a way of interpreting the need for change. One sort of answer to this last question, for example, might be, 'Well, she'd need to improve her after sales, and show a lot more interest in learning the various product lines. That's more of an issue than getting her to be relaxed and pleasant with the customers.'

This kind of exploration is particularly useful if you are trying to make the interviewee's tacit knowledge about the job explicit, asking her to think about the way she views job expertise in a reflective way.

Convey your wisdoms and insights gently, check them, and build on them! This can sometimes be difficult to do, since principal components analysis does require some complicated statistical knowledge which it's difficult to share neatly and elegantly with the other person in the course of your interview. That's why my own choice of analysis technique is cluster analysis as described in Section 6.2 above: the inferences it affords are more easily explained to people who don't have a grounding in statistics.

6.4 CONCLUDING IMAGES

You'll have noticed that the results of both techniques, cluster analysis and principal components analysis, are compatible with each other in the examples we've looked at. And so they should be. They're simply two different ways of doing the same thing, which is to say something about the relationships between the ratings in the grid, and thereby to suggest something about the way in which the elements and constructs are structured in the system the interviewee uses to make sense of the topic in question.

I find the following analogy helpful. Think of the elements of a grid as being like stars in the night sky (see Figure 6.5). You can make statements about the position of the stars by pointing out that they group into constellations. That's like a cluster analysis. Or you could, as an alternative, describe the same position with reference to two lines at right angles to each other which you mentally project onto the heavens. This is exactly what astronomers do, and the lines in question are called the *vernal equinox* and the *celestial equator*. The position of a star is then given in terms of its *right ascension* and its *declination*, which are units 'along' these lines. And that's like a principal components analysis. (Well, -ish. Not quite as close an analogy, as any statistician will tell you. Or maybe they're both rather baggy similes. But never mind, they get us away from numbers for a moment of relaxed and fuzzy contemplation.)

Perhaps the main point to remember is that both constellations and the vernal equinox/celestial equator are useful inventions. Depending on rather more complex social agreements about observational and analytic conventions than those which underlie the simple initial observation of the stars themselves, they don't exist in quite the same way that the stars do. They exist in the minds of the beholders, as they gaze at the night sky and make sense of the grand sweep of the heavens. So it is with clusters and principal components, as ways of understanding the relationships between elements and constructs which the interviewee has presented.

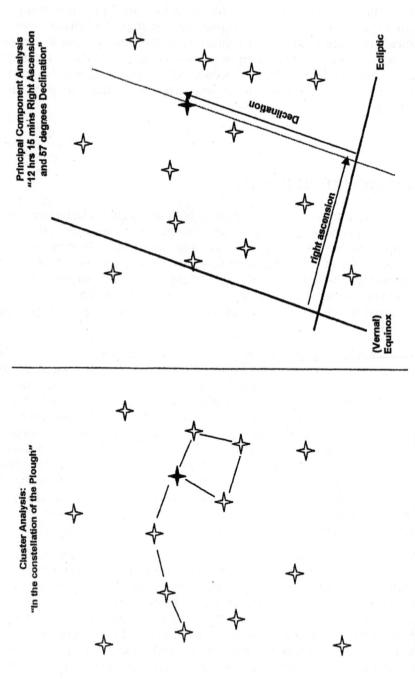

Figure 6.5 Two systems for showing star positions

THINGS TO DO

Exercise 6.1 Relationships Among Elements

(a) Using Table 6.15, work out the sums of differences for all the element pairings in the grid. (Just follow steps 1 to 4 in Section 6.1.1.) Write in the sums of differences in the appropriate row and column of the bottom half of the table (so, for example, the sum of differences for element T1 compared to element T2 is 18, and this value has been written down for you, in the 'T1 against' row and the 'T2' column of the bottom half of the table).

(b) Confirm for yourself that the most similarly rated elements are T1 and T3 (smallest sum of differences), and that the least similar elements are T1 and T4 (largest sum of differences), as I asserted in discussing step 4 of the procedure above.

(c) Which of the trainers does the interviewee construe most similarly to her- (for the sake of argument) self?

Table 6.15 An extract from a grid interview with a young training officer on 'trainers I have known', together with element difference scores

1	T1	T2	T3	T4	Self	5
Prepares thoroughly	5	2	5	3	2	Seat-of-pants speaker
Energetic, moves about	1	2	1	5	1	Just stands there stolidly
Intellectual	3	1	3	5	2	Pedestrian
Language articulate, precise, and concise	5	1	4	2	3	Language shambolic, appeals to intuition
Makes it seem so obvious and clear	3	1	2	5	3	You have to work to understand his point
Tells jokes	1	5	2	4	3	Takes it all very seriously
Overall, enjoyed his courses	1	3	2	5	2	Overall, didn't enjoy his courses

Simple element analysis	T1	T2	T3	T4	Self

Sums of differences

		T1	T2	T3	T4	Self
T1 against	–		18			
T2 against		–				
T3 against			–			
T4 against				–		
Self against					–	

Now check your answers in Appendix 1.6.

Exercise 6.2 A Simple Decision Task

You have won a modest prize in the national lottery and decide to buy a new computer in the £1000–£1500 price range. You look through the usual magazines and do a quick grid while you're doing so, to help yourself to focus systematically on the factors mentioned there.

(a) When you've finished this, you realise that you can boil all this down to a simple choice by adding a 'my ideal computer should...' column to the grid. You do a simple element relationship check (do it now, using Table 6.16!) and decide to purchase the computer whose ratings are closest to the ideal. Looking at the following extract from the grid in question, which should you buy?

Table 6.16 An extract from a grid on 'Computers I might buy', together with element difference scores

| | | Mac | iMac | | | |
1	PC	G3	G4	eMac	Ideal	5
Looks boxy and 'standard'	1	2	5	4	5	The looks are to die for
Large range of software	1	2	4	2	1	Smaller range of software
Slow performer	1	3	5	2	5	Fast
Easy to set up	5	1	1	2	1	Difficult to set up
Good build quality	5	2	1	3	1	Flimsy build
Easy to upgrade	2	3	1	1	1	Upgrade is a dealer job
Difficult to move	1	1	4	5	5	Transportable

Simple element analysis

| | | Mac | iMac | | |
	PC	G3	G4	eMac	Ideal
Sums of differences					
PC against	–				
Mac G3 against		–			
iMac G4 against			–		
eMac against				–	
Ideal against					–

(b) What are the main reasons why the least favoured computer isn't chosen? (Find the constructs which show the largest differences when the computer in question is compared to the ideal.)

In this example, I suppose that the outcome is clear. But step through the calculations anyway, writing the sums of differences into the lower half of the table, to practise what you'd need to do in a more realistic situation of, perhaps, 10 or 15 alternatives (elements) to choose from, and 8 to 15 or so constructs used to think about those alternatives

Check your answer against Appendix 1.7.

Exercise 6.3 Turning Element Differences into % Similarities

This gives you more practice in thinking about element differences as % similarities. Look at the sums of differences you calculated in Exercise 6.2 (Table 6.16). Better still, work with the correct values for that exercise, given in Appendix 1.7.

(a) Look at each entry in the lower half of Table A1.4 in Appendix 1.7 (the section headed 'Simple element analysis'). Apply the formula to each sum of element difference:

$$\% \text{ element similarity} = 100 - \{[SD/(LR - 1)] \times 100\}$$

(b) Check each result by looking it up in Appendix 1.8. (If the check shows that your calculation is wrong, you've probably worked out the formula in the wrong order. Go back to step 7 in Section 6.1.1 and follow the bullet points for expressing a sum of differences as a percentage, step by step.)

(c) Is the element which shows the least difference from the Ideal in Table 6.16, the same one that has the highest % similarity score?

Your final table should look like Table A1.5 in Appendix 1.8.

When you're finished, congratulations! You know all there is to know (for the time being) about element relationship calculations.

Now go on to Section 6.1.2 on construct relationships.

Exercise 6.4 Relationships Among Constructs

Table 6.17, opposite, contains the same grid which you used in Exercise 6.2: the decision exercise in which you decided which make and model of computer came closest to your ideal. You decided *what* you wanted; now, is there anything interesting about *how* you want things? (computers, at any rate).

(a) Work out the sums of differences between C1 and C2, C1 and C3, C1 and C4, etc., and then C2 and C3, C2 and C4, etc., filling in the values in the upper right of the table. The first line (relationships between construct 1 and the remainder) has been done for you. Check that you agree.

(b) Now reverse the ratings, construct by construct, and work out the sums of differences between C1 reversed and C2 *unreversed*; C1 reversed and C3 *unreversed*; C1 reversed and C4 *unreversed*, etc. Then go on to C2 reversed and C3 *unreversed*; C2 reversed and C3 *unreversed*, etc., to the end. Fill in the results in the bottom left of the analysis half of the table. Again, the sums of differences for construct 1 reversed and the remainder unreversed have been done for you.

(c) Which two constructs are the most highly matched? (Check the sums of differences you wrote into the unreversed *and* the reversed parts of the table!)

When you've finished, check your answers
against the table shown in Appendix 1.9.

Exercise 6.5 Turning Construct Differences into % Similarities

This won't take long: take each of the sums of differences in the right-hand side of Table 6.9, and turn them into % matching scores which you enter into the corresponding places in Table 6.10. You could use Appendix 4 to look up the values (using the column for six elements, since that's how many elements there are!); but do calculate some of the values, using the formula, by hand. Go on, it's good for the soul.

The answers are provided in Appendix 1.10.

Table 6.17 An extract from a grid on 'Computers I might buy', together with construct difference scores

		Mac		iMac					Simple construct analysis						
												UNREVERSED			
1	PC	G3	G4		eMac	Ideal	5		Against C1	Against C2	Against C3	Against C4	Against C5	Against C6	Against C7
C1 Looks boxy and 'standard'	1 (5)	2 (4)	5 (1)	4 (2)	5 (1)	5	The looks are to die for	R	–	7	3	15	13	13	3
C2 Large range of software	1	2	4	2	1	1	Smaller range of software	E	9	–					
C3 Slow performer	1	3	5	2	5	5	Fast	V	13		–				
C4 Easy to set up	5	1	1	2	1	1	Difficult to set up	E	3			–			
C5 Good build quality	5	2	1	3	1	1	Flimsy build	R	3				–		
C6 Easy to upgrade	2	3	1	1	1	1	Upgrade is a dealer job	E	5					–	
C7 Difficult to move	1	1	4	5	5	5	Transportable	D	17						–

Exercise 6.6 Finding Your Way Round a Principal Components Analysis Plot

(a) In Figure 6.3, which construct lies closest to the axis representing a principal component?

(b) Which construct shows the least variance along its component?

(c) Which construct shows the most?

(d) If element 6 represented myself, element 5 my partner, and element 3 my ideal self, which of us is closest to that ideal?

Check your answers in Appendix 1.11.

THINGS TO READ

If you didn't read it at the end of the previous chapter, now is the time for Jankowicz & Cooper (1982), as a good account of the ways in which relationships between elements, and relationships between constructs, are discussed between the interviewer and the interviewee in a counselling setting. If you have read the former work, then get hold of Mildred Shaw's *On Becoming a Personal Scientist* (London: Academic Press, 1980) and read that instead. It's a classic presentation of the cluster-analysis technique, and does an excellent job of computer-assisted analysis without losing sight of the basic rationale for simple relationships analysis that does not depend on computerisation but can, as you'll recall from Section 6.1, be done entirely by hand!

If you haven't done so already, now is the time to become better acquainted with one of the software packages mentioned at the start of this chapter. (I'm assuming that to make reasonable sense of Sections 6.2 and 6.3, you've already accessed and used some grid software.) Take a thorough look round the WEBGRID site at *http://tiger.cpsc.ucalgary.ca.1500/* (this is free software!). Or access one of the other, commercial packages listed in Scheer (2003).

CHAPTER 7

ANALYSING MORE THAN
ONE GRID

In the previous two chapters, we addressed the issues involved in analysing single grids, and provided opportunities to practise the techniques involved. In reflecting on the activity, you'll remember that, in Section 5.2, I emphasised that all knowledge is socially defined, and stressed the importance of being able to communicate your understanding of the interviewee's construing to other people. This becomes particularly important when you're dealing with several grids at a time.

If the grids consisted entirely of *supplied* constructs, and the constructs were identical across all the grids with just the ratings being different (see Section 4.2.7), you'd have no problem in analysing them. You'd treat each grid as a set of rating scales which just happen to have been printed close together; and you'd analyse the whole set as you would any set of rating scales. You'd work out the average rating in each cell of the grid across all the grids, or you might prefer to calculate the sum of the ranks and rank these sums – whatever you're accustomed to do with rating scales. But, to the extent that *different* constructs appear in the different grids (and, to my mind, that's much more interesting and, indeed, is the whole point of all this work with repertory grids!), the results would be meaningless.

So how can you aggregate the different meanings presented? The constructs are all different, having been elicited rather than supplied! Somehow, you have to summarise the various meanings present in all the grids for the sample as a whole; but, at the same time, you need to preserve as many of the different interviewees' personal meanings as possible.

We assume, first of all, for the sake of simplicity, that the elements are identical for all of the respondents, or have been elicited by using identical elicitation categories (see Section 3.2.2 and Table 3.1). That leaves us free to deal with the differing constructs, classifying the different types of constructs used by all the interviewees.

Content analysis is the technique in question. A variety of different approaches is available to you, and the exact approach you take depends on two distinct factors: how you intend to put the information together, which is a matter of **design**, and the number of grids you have to deal with, which is a matter of **sample size**.

7.1 THE NATURE OF THE PROBLEM

Let's tackle the issue of sample size first of all: the number of respondents whose grids you wish to aggregate.

7.1.1 Sample Size

You may be doing an inventory of the differing views of teachers in a rural primary school, interviewing them about the different ways they have of maintaining classroom control. Since there are only four teachers in the school, you plan to describe each of the four grids in order, using the techniques described in Chapters 5 and 6. So long as you're systematic about it, sign-posting what you're doing, providing bulleted summaries, and perhaps using a standard framework within which you can indicate similarities and differences between the various grids, you'll be able to report all the relevant information in a way which is sensible and easily digested by your readers.

This approach is very straightforward. In each case, you work through the same set of analysis techniques chosen from Chapters 5 and 6. What you do with one grid, you do with the others. Then, if it makes sense, you compare the main points of information from each grid with each other grid. You'll find yourself comparing and contrasting, and perhaps drawing inferences from the interviewee's individual background and experience, to cast light on the ways in which they construe similarly, and differently, to the other people in the sample. Fine!

Suppose, however, that your audit covered all 50 teachers employed in a comprehensive school. What then? Making sense of more than three or four grids at a time is rather more complicated. The amount of information you're dealing with grows exponentially with each new interviewee (because at some point you're probably making comparisons among *all* the interviewees), and your reader ends up being unable to see the wood for the trees well before the total of 50 people has been reached!

It looks as though you'll need to sacrifice some detail in *each* of the grids, while recognising trends that are common to *all* of them. A content analysis will do just that, summarising the different meanings in the interviewees' grids by categorising them, counting the similarities and differences within each category.

Section 7.2 provides you with a generic approach to content analysis, which drops some of the information in all of the grids in the interests of clarity, while concentrating on the essentials which you wish to communicate as representative of the sample of interviewees as a whole.

Section 7.3 provides a variant of content analysis suited to samples of around 15 people and over, which makes use of a substantial proportion of the information present in the whole sample of grids while remaining true to its individual provenance. A running example is used to illustrate the procedure.

In both situations, your unit of analysis is not the individual grid, but the individual construct.

7.1.2 Research Design

In this context, design is the carefully planned 'arrangement of conditions for analysis and collection of data in a manner that aims to combine relevance to the research purpose with economy of procedure' (Selltiz et al., 1981).

In any situation, do you want to know whether your male interviewees construe the topic differently to the females? Then, whatever else you do when you categorise the constructs, you're going to need to keep the males' constructs separate from the females'.

Or, suppose you're working with a company's marketing and sales department, and you suspect that your sales staff – who have direct contact with the customers – think about the products and the discounts they can give on sales differently from the staff back in the office. Then you'll have to aggregate the constructs separately for the two groups (sales force and non-sales force) and see what differences there might be.

You're essentially grouping your respondents according to one or more variables of interest, and then seeing how each separate group construed the topic in question. This means that you have to label, code, or otherwise identify each interviewee's constructs as you elicit them, so that you can identify which subgroup they belong to during the content analysis. It also means that you need to think through how you intend to analyse the information in the grids as you put the individual grids together, and this needs *doing in advance* – before you start on the interviews, and not after!

We'll look at how to do a generic content analysis in Section 7.2, and then see how subgroups can be handled.

Finally, the systematic use of a supplied, 'overall assessment' construct with the full sample of respondents lies at the heart of the procedure presented in Section 7.3. It is this matching of ratings on this supplied construct with all the elicited constructs which makes it possible to make use of a substantial proportion of the personal information in each of the grids being content-analysed.

7.2 GENERIC APPROACHES TO CONTENT ANALYSIS

Content analysis is a technique in which the constructs of all the interviewees are pooled, and categorised according to the meanings they express. The categories are derived either from the constructs themselves, by looking at them systematically and identifying the various themes they express ('bootstrapping'), or from a standard category system which you have encountered in the literature, or which stems from some theory with which you're working.

7.2.1 Bootstrapping Techniques

By this is meant any approach in which a category system is developed on the hoof, in the course of categorising the items being dealt with. Holsti's original account (Holsti, 1968) is definitive and should be referred to for background information about content analysis in general social research; Neuendorf's work (2002) looks set to replace Holsti in due course. The following core procedure summarises the basics in as much detail as you require.

Firstly, a decision is taken on what constitutes the *content unit*, or basic unit of analysis. What's the basic unit being categorised: how large or small should the basic idea be? And less obviously but equally important, the *context unit*: where should the basic idea be located: should we scan the phrase, the sentence, and the paragraph in a search for it? Should we stick to the same context unit, such as the sentence, throughout, or can we use the sentence at times, and a whole paragraph at other times ('This sentence is basically about X'; 'These next few sentences are basically padding, but I can see that the whole paragraph is about Y')?

You'll be relieved to hear that when you content-analyse a repertory grid, these questions have already been resolved for you during construct elicitation. Each construct is your basic unit of analysis and, in Holsti's terms, the construct is both the content unit and the context unit. In other words, each and every construct is regarded as expressing a single unit of meaning. Of course!

The Core-Categorisation Procedure

Each item being categorised is compared with the others, and then:

(1) **If an item is in some way like the first item, the two are placed together under a single category created for them at that very moment.**

(2) **If an item is different to the first item, they're put into separate categories.**

(3) **The remaining items are compared with each of the categories and allocated to the appropriate one if an appropriate category exists.**

(4) **A new category is created if required; when a new category is created, the possibility that existing categories need to be redefined (combined or broken up, with their items reallocated accordingly) is considered and effected as necessary.**

(5) **This process continues until all the items have been classified.**

(6) However, a small number are usually unclassifiable without creating categories of just one item, which would be pointless, so **all unclassifiable items are placed in a single category labelled 'miscellaneous'.**

(7) If more than 5% of the total are classified as miscellaneous, consider redefining one or more existing categories so that, at the end, **no more than 5% of the total are categorised as 'miscellaneous'.**

Now, with one proviso, this caters for our first need. By recognising similarities and dissimilarities in the interviewees' items as they specified them, we've aggregated the meanings in the whole sample while classifying some individual meanings as similar, and others as different. We've accommodated differences in meaning and intention on the part of individual interviewees. (We have, however, lost a lot of information, for none of the *ratings* have been taken into account. We'll see that Section 7.3 deals with this difficulty.)

The proviso is obvious. The categories we have devised are simply our own opinion. But your category system is simply your own way of construing your interviewees' constructs: other people might not see the same kinds of meaning in the constructs, and might disagree! Yet the whole point of this chapter, you'll recall, is to make statements which communicate meanings effectively to other people. Something's wrong if we can't agree on the category to which a particular construct belongs.

To guard against this problem, every content analysis needs to incorporate a reliability check. This is a procedure which ensures that (though one has every right to a private interpretation – remember Section 5.3?) the category system shouldn't be wildly idiosyncratic, if it is to make sense to other people. There's more on this later, in the section on reliability.

> Don't forget that there are several different forms of reliability. Hill (1995: 105–106) reminds us that in content-analysis terms, three kinds exist. Firstly, there is *stability*, the extent to which the results of a content analysis are invariant over time. Are your category definitions robust enough that, if you were to repeat the core procedure all over again, you would end up with the same categories, and within the same constructs under each category? After all, you're supposed to be recognising similarities in meaning in a set of constructs. So long as you're working with that particular set, the meaning you recognise should be the same on both occasions.
>
> Secondly, there is *reproducibility*, the extent to which other people make the same sense of the constructs as you do. If meaning is socially defined, if you are to avoid laying your own idiosyncracies onto the data, your content analysis needs to be reproducible.
>
> Finally, there is sheer *accuracy*. How consistently are you applying your category definitions, once you have fixed them as a standard to aim at?
>
> In practice, it is sometimes difficult to distinguish between these three sources of unreliability; however, you will notice as you use the procedures outlined below that all three confront you as you make decisions about category definitions, and about the allocation of constructs to categories. The procedures described have been devised to reduce unreliability under all three headings.

This is all a little abstract. Let's pin it all down. Firstly, what *are* the items we're talking about? In fact, the generic procedure can be applied to either elements or constructs, though usually it's the latter. Thus, a discussion of the *elements* provided by all the interviewees in a group, getting the group members to categorise them themselves by means of the procedure outlined above, is often a good way of getting people to examine, debate, and challenge their ideas about the topic, particularly in a training setting (see Section 9.2.1, step 2 of the partnering procedure outlined there, for an example of this activity in a personal change setting).

For general research purposes, though, it's the *constructs* which are the items being categorised, and the remainder of this chapter will deal with construct content analysis only. First, let's look at the generic procedure, and then deal with the matter of reliability.

The Generic Content-Analysis Procedure

(1) Identify the categories.

(2) Allocate the constructs to the categories following the core procedural steps 1 to 7 above. You'll notice that this results in a set of categories which are mutually exclusive, and completely exhaustive: all your constructs are accounted for. A convenient way of doing this is to transcribe each construct from all the grids onto its own file card, coding the card to identify which interviewee provided the individual construct, and which of his/her constructs it is, in order of appearance in that interviewee's grid. (Thus, the code 5.3 would indicate that the construct in question was the third construct in the fifth interviewee's grid.)

Now go through steps 1 to 7 above, placing the cards into heaps, each heap constituting a different category. If you lay all the cards out on a large table, you can see what you're doing, and shuffle cards around as you identify categories, allocate cards to them, change your mind and create new categories, and so on.

(3) Tabulate the result. In other words, record which constructs have been allocated to which categories. On a large sheet of paper (flip-chart paper, especially if it has been ruled as graph paper, is ideal), create a set of rows, one for each category. Create a column on the left, and in it, label each row with its category name. Now create a new column and use it to record a short definition of that category. In a third column, record the code numbers of all the constructs that you allocated to that category.

(4) Establish the reliability of the category system (ignore this for the moment; see the discussion below).

(5) Summarise the table; first, the meaning of the category headings. What kinds of categories are these? What sorts of constructs have we here? Use the column 2 information to report on the distinct meanings available in the whole set of constructs.

(6) Summarise the table: next, find examples of each category heading. Are there constructs under each category which stand for or exemplify that category particularly well? Are there perhaps several such constructs, each summarising a different aspect of the category? Highlight the code numbers of these constructs among the list in column 3. You'll want to remember these and quote them in any presentation or report that you make, since they help other people to understand the definitions you have proposed in step 4.

(7) Summarise the table; finally, find the frequency under the category headings. In a fourth column, report the number of constructs in each category. Which categories have more constructs and which have fewer? Is this significant, given the topic of the grid? For reporting purposes, when you have to list the categories, consider reordering them according to the number of constructs allocated to them.

Table 7.1 provides an example, taken from a study I once did of fraud and security issues in the Benefits Agency (Jankowicz, 1996). For the moment, ignore the two rightmost columns (the ones headed 'Prov.' and 'Met.'). Notice how, in step 3, I've expressed the definitions of each category as bipolar constructs (in the second column). Next, the codes which stand for each construct are listed; I haven't listed them all in this example since there isn't the space on the page! The 'Sum' column shows how many constructs were categorised under each heading, and below that, the percentage of all the constructs that this figure represents (for example, in the first row, 57 constructs, this being 19.1% of all the constructs, came under the first category). This table is in fact a summary, and was accompanied by a set of tables which listed the constructs themselves, as well as their codes. You might argue that it's the constructs themselves, and not the code numbers standing for them, that matter, and you'd be perfectly right. However, a table like Table 7.1 provides a useful summary, and the third column is, in fact, a necessary discipline in checking the reliability of the content-analysis process (see steps (4.1) to (4.7) below), so you might as well take this column seriously!

Design Issues: Differential Analysis

If you have some hunch or hypothesis which you want to check by your analysis, you need to create additional columns in Table 7.1 at step 7, one for each subgroup into which you have divided the sample. You will then count the number of constructs under each category, subgroup by subgroup, thereby carrying out a 'differential analysis'. This is very straightforward. It simply reports whether the constructs from the members of one subgroup are distributed differently across the categories than the constructs from other subgroups, working with the percentage figures in each category. (Where the total number of constructs provided by each subgroup varies, you'll need to change all the figures into percentages of each subgroup's total, so that you can compare between subgroups.)

For example, *do* younger interviewees think differently to the older ones (in terms of the percentage of their constructs they allocated to particular categories)? Does a sales force think differently about the price discounts

Table 7.1 Content-analysis procedure, Benefits Agency example

Category	Definition	Construct	Sum %	Prov.	Met.
Deliberateness of action and intent	Knowing what's right and ignoring it; lawbreaking; deliberate fraud; errors of commission *versus* bypassing procedures; making technical errors; mistakes and errors of omission	2.1 17.1 18.2 35.1 etc.	57 19.1	47 21.1	10 13.3
Friendship and other external pressures	Divulging information to a 3rd party; collusion *versus* acting alone; no 3rd party involved	46.1 31.1 etc.	39 13.3	29 13.0	10 13.3
Pressure of work	Shortcuts to gain time or ease workflow; pressure of targets; negligence *versus* reasons other than workflow; breaches of confidence; deliberate wrongdoing	16.1 44.1 13.1 etc.	34 11.4	26 11.7	8 10.7
Internal versus external involvement	Staff member is the agent in doing/condoning the offence *versus* claimant the agent in the offence	1.2 17.2 35.2 etc.	33 11.1	27 12.1	6 8.0
Risk, proof and obviousness	Definite and easy to prove; clear feeling there's something wrong; rules clearly broken *versus* unsure if fraud occurred; no rules broken	1.1 4.5 34.5 etc.	32 10.7	25 11.2	7 9.3
Systems and security procedures	Using information improperly; cavalier attitude to checking; misuse of IT procedures *versus* accidental outcomes of IT system; inadequate clerical procedures	3.1 12.2 39.3 etc.	31 10.4	21 9.4	10 13.3
Who gains	Employee reaps the benefit of fraud; less personal need or motive *versus* claimant reaps the benefit; personal problems provide a motive	10.5 25.2 47.6 etc.	27 9.1	20 8.9	7 9.3
Money versus information	Personal cash gains; clear overpayments *versus* provision of information	4.1 11.4 etc	21 7.1	14 6.3	7 9.3
Outcomes	Severe consequences or repercussions *versus* fewer/less severe consequences	33.5 44.5 etc.	8 2.7	3 1.3	5 6.7
Training issues	Not preventable by training *versus* preventable by improved training	7.7 36.3 etc.	4 1.3	2 0.9	2 2.7
Where it happens	Occurs in the agency office *versus* occurs in claimant's home or similar	7.4 9.6 etc.	3 1.3	0 0	3 1.3
Miscellaneous		3.6 etc.	9 3.0	6 2.7	3 4.0
Totals			298 100.2	223 99.9	75 99.9

Source: *Reproduced from the Analytical Services Division, Department of Social Security.*

available to them than the sales office staff who set the discounts but never meet real clients?

Take a third example. Perhaps, as a manager in a department of a municipal administration, you suspect that clerical officers who have had private-sector experience before deciding to work in local government have a systematically different way of thinking about their jobs than clerical officers who have always worked in local government. You feel there may be two distinct types of clerical officer, and if this is the case, the implications (to do with their attitude to the public as customers; to issues of supervision; and to the way they exercise initiative) may be wide-ranging.

The following steps can now be completed.

(8) Complete any differential analysis which your investigation requires. Create separate columns for each group of interviewees you're interested in, and record the constructs separately for each of them. Count the constructs from each group in each category, and see! Does each group of respondents think systematically differently?

In the Benefits Agency study reported in Table 7.1, the Agency wished to see whether there were any differences in the construing of employees in busy metropolitan offices as distinct from quieter provincial offices, and the sampling was designed to pick this up. Table 7.1 shows the relevant information in the columns headed 'Prov.' and 'Met.'. Since there were differing numbers of interviewees in each location, each providing grids showing differing numbers of constructs, the entries in each category were turned into percentages of the total number of metropolitan and provincial constructs. Each entry in the 'Prov.' column shows the number of constructs in that category mentioned by provincial employees, and, below, the corresponding percentage of all the provincial employees' constructs. Ditto for the 'Met.' column.

As you can see, though there were some differences, these weren't dramatic. 'Deliberateness of intent' was mentioned especially frequently by provincial employees (21.1% of their constructs in this category). Metropolitan employees saw this as important (13.3% categorised under the same heading) but were equally concerned about 'friendship and other pressures' (13.3%) and 'systems and security procedures' (13.3%).

(9) Complete any statistical tests on this differential analysis as required. If you're familiar with null hypothesis testing, you'll have noticed that this table consists of frequency counts under mutually exclusive headings. Any differential analysis in which you're involved turns the content analysis into an X by Y table where X is the number of categories (rows) and Y is the number of distinct groups (data columns; Y equals 2 in the case of the clerical officers example above). This is exactly the kind of situation which lends itself to the chi-square statistic (or Fisher's Exact Probability Test, depending on the number of expected values in each cell). Other tests dependent on a comparison of the order of frequencies in each column may occur to you. If you aren't familiar with these statistical tests and this last step doesn't convey any meaning to you, just ignore it.

Reliability

You may have noticed that we omitted one crucial step from the procedure. As you remember from our earlier discussion, content analysis can't be idiosyncratic. It needs to be reproducible, and to make sense to other people. And so, all content analyses should incorporate a reliability check. This is an additional twist to the procedure, and takes place during the tabulation stage.

Let's work with a running example. This is an (invented) study of the factors which a publishing company's sales reps believe are important in achieving sales. Imagine, if you will, that 50 sales reps have each completed a repertory grid, taking eight recently published books as their elements.

Run through steps 1 to 3 as above, using the core-categorisation procedure described earlier.

(1) Identify the categories.

(2) Allocate constructs to those categories.

(3) Tabulate the result.

(4) Establish the reliability of the category system.

> **(4.1) Involve a colleague: ask a colleague to repeat steps 1 to 3 independently, producing a table, like your own, which summarises his/her efforts.** Now, the extent to which these two tables, yours and your collaborator's, agree indicates how reliable your procedures have been.

> **(4.2) Identify the categories you both agree on, and those you disagree on.** You can assess this by drawing up a fresh table, whose rows stand for the categories you identified, just as you did before; and the columns stand for the categories *your collaborator* identified. This is a different table to either of the content-analysis tables which you and your collaborator have filled out. Its purpose is to compare the two separate ones. For the sake of clarity, let's call it the **reliability table**. Here's our worked example, shown as Table 7.2.

Jot down the definitions of the two category sets; discuss the categories, and agree on which ones mean the same. Now rearrange the rows and

Table 7.2 Assessing reliability, step (4.2), before rearrangement

Collaborator / Interviewer	1 Sales price	2 Nature of purchasers	3 Current fashion	4 Coverage	5 Trade announcements	6 Layout and design	7 Competition	8 Advertising budget
1 Popularity of topic			5.8					
2 Buyer characteristics						6.1		
3 Pricing decisions								
4 Design								
5 Contents								
6 Competitors								
7 Promotion					7.4			4.1

Example of initial content-analysis categories from a study of the factors which a publishing company's sales reps believe to be related to the volume of sales they're able to achieve. This example is developed in Tables 7.3 to 7.6. The reliability table will be used to record how the interviewer, and the collaborator, have categorised all of the constructs. As an example, four constructs have been placed into the table. So, for example, the interviewer has put construct 6.1 into the 'buyer characteristics' category. The collaborator seems to disagree about its meaning, having put it under the 'layout and design' category.

columns of the reliability table so that categories which you and your collaborator *share* are placed in the same order: yours from top to bottom at the left of the table, and your collaborator's from left to right at the top of the table. In other words, tuck the shared categories into the top left corner of the table, in the same order across and down, with the categories that you don't share positioned in no particular order outside this area (see Table 7.3).

(4.3) Record your joint allocation of constructs. Working from your two separate content-analysis tables prepared in step 3, record the position of each of your constructs into the reliability table. How did you categorise the construct, and how did your collaborator categorise it: which row and column, respectively, was it put into? Write the construct number into the appropriate cell of the table. Table 7.3 shows just four constructs which have been allocated in this way, as an example, while Table 7.4 shows a full data set of constructs recorded in this way.

As you can see, there are two parts to the reliability issue. Can you agree on the category definitions; and, when you have agreed, are you both agreed on the allocation of the constructs to the same categories? The rearrangement of the reliability table, as shown in Table 7.3, is a useful exercise, since it forces you both to think about your category definitions. It also provides you with a measure of the extent to which you can allocate constructs consistently, as follows.

(4.4) Measure the extent of agreement between you. Think about it. If you were both in perfect agreement on the allocation of constructs to categories, all of your constructs would lie along the diagonal of the reliability table (the shaded cells); to the extent that you disagree, some constructs lie off the diagonal. So your overall measure of agreement is as follows:

- the number of constructs which lie along the diagonal

- in all the categories you were both agreed on (the categories which lie above and to the left of the two heavy lines drawn in Table 7.3)

- as a percentage of *all* of the constructs in the *whole* table.

Work out this figure, and call it index A. Now, repeat this calculation but express the number as a percentage of the constructs, not in the whole reliability table, but just those which have been allocated to categories you both agree on. Call this index B.

Table 7.5 provides you with a complete worked example. Index A is 54%: you've only agreed on just over half of what the constructs mean! Index B is, as it must be, larger, at 64%: when you confine your attention to categories which mean the same to both of you, you have a better result.

Table 7.3 Assessing reliability, step (4.2), after rearrangement

Collaborator ↓ Interviewer →	1 Current fashion	2 Nature of purchasers	3 Sales price	4 Layout and design	5 Coverage	6 Competition	7 Trade announcements	8 Advertising budget
1 Popularity of topic	5.8							
2 Buyer characteristics				6.1				
3 Pricing decisions								
4 Design								
5 Contents								
6 Competitors								
7 Promotion							7.4	4.1

1. Discussion of the definitions showed that the interviewer's 'popularity of topic' category is the same as the collaborator's 'current fashion'; the interviewer's 'buyer characteristics' is the same as the collaborator's 'nature of purchasers' category; 'pricing decisions' is the same as 'sales price'; 'design' is the same as 'layout and design'; 'contents' is the same as 'coverage'; and 'competitors' is the same as 'competition'. The interviewer has one category not used by the collaborator, 'promotion'; and the collaborator has two categories not used by the interviewer, 'trade announcements' and 'advertising budget'.

2. The categories have now been reorganised so that the commonly shared ones are at the top left of the table. The way in which both the interviewer and collaborator have categorised the constructs is now recorded by placing construct codes into their appropriate cells; just four examples, the same ones which appeared in Table 7.2, are shown above.

3. Construct 5.8, 'there's a demand for a textbook like this – no demand for this topic', was categorised under 'popularity of topic' in the interviewer's analysis, and as 'current fashion' in the collaborator's analysis, so it's placed in row 1, column 1, in this table: a construct on which both are agreed. Construct 6.1, 'ring-bound covers: bookshop buyers don't like – conventional cover: bookshop buyers will accept', was categorised under 'buyer characteristics' by the interviewer but under 'layout and design' by the collaborator. Construct 7.4, 'advertised heavily in the trade press – not advertised in the trade press' was placed in the 'promotion' category by the interviewer, but in the 'trade announcements' category by the collaborator. Construct 4.1, 'big advertising budget – small advertising budget' was categorised under 'promotion' by the interviewer but under 'advertising budget' by the collaborator.

Table 7.4 Assessing reliability, step (4.3)

Collaborator / Interviewer	1 Current fashion	2 Nature of purchasers	3 Sales price	4 Layout and design	5 Coverage	6 Competition	7 Trade announcements	8 Advertising budget
1 Popularity of topic	2.3, 5.8, 3.5, 5.3		1.4			3.2		
2 Buyer characteristics		1.1, 2.5, 3.7, 5.7		4.6, 6.1	1.6, 6.4	6.6		
3 Pricing decisions		7.1	1.2, 3.1, 4.4, 5.5, 6.3, 7.7	7.3	6.2			7.2
4 Design				1.5, 4.5, 7.5				
5 Contents	7.8				4.3, 5.9, 7.6	3.6, 5.2		
6 Competitors			7.9			2.1, 1.3, 2.4, 3.3, 4.2, 5.1, 6.5		
7 Promotion			7.4				1.7, 5.6, 6.7	2.2, 4.1, 3.4, 5.4

All of the constructs in the publisher's example are shown here, identified by their code number.

Table 7.5 Assessing reliability, step (4.4)

Collaborator / Interviewer	1 Current fashion	2 Nature of purchasers	3 Sales price	4 Layout and design	5 Coverage	6 Competition	7 Trade announcements	8 Advertising budget	Total
1 Popularity of topic	4		1			1			6
2 Buyer characteristics		4		2	2	1			9
3 Pricing decisions		1	6	1	1			1	10
4 Design				3					3
5 Contents	1				3	2			6
6 Competitors			1			7			8
7 Promotion			1				3	4	8
Total	5	5	9	6	6	11	3	5	50

1. Index A: number of constructs along the diagonal for the categories agreed on, as a percentage of all the constructs *in the table*:
   $4 + 4 + 6 + 3 + 3 + 7 = 27$;
   50 constructs in total;
   $100 \times 27/50 = 54\%$

2. Index B: number of constructs along the diagonal for the categories agreed on, as a percentage of all the constructs *in the categories agreed on*:
   $4 + 4 + 6 + 3 + 3 + 7 = 27$;
   42 constructs in the categories agreed on ($5 + 5 + 9 + 6 + 6 + 11$, or, of course, $6 + 9 + 10 + 3 + 6 + 8$; it's the same!)
   $100 \times 27/42 = 64\%$

But it's still not good enough; *a benchmark to aim at is 90% agreement, with no categories on whose definition you can't agree*. So:

(4.5) Negotiate over the meaning of the categories. Look at which categories in particular show disagreements, and try to arrive at a redefinition of the categories as indicated by the particular constructs on which you disagreed, so that you improve on the value of Indices A and B. Argue, debate, quarrel, just so long as you don't come to blows. Break for lunch and come back to it if necessary!

For example, in Table 7.5, even without knowing what the constructs are, you can hazard a guess that the interviewer and collaborator will be able to agree on a single category, 'promotion', since announcements in the trade press, and advertising, might both be regarded as forms of promotion. This single redefinition would be sufficient to create a total set of seven categories which accounted for all the constructs and on which both were agreed.

Even if nothing else changed, a redrawing of Table 7.5 (see the result in Table 7.6) shows an improvement to 68% agreement. It is likely that this discussion will clarify the confusion which led to construct 7.2 being categorised under 'pricing decisions' by the interviewer, raising the index to 70%. Further discussion, concentrating on the areas of disagreement, would tighten up the definitions of the other categories. The aim is to get as many constructs onto the diagonal of the table as possible!

(4.6) Finalise a revised category system with acceptably high reliability. The only way of knowing whether this negotiation has borne fruit is for each of you, interviewer and collaborator, to repeat the procedure. Redo your initial coding tables, working independently. Can you both arrive at the same, including categorisation of the constructs to the carefully redefined categories?

Repeat the whole analysis again. That's right! Repeat step 2 **using these new categories**. Repeat steps 3 and 4, including the casting of a new reliability table, and the recomputation of the reliability index.

This instruction isn't, in fact, as cruel as it may seem. The categorisation activity is likely to be much quicker than before, since you will be clearer on category definitions and **you will be using only agreed** categories. It is still time-consuming, but there is no alternative if you care for the reliability of your analysis.

(4.7) Report the final reliability figure. The improved figure you're aiming for is 90% agreement or better, and this is usually achievable.

There are more accurate measures of reliability, including ones which provide a reliability coefficient ranging between −1.0 and +1.0, which may be an obscure

Table 7.6 Assessing reliability, step (4.5)

Collaborator / Interviewer	1 Current fashion	2 Nature of purchasers	3 Sales price	4 Layout and design	5 Coverage	6 Competition	7 Promotion	Total
1 Popularity of topic	4		1			1		6
2 Buyer characteristics		4		2	2	1		9
3 Pricing decisions		1	6	1	1		1	10
4 Design				3				3
5 Contents	1				3	2		6
6 Competitors			1			7		8
7 Promotion			1				7	8
Total	5	5	9	6	6	11	8	50

1. The collaborator's category no. 7, 'promotion', is the result of combining the previous two categories: 7, 'trade announcements' and 8, 'advertising budget'.

2. Index A: number of constructs along the diagonal for the categories agreed on, as a percentage of all of the constructs in the table:

$4 + 4 + 6 + 3 + 7 + 7 = 34$

50 constructs in total

$100 \times 34/50 = 68\%$

3. (As all the categories are now agreed on, index A is identical to what was earlier called index B.)

characteristic to anyone other than a psychologist or a statistician, who is used to assessing reliability in this particular way. Probably the most commonly used statistic in this context is Cohen's Kappa (Cohen, 1968). However, if having a standard error of the figure you have computed matters to you, then the Perrault–Leigh Index is the appropriate measure to use: see Perrault & Leigh (1989).

The value of Cohen's Kappa or the Perrault–Leigh Index which you would seek to achieve would be 0.80 or better. This is the standard statistical criterion for a reliable measure, but, if you're conscientious about the way in which you negotiate common meanings for categories, a highly respectable 0.90 is typical for repertory grid content analyses.

And that's that: with the completion of step 4 of our procedure, you'd continue with the remaining steps, 5 to 9, taking comfort that the categories devised in steps 5 to 9 were thoroughly reliable.

All of this seems very pedantic, and for day-to-day purposes, most people would skip the reanalysis of step 4.5. However, if you were doing all this as part of a formal research programme, especially one leading to a dissertation of any kind, you'd have to include this step, and report the improvement in reliability (it is conventional to report both the 'before' and the 'after' figure, by the way!).

Well and good; but haven't you forgotten something? When you present the final results at steps 5 to 7 (the content-analysis table, with its subgroup columns for differential analysis as required), *whose* content-analysis table do you present: yours, or your collaborator's? You've increased your reliability but, unless you've achieved a perfect 100% match, the two tables, yours and your collaborator's, will differ slightly. Which should you use? Whose definition of reality shall prevail?

In fact, you should use your own (what we've been calling the interviewer's content-analysis table), rather than your collaborator's. *You* designed the whole study and it's probably fair for any residual inaccuracies to be based on your way of construing the study, rather than your collaborator's. (Though if someone were to argue that you should spin a coin to decide, I could see an argument for it based on Kelly's alternative constructivism: that one investigator's understanding of the interviewees' constructs is as good as another's, once the effort to minimise researcher idiosyncrasy has been made!)

Okay, this is a long chapter: take a break! And then, before you continue, please do Exercise 7.1.

7.2.2 A Design Example

I'd really like to set you an exercise with a realistically sized sample, with answers presented in Appendix 1, as I've done for the other procedures outlined in the previous chapters! However, it just isn't possible to provide you with the data from 20 grids, and all the associated paraphernalia. (Exercise 7.1 will have to do. At least it focuses attention on what's involved in reliability checking.) Hence the level of pedantic detail I've gone into in Section 7.2.1, to try to ensure that the procedure is readily understandable. The best way to learn a procedure is to do it, and when you do, you'll find that everything falls into place.

Instead, let me provide you with a case example which addressed the same problem of how best to analyse a large number of grids, using a somewhat different approach and with slightly different design decisions being adopted. An examination of some slightly different answers adopted to the questions we're addressing should help to establish the principles of what we're doing. It's worth examining in detail, as a further example of the sampling and design options involved in content analysis.

Watson et al. (1995) were interested in the tacit, as well as the more obvious, knowledge held by managers about entrepreneurial success and failure. This suggested the use of a personal construct approach, since constructs, being bipolar, are capable of saying something about both success *and* failure. (In fact, this issue was so important to the researchers that they took a design decision to work with two distinct sets of constructs, those dealing with successful entrepreneurship, and those dealing with unsuccessful entrepreneurship, doing a *separate* content analysis of each.)

Theirs was a large study. They identified 27 different categories for 570 constructs relating to success, and 20 categories for 346 constructs relating to failure, in a sample of 63 small-business owner-managers.

The top five categories assigned to successful entrepreneurship were 'commitment to business', 'leadership qualities', self-motivation', 'customer service', and 'business planning and organising', between them accounting for 42% of the success-related constructs. The top five categories assigned to unsuccessful entrepreneurship were 'ineffective planning and organisation', 'lack of commitment', 'poor ethics', 'poor money management', and 'lack of business knowledge and skills', accounting for 32% of the constructs which related to business failure.

Other variants on the approach outlined in Section 7.2.1 above are as follows. Their constructs were obtained, not through grid interviews, but by asking their respondents to write short character sketches of the successful entrepreneur, and the unsuccessful entrepreneur, together with their circumstances, market, etc. The content analysis followed the classic Holsti approach towards the identification of content units and context units. Notice, since constructs had to be identified from connected narrative, rather than being separately elicited by repertory grid technique, there wasn't a pre-existing and obvious content unit. You'll recall that grid-derived constructs provide you with a predefined unit of meaning. So, in that sense, their analysis was more difficult and much more time-consuming than the one I've outlined above.

Their categorisation procedure was carried out twice, on what were two distinct sets of data: the constructs about successful entrepreneurs, and the constructs about unsuccessful entrepreneurs. Thus, the differential analysis I have indicated as step 8 is, in their case, not an analysis, immediately amenable to statistical testing, of one single table divided up into groups of constructs, but a looser analysis 'by inspection' of differences between the two complete data sets. It's clear, however (see Watson et al., 1995: 45), that the two solid and comprehensive sets of constructs constitute a database which is available for further analysis in a variety of ways. For example, they have carried out cluster analyses of both their data sets, although the details of the procedure they followed are not reported.

Their reliability check was a careful and detailed six-step procedure in which two independent raters:

- sorted constructs written onto cards into categories

- privately inspected and adjusted their category definitions

- negotiated over the meanings

- privately adjusted their category definitions again

- renegotiated

- finally agreed the definitive category set.

These categories were 'approximately the same' as a result, although no computation of a reliability index or coefficient was reported.

In Conclusion

If we stand back from the details of this generic bootstrapping technique for a moment, one characteristic, in particular, is worth noting. The generic technique as I've described it, and as applied in their own way by Watson et al. (1995), emphasises the meanings present in the constructs, but discards information about the ways in which interviewees use those constructs. There were no ratings available in Watson's study since the constructs were obtained from written character sketches rather than from grids.

But where ratings are available, as in the procedure outlined in Section 7.2.1, it seems a shame not to use them to capture more about the personal meanings being aggregated in the analysis. What a pity to disregard the individual provenance which leads one person to rate an element '1' on a given construct, and another person to rate the same element '5' on a construct which the content analysis has demonstrated means the same to both people!

But how can this be done? It's rather a tall order, you might argue. Though there's an overlap in meaning for different interviewees, they don't each use the same set of constructs, so how can one make use of the ratings in a regular and ordered way? Well, the content-analysis technique presented in Section 7.3 does just that. In the meanwhile, we need to consider a further generic approach.

At this point, you may feel you'd like to get away from my artificial examples, and case examples like the one above, and essay a content analysis of your own. Exercise 7.2 gives you the opportunity to do so.

7.2.3 Standard Category Schemes

Pre-existing, standard category schemes come from two alternative sources:

• they're the result of a previous bootstrapping exercise by yourself or someone else; or

• they're drawn up following a category system based on pre-existing research, theory, or assumptions which are felt to be relevant to the topic.

In either case, step 1 of the content-analysis procedure outlined in Section 7.2.1 has already been carried out for you. The categories already exist, and you use the scheme in your analysis from step 2 onwards. That is, you code, tabulate, and carry out a differential analysis as required. The reliability check of step 4 is probably unnecessary if the pre-existing categories are already known, from previous research, to provide a reliable way of summarising the topic in question, but you still need to be conscientious about the consistency with which you assign the constructs to the categories, and you might want to do the 'second run-through', as I indicated in step (4.6) above.

Bootstrapped Schemes

After going to all the trouble involved in bootstrapping a category scheme, one's inclined to put it to further use! Now that it's pre-existing, as it were, it's useful to put it to work in order to categorise new constructs should your circumstances require a fresh set of interviews. This would seem entirely appropriate if the topic remained the same from the first to the second occasion, and you were satisfied that the new interviewees were, as a sample, from the same population, so far as thinking about the topic is concerned. Nevertheless, you'd probably want to review the literature relevant to your topic area, to draw on some background theory to which you could appeal in establishing this.

Many of the personnel-psychology applications of grid technique (e.g., Jankowicz, 1990) depend on an initial job-analysis grid in which the different ways in which effective employees do their jobs are expressed in the form of constructs, and then categorised. This scheme can then be used to devise standard scales for use in the development of

- competency frameworks

- performance-appraisal questionnaires

- training needs analyses

- personal development need identification.

After a bootstrapping approach has been used to devise the original category scheme using the constructs of a group of employees, the categories might subsequently be applied to other groups of employees, if it is established that the jobs done by the original, and the new, groups of employees are similar. Section 7.3 provides further examples of applications in job analysis, and development of employee-appraisal questionnaires.

Theory-Based Schemes

Perhaps the best-known standard category system is Landfield's (Landfield, 1971). Twenty-two distinct categories, ranging over such themes as 'social interaction', 'organization', 'imagination', 'involvement', and 'humour', are offered, together with a set of detailed guidelines to their use; and careful definitions of what is, and what isn't, an example of each category are provided. While this system has been used mainly in clinical work (Harter et al., 2001, give a recent case example), it is sufficiently general to be helpful in a variety of personal and interpersonal situations.

More recently, Feixas et al. (2002) have developed a 45-category system divided into six overall themes, dealing with moral, emotional, relational, personal, intellectual/operational, and value and interest-related constructs. Superficial constructs (which I assume would include some types of propositional construct: see Section 5.3.3), figurative constructs involving comparisons with particular other individuals, and constructs applicable to particular relationships have been excluded from the scheme. Great care has been taken to ensure the reliability of the scheme, and the level achieved, for what is a generic system, is comparable to the levels of reliability achievable with the more specific category systems obtained by bootstrapping (as outlined in the previous section). For those of a statistical inclination, a mean percentage agreement figure of 87.3%, corresponding to a Cohen's Kappa of 0.95 on the six themes and 0.89 on the 45 categories, and to 0.96 and 0.93, respectively, using the Perrault–Leigh Index, are reported.

Viney has provided scales for assessing cognitive anxiety (broadly, uncertainty-related anxiety) by drawing on Kelly's personal construct theory to revise earlier scales constructed in the psychoanalytic tradition (Viney & Westbrook, 1976).

Duck (1973) has devised a category scheme for assessing interpersonal relationships, based on a personality-role-interaction classification. Other schemes for categorising constructs commonly used in social settings are briefly described in Winter (1992: 31–32).

Combining Bootstrapping and Theory-Based Approaches

Finally, Hisrich & Jankowicz (1990) provide an example of a pilot study in which bootstrapping and the use of a pre-existing scheme were combined. It was known from previous theory and research that when they take an investment decision, venture capitalists pay attention to three main characteristics of the proposal: the managerial expertise in the company seeking funds (MacMillan et al., 1987), the market opportunity, and the cash-out potential (Tyebjee & Bruno, 1984; MacMillan et al., 1987) for the whole venture. Hisrich & Jankowicz (1990) followed the bootstrapping procedure to arrive at nine categories classifying 45 constructs used by five venture capitalists. They found that these reflected three superordinate headings:

- 'management' (which fits into what is known about managerial expertise)

- 'unique opportunity' (a match with what is known about the importance of market opportunity in the literature)

- 'appropriate return', which, as its component constructs indicate, is synonymous with 'cash-out potential'.

This was a small-scale pilot study, with only 45 constructs in total. However, as Table 7.7 shows, the value in doing a bootstrapping content analysis, rather

Table 7.7 Categories summarising factors assessed in venture capital decision-making

Constructs	No.
Management Personal traits of the proposer Experience of the proposer Management team characteristics Continuity of the company/market	22
Unique opportunity Product-market uniqueness	9
Appropriate return Funding base and risk	5
Other The proposal itself Use of technology Market location	9
Total	**45**

Source: Reproduced by permission Hisrich & Jankowicz (1990).

than relying entirely on the pre-existing analytic framework, is indicated by the fact that nine of the constructs could not be accommodated within the pre-existing scheme. The nature of the proposal itself, the way in which it uses technology, and the geographical location (local versus distributed) also play a part, in ways which the pre-existing category scheme did not allow for.

7.3 HONEY'S CONTENT ANALYSIS

We seem to have solved the problem outlined at the start of this chapter: how to say something about the different meanings being expressed in a set of grids, making general statements about the sample as a whole, while reflecting the particular meanings being offered by individual interviewees as they express their personal and, at times, idiosyncratic knowledge.

But we've done so at a cost. We haven't been able to use any of the *ratings* of elements on constructs available in the original grids. Somewhere in the whole set, we've retained each person's constructs; but we've lost what each person was telling us about the topic by means of those personal constructs. This is the price we've paid for starting with individuals' constructs, rather than using a standard set of constructs supplied to all the interviewees on which ratings could be taken, totalled, averaged, and so on. We've lost a considerable amount of the information available in each grid.

7.3.1 Rationale

However, there is a technique, first developed by Honey (1979), which achieves what, at first sight, appears to be impossible. It aggregates different constructs across a sample and provides a way in which we can make use of some of the individual meanings being conveyed by each person's ratings.

The technique assumes that what we're interested in is each individual's personal understanding of the topic in question, and treats each construct offered by the individual as more closely related, or less closely related, *to the overall issue s/he has in mind when thinking about the topic.*

> This makes a lot of sense. Kelly's theory asserts that constructs are organised into a system, with some constructs being superordinate to others (the Organisation Corollary), and, you'll recall, we make use of this property when we seek to elicit more specific constructs by laddering downwards (see Section 4.4.1). Some constructs are crucial and central to the individual's knowledge and views about the topic, while others, while relevant, are somewhat more peripheral. Moreover, we expect some kind of consistency among the constructs a person uses. So, for example, if an interviewee were to characterise an individual as 'unreliable' and at the same time 'dependable', we would be surprised, and look for a rationale. We expect constructs to hang together, to express a coherent point of view, and to tell a consistent story.

> But Kelly also mentions that the different ways we have of making sense of different situations may not necessarily be compatible with each another (Fragmentation Corollary). A person's construct system isn't a monolithic structure. And so it is very reasonable to expect that some constructs are particularly related to any issue being construed, carrying more meaning about the topic in question. Others, while relevant, might flesh out the meaning, adding grace notes, as it were, without being 'what the whole thing is really all about'.

In Honey's technique, 'what the individual has in mind when thinking about the topic' is summarised by *supplying* a construct: an 'overall summary' construct designed to sum up the interviewee's individual stance to the topic as a whole. (See Section 4.2.7 on supplied constructs and their uses. Refresh your memory now, before reading on!)

Thus, a grid designed to capture the reactions of a set of trainees to the different sessions of a course which they attended, in order to make improvements in the course, might involve a supplied construct which assessed the extent to which they felt they learnt: 'overall, learnt a lot – overall, didn't learn much'. A grid which assessed the knowledge in a company's sales team about which approaches worked best in selling to their customers might conclude by asking each salesperson to rate each approach on 'overall, more effective – overall, less effective'. A grid about personal friendship using the names of friends and acquaintances as the elements might require the interviewee to rate all of them on the supplied construct, 'overall, a closer relationship – overall, a more distant relationship'. Table 7.8 provides some further examples.

Honey's content analysis aggregates constructs across the sample, as in Section 7.2.1, but labels each construct with two indices reflecting the extent to which the ratings on the *particular* construct match the ratings on the *'overall'* construct. The first index is our familiar % similarity score, as outlined in Section 6.1.2. One hundred per cent means that the ratings on the individual construct are identical to the ratings on the overall construct; 70% means that the ratings are less similar, and so on.

The second index reflects the fact that people differ in their typical % similarity scores. When we compare the ratings elicited from one interviewee on all of the constructs in the grid, we may find that they typically reveal a relatively narrow range of % similarity scores. The highest may be 100% and the lowest perhaps 80%. A second person, however, might be inclined to see many different, and relatively unrelated, aspects of the issue when thinking about the topic, and so her highest % similarity score may be 85% and the lowest, 55%. To the extent that different people have different ranges of % similarity scores for any topic, we can talk of different personal metrics. At 85%, what feels very similar for the second person may lie towards the bottom of the range of similarity for the first person.

And so, Honey's procedure acknowledges that % similarity scores are relative, and as well as noting their *actual* percentage value, notes whether that value is placed among the high, the intermediate or the low (H-I-L) values (what Honey calls the 'top-and-tail data' *for that particular individual.*

Okay. So, taking both indices (% similarity and the H-I-L index) into account (see below for the detail), it's clear that some constructs will match highly with the supplied 'overall' construct. In other words, they will represent what that particular individual felt and thought, overall, very well. Others, however, will match less highly with the 'overall' construct; that is, they will represent what the individual felt and thought about the topic, overall, somewhat less strongly.

The aggregated set of constructs for the sample as a whole will, in other words, represent the categorised views of *all* the individuals in the sample, but will also preserve information about *each* individual's views in terms of how he or she severally, personally, *idiosyncratically* if you will, thought about the topic.

Table 7.8 Examples of 'overall' constructs in Honey's content-analysis technique

Topic	Elements	Possible qualifying phrase '...from the point of view of...'	Supplied construct 'overall...'
Lecturer effectiveness	Lecturers, rated by a sample of students	...What they *do* that makes them more, or less, effective as lecturers	...More effective – less effective
Counselling style	Different types of 'helper': 'a friend', 'a counsellor', 'a parent', 'a priest'	...What they do and how they do it that makes them more, or less, approachable to a person seeking help	...More approachable – less approachable
Being an effective clerical officer	Different clerical officers, including some more effective and some less	...How they do their job which makes them good at it, or less good at it	...More effective clerical officer – less effective clerical officer
Understanding creative block in the figurative arts	Several of their own paintings as nominated by each artist	...What was going on which made them easy to paint, or led to getting 'stuck'	...More straightforward – more problematic
Thinking about what friendship means to you	People you know, ranging from 'best friend' to 'disliked acquaintance'	...What it is about them that makes for friendship – or otherwise!	...A real friend – rather less so

1. In each case, your analysis will identify the constructs, in their categories, which each interviewee has particularly in mind when thinking about the issue involved in the topic, as that issue is summarised by the 'overall' construct. Thereby specifying what 'effectiveness', 'approachability', and so on mean in particular to him or her.

2. Notice how the 'overall' construct summarises the issue at stake, as previously highlighted by the qualifying phrase. (Glance again at the rationale for the use of qualifying phrases in Sections 3.2.1 and 3.2.3. Table 3.2 is worth another look too.)

And it will take into account both the % similarity value and the individual's personal metric!

This is tremendous. It's pure gold. I have taken my hat off to Peter Honey for a quarter-century now, and shall continue to do so for another 50 years at least. I hope you can see why. While strongly advocating procedures for ensuring reliability, he doesn't go into reliability measurement in any great detail; I have added that, below, together with some grace notes of my own. But the overall thrust is his; he gives us exactly what we need when we seek to aggregate large samples of respondents.

7.3.2 Procedure

The procedure is similar to the bootstrapping one outlined in Section 7.2.1, and looks as follows. You may find a glance at Figure 7.1 is helpful as you go through the steps below. It's a grid completed by one of our sales staff in the publisher's example shown in Tables 7.2 to 7.6.

(1) Obtain ratings on a supplied 'overall' construct. Make sure, when you elicit each grid, that you supply a construct which serves to sum up the interviewee's overall stance on the topic. Ask the interviewee to rate all the elements on this supplied construct, as well as on the elicited constructs.

(2) Compute sums of differences for each construct against the 'overall' construct. Use the procedure defined in Section 6.1.2, 'simple relationships between constructs'. Note: you're doing this for every construct against the 'overall' construct *only*. For the purposes of our present analysis, you *don't* have to work it out between each construct and each other construct. Bearing in mind that you have to check for reversals (that you might get a smaller sum of differences between a given construct and the 'overall' construct if one of the two is reversed), the quickest way of completing this step is to compute the sum of differences

  (a) between 'overall' construct and the first construct

  (b) between 'overall' construct (reversed) and the first construct (unreversed, of course)

  (c) note the smaller of the two sums of differences.

Repeat for the 'overall' construct and each of the other constructs.

Doing it this way makes sure that you only have to reverse one set of ratings, those for the 'overall' construct; and, in fact, this part of the procedure is much quicker to do than to describe! (Glance at the very bottom row of ratings in Figure 7.1).

Topic: Factors related to book sales

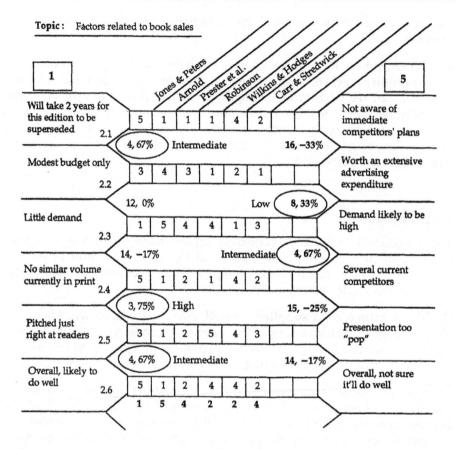

Following step 2 of the procedure, the sums of differences are shown below each construct, on the left. The reversed sums of differences are shown **in bold** on the right; you only need to reverse one set of ratings, for the 'overall' construct, in order to calculate them. The reversed ratings are shown **in bold** at the bottom. For each construct, the lower of the two values (unreversed, reversed) has been chosen and circled.

Following step 3, these sums of differences have been turned into % similarity scores.

Following step 4, the constructs have been divided into three sets, high, intermediate, and low, as evenly as possible.

Following step 5, the constructs have been labelled (2.1, 2.2, 2.3, etc.) to ensure subsequent identification. The grid sheet can now be cut up into strips, ready for categorisation.

Figure 7.1 Using Honey's technique

(3) Ensure comparability with other grids. In other words, turn these sums of differences into % similarity scores.

(4) Take the individual's personal metric into account. Look at these % similarity scores. Within each grid, divide the constructs as best you can into the highest third, intermediate third, and lowest third. ('As best you can'. In

Figure 7.1, 67%, 33% reversed, 67% reversed, 75%, and 65% don't divide into three equal groups!)

(5) Label each construct with both indices. At this stage, as with the bootstrapping technique, it's convenient if you transfer each construct onto a separate file card, and note which interviewee it came from. Or simply cut the grid sheet into strips, each construct on a separate strip; but be sure to indicate which interviewee's construct it is! Give each construct its unique number, as suggested in Section 7.2.1 (construct 16.4 would be the fourth construct from interviewee number 16, for example). Now check that the % similarity scores have been written in below each construct. Next, mark it H, I, or L depending on its % similarity score value in comparison with the other constructs *which that particular interviewee* used. Now, back to the content-analysis procedure.

(6) Identify the categories.

(7) Allocate the constructs to the categories, following the core-categorisation procedure (see Section 7.2.1).

(8) Tabulate the result.

(9) Establish the reliability of the category system, following exactly the same procedures you used in steps 4.1 to 4.7 in Section 7.2.1. You get your colleague's help in going through steps 6, 7, and 8, working with the constructs after they've been labelled with their % similarity scores and their H-I-L indices, but before doing anything else. There's no point in summarising the table and doing differential analyses if the category system isn't reliable.

(10) Summarise the table: first, the meaning of the category headings; that is, define the category headings.

(11) Summarise the table: find examples of each category heading. Here's where the power of Honey's approach reveals itself.

> **(11.1) Within each category, order the constructs from top to bottom with respect to their % similarity scores.** Those at the top have identical or near-identical scores (that is, they represent 'what the interviewee particularly had in mind in thinking about the topic', even though, within their category, of course, they may be different in meaning, covering some different aspect of that category). Those at the bottom, those with the low % similarity scores, will be less salient (bulking less, as it were, in that particular interviewee's thinking so far as the topic is concerned).
>
> **11.2) Looking at all the constructs within a category, identify personally salient constructs on which there is consensus in the group.**
>
> - If the H-I-L indices are high, the idea behind that particular construct is important for the people in your sample as individuals. And if many individuals in your sample have that construct, then certainly, hang on

to it, since it's saying something about the thinking of your sample as a whole as well as each individual member!

- If the H-I-L indices are mixed, the idea behind that particular construct reveals no particular consensus. In the sample as a whole, there's a certain ambivalence about the construct's relevance or importance to the topic. And particularly, if you notice that two or more constructs which express essentially the same meaning, *obtained from the same person*, have mixed H-I-L indices, set the constructs aside. There's no point in preserving ambiguity or ambivalence here.

- If the H-I-L indices are low, it looks as though the sample as a whole agree that the construct doesn't relate particularly well to the topic in general. Note this.

Table 7.9 shows the result of this step for our running example.

(11.3) If there are subthemes within a category, group them according to the meaning being expressed. The final result will reflect your overall purposes in doing a content analysis; but, typically, you would aim to end up with 40% to 80% of the original number of constructs which show the consensus you're looking for. (Of course, if there was little consensus, you'd say so!) The result will be a table in which the columns are categories, each one divided into two subcolumns, in the first of which the chosen constructs appear, and, in the other, the % similarity scores and the H-I-L index.

(12) Summarise the table: state the frequency under the category headings. How many constructs are there in each category (and subcategory, if relevant) at this stage? Report the number, and if this varies markedly from the original number of constructs in each category at the start of step 10, assess and discuss the significance. On what kinds of issues is there a consensus, and on which ones don't people agree?

This is a good point at which to calculate any sums, averages, and so on. You might, for example, use the % similarity scores to provide a 'mean importance score' of each category for the sample as a whole, if this makes sense in your analysis.

(13) Complete any differential analysis which your investigation requires, as before, when you bootstrapped. If you tag each construct according to the different subsamples of interviewee, or cross-tabulate them in different rows of your table, you may see differences among the subsamples in terms of:

- the number of constructs in different categories

- the relative importance (the H-I-L indices and/or the mean % similarity scores).

So, for instance, suppose in our running example, you knew that interviewees nos 5, 6, and 7 had only had sales experience, whereas interviewees nos 1, 2, 3, and 4 had worked in the office before joining the sales force. Would the fact that there are more constructs from interviewees 5, 6, and 7 in the 'pricing decisions' category be meaningful?

> But be careful! This example has only 50 interviewees since it is invented for illustrative purposes. A real data set would have at least 200 items. In point of fact, in *this* example, it would be dangerous to come to any differential conclusions because the subsamples of sales staff with office experience, and without, are rather small. For instance, four of the 10 constructs under the 'pricing decisions' category which we are using to make a point in our differential analysis come from just one interviewee, no. 7. We have to avoid a conclusion that the bee in one interviewee's bonnet does indeed typify the views of the other interviewees in the subgroup!

> As with any form of sampling, idiosyncrasies that do not reflect population characteristics are more probable in a small sample than a large one. If you want to conduct a differential analysis, make sure that you have sufficient constructs to represent each subgroup.

Okay. And, while on this statistical theme, note the following step.

(14) Complete any statistical tests on this differential analysis, as before.

> *Before moving on, make an attempt at Exercise 7.3. This gets you to practise steps 1 to 8 of the Honey procedure.*

7.4 IN CONCLUSION

Content-analysis procedure, and particularly, the reliability check, are very time-consuming. Do we really have to follow them?

Well, what can I say? If accuracy and reliability matter to you, then the sane answer has to be 'yes', especially if, in the case of a dissertation based on repertory grid technique, your work is to be judged against scholarly standards by other people. And if accuracy and reliability don't matter to you, should you really be using repertory grid technique in understanding other people?

Finally, I should mention that I have not described one very interesting bootstrapped content-analysis technique that aggregates individual interviewees' grids while capturing information about the structure of their

Table 7.9 Content-analysis procedure: factors related to book sales as seen by publisher's sales staff

Category	Constructs	No., %	% Similarity	H-I-L value
Pricing decisions	1.2 Affordable – less affordable at that size		92	H
	3.1 Easily produced – difficult to produce at a reasonable price		83	H
	4.4 For the under-£20 market – will sell at £25		100	H
	5.5 Easy to price – standard of illustration may make it too expensive	10,	83	I
	6.2 Looks like good value – looks too cheap to be worth the price	20	75	I
	6.3 Under £20 and soft cover only – would need to sell for £35		92	H
	7.1 Cheap and cheerful – only libraries could afford it		100	H
	7.2 Well advertised, could sell at that price – can't produce it at the price that would reach the buyer		92	H
	7.3 Affordable illustrative materials – requires a level of illustration we couldn't provide at the price		100	H
	7.7 Would sell at a higher price than normal for its market – would its market buy something at the low price required?		58	L
Buyer characteristics	1.1 Well suited to the younger market – not our sort of customer		100	H
	1.6 Appeal to intelligent lay reader – appeal to specialists		75	I
	2.5 Pitched just right at readers – presentation too "pop"		67	I
	3.7 A healthy undergraduate market – more postgraduate	9,	83	H
	4.6 Attractive, our sort of market – aimed at a more conservative sort of customer?	18	92	H
	5.7 A good standard coverage – too narrowly focused for our market		83	I
	6.1 Conventional cover, buyers will accept – ring-bound covers: buyers don't like		50	L
	6.4 Deals with the topics our market likes – some expected topics missing		92	H
	6.6 Our sort of book – not sure if it's for our readers		58	L
Competitors	1.3 No current authors competing – several other competitors		90	H
	2.1 Will take 2 years for this edition to be superseded – not aware of immediate competitors' plans		67	I
	2.4 No similar volume currently in print – several current competitors		75	H

Category	Item	Weight	Score	Rating
	3.3 Competition outdated – competition strong	8, 16	50	L
	4.2 New edition needed urgently to compete – no new editions planned by competitors		83	I
	5.1 Can sell more of this book than other publishers can of theirs – can't		75	L
	6.5 No competition – lots of competition		92	H
	7.9 Cheaper than our nearest competitor – competitors' pricing policy enables them to compete effectively		66	L
Promotion	1.7 Aimed at the trade – general advertising	8, 16	66	L
	2.2 Worth an extensive advertising expenditure – modest budget only		33	L
	3.4 Will do well in long run without expensive advertising – will need constant support to do well		83	H
	4.1 Big advertising budget – small advertising budget		83	I
	5.4 Modest advertising via direct mailing – extensive advertising using all promotional means		100	H
	5.6 Some conference promotions – trade promotions only		83	I
	6.7 Advertised heavily in trade press – not advertised in trade press		75	I
	7.4 Will sell at this price without promotion – not worth promoting extensively, will sell anyway		70	I
Popularity of topic	1.4 Likely to sell – low volume	6, 12	92	H
	2.3 Demand likely to be high – little demand		67	I
	3.2 Current demand – demand well satisfied by others		67	I
	3.5 Will walk off the shelf – slow sales likely		83	H
	5.3 Will sell well – won't sell		100	H
	5.8 We're doing well with this topic – our firm doesn't do well with this topic		75	L
Contents	3.6 Good basic read – too much like a reference text to compete well	6, 12	67	I
	4.3 Covers the ground well – essential bits missing		92	H
	5.2 A good standard coverage – too narrowly focused for our market		75	L
	5.9 Standard topics there as expected – missing essential contents		100	H
	7.6 Reads well – difficult to read		66	L
	7.8 Coverage ensures its likely to become a standard – flavour of the month		92	H
Design	1.4 Illustrations well laid out – cramped appearance	3, 6	75	M
	4.5 Nicely packaged – likely to fall apart		70	L
	7.5 Well proportioned – wrong size for this sort of book		66	L
Totals		50, 99		

construct system about a given topic in a way that includes details of personal values, and about the implicational connections between constructs at several levels of detail. Hill's content-analysis technique (Hill, 1995) depends on an understanding of constructs as values, a topic which I wish to examine in Chapter 8, and you might like to read that chapter first before turning to Hill.

THINGS TO DO

It's difficult to practise a full content analysis by means of a worked exercise, since you need lots of data and several grids to do anything useful. The following exercises focus attention on different stages of the process.

Exercise 7.1 Identifying Categories

(a) Take a look at these 19 constructs, a very small subset of comments overheard at a wine tasting.

Consistent quality – quality inconsistent

Smooth – petillant

Unreliable – always reliable

A long finish – little if any finish

Fruity – grassy

Musty and stale – fresh and bright

Expensive – cheap

Needs to rest and air – drinkable straight on opening

Scented and flowery – deep and heavy

Cloudy – clear

Deep colour – colour rather shallow

Yeasty – clear of yeast

Chocolate overtones – citrus overtones

Heady – light

Sweet – dry

Ready for immediate drinking – will benefit from laying down

Old and brown – young and fresh

Robust with tannin – gentle, without tannin roughness

Overpriced – a bargain.

(b) Devise a simple scheme of four or five categories, and then allocate the constructs to those categories.

(c) Find a friend who claims to know a lot about wine, and ask him or her to devise their own set of categories, allocating the constructs to them.

(d) Now place the two data sets into a single reliability table, along the lines described in Section 7.2.1, step 4.2. Discuss the similarities and differences. Then recast the table, laying it out so that, however they're labelled, the categories which you're both agreed on run from left to right and top to bottom of the table. (In other words, turn a table that looks like Table 7.2 into one arranged like Table 7.3.)

(e) Argue until you have agreed a set of common categories, and jot down the definitions.

(f) Finally, both of you repeat the analysis, independently, but using this single set of categories. Is the result an improvement over step (d)? (Work out the percentage similarity score for the 'before' and the 'after' table and see.)

I can't provide you with any answers against which you might check your working, since I don't know what categories you and your collaborator might devise! However, in case you can't find a collaborator, and want to practise setting up the reliability table as in step (d), you may get a feel for this stage of a content analysis if you look at a sample category scheme which I have provided as Appendix 1.12.

Exercise 7.2 Practising Content Analysis: D-I-Y

Take a small data set of your own, 50 constructs or so, before you first commit yourself to a full-sized set of 400! Run through the various steps described in Section 7.2.1. Once you've completed them, you'll recognise that the procedures are fairly straightforward, and certainly much less confusing than they might appear at first glance.

When you've finished, continue this chapter by
returning to Section 7.2.3.

Exercise 7.3 Preparing Grid Data for Honey's Technique

Here's a little refresher in the calculation of sums of differences, checking for reversals, and working out % similarity scores. As a reminder of what you need to do in Honey's content-analysis technique, you're asked to compute these against the supplied 'overall' construct, and to prepare your grid for content analysis.

As a senior manager in the oil business, you appreciate the value of experience in your project managers, but you know that experience isn't just a matter of age; some of your younger engineers run their projects just as well as the older ones. You decide to capture the knowledge and expertise they have that makes the difference between success and failure in project management. Eight project managers of varying expertise (as defined by checking the records of all the projects they've managed in the last 10 years) are your elements, presented anonymously to 20 senior project managers who have managed major projects in the past themselves, while being responsible for other project managers at present.

Just one of the grids, from respondent no. 8, is shown below as Figure 7.2. It is already marked into strips ready for content analysis. Before you do this, you have to write onto each strip:

(a) The sums of differences between each construct and the 'overall' construct.

(b) The corresponding % similarity score (work it out from the formula in Section 6.1.2, step 7, or, much easier, just look it up in Appendix 4).

(c) Both of the above, reversed.

(d) For each construct, choose the lower of the two values (reversed/unreversed) and circle it.

(e) Mark each construct with 'H', 'I', or 'L' depending on whether it is in the highest third, intermediate third, or lowest third of % similarity scores in this interviewee's grid.

Appendix 1.13 shows you what your result should look like.

THINGS TO READ

A good way of complementing your knowledge of Honey's technique is to read his original paper:

- Honey, P. 'The repertory grid in action'. *Industrial and Commercial Training* 1979, 11, 452–459.

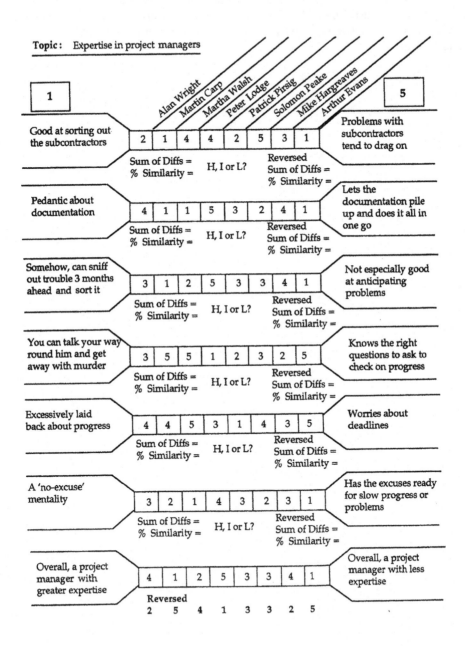

Figure 7.2 Exercise with Honey's technique

And while you're ordering that item through inter-library loan, why not order the October and December issues of the journal as well? (That's 1979, 11, 10 and 1979, 11, 12.) Each contains another article, presented in the same, user-friendly way, showing a different way of using grid technique.

CHAPTER 8

WORKING WITH PERSONAL VALUES

This chapter provides you with a way of assessing personal values. It draws on an important set of assumptions in personal construct theory, in relation to a rather large field of research relating to cognitive structure: to the mental frameworks or maps that people construct for themselves, and the ways in which these structures hang together.

8.1 CAPTURING PERSONAL VALUES

The last time you elicited a repertory grid, you may have noticed that some constructs seemed to be rather more important to your interviewee than others. Just a feeling you got from the energy with which s/he expressed them, or from the kinds of implications that seemed to follow from the way in which s/he used them.

You may have deliberately used the techniques of **laddering down** (introduced in Section 3.2.3 and developed in Section 4.4.1 as a way of expressing constructs in more specific, behaviourally defined detail) and of **pyramiding** (outlined in Section 4.4.2 as a way of identifying a variety of different, more detailed aspects of a given construct: while you're at it, take another look at Figure 4.1). You might have wondered: if constructs can be laddered *down* so that they're more precise and detailed, can they be laddered *up* to arrive at more general variants? If constructs can 'contain' more specific ones, can they themselves be contained within superordinate ones; is there a hierarchy operating?

Indeed there is, and it's given an important status in Kelly's personal construct theory. Namely, personal constructs do not operate in isolation from each other, but form an integrated system. He expressed this formally as the 'Organisation Corollary': 'Each person characteristically evolves for his experience in anticipating events, a construction system embracing ordinal relationships between constructs.' You can look at this in two ways, in terms of implied *meaning*, or in terms of *structure*.

A construct can be superordinate, because, when a person uses it to make a particular statement about a set of elements, s/he is also making a number of other, implied, statements which follow from it.

warm   –   cold

friendly – unfriendly   untrustworthy – trustworthy

Here, for example, in a grid whose topic is 'people I know', you've pyramided the superordinate construct 'warm–cold' into two subordinate constructs, so you discover that for this individual, the meaning of 'warm' implies friendliness and trustworthiness; or, conversely and equivalently, the meaning of 'cold' implies unfriendliness and untrustworthiness.

Now, if your interviewee changed their mind about a particular person's standing on the 'warm–cold' dimension, s/he might give a different rating on the 'friendly–unfriendly' and 'trustworthy–untrustworthy' constructs as well. *To the extent that* change in one construct is implied by change in another, there is a *structural* connection between the constructs. So, if you asked your interviewee which construct would change if ratings on 'warm–cold' changed, s/he might reply, 'Well, by and large, people who're warm tend to be friendly, but the connection to their trustworthiness isn't as strong; sometimes warm people can be untrustworthy, after all'. This is actually a complex issue, and I'm choosing my words with some simplification. It hinges on the extent to which there are different 'flavours' of contrasting implicit poles for any single emergent pole. If you want to pursue this further, read Riemann (1990) for an empirically based study, or Yorke (1978) for some implications for educational research. However, let's keep it simple for the moment.

There is a well-developed form of grid called an 'Implications grid', which can be used to identify the shape of the data structure, and hence the way in which meanings are organised in a person's construct system. It was first described by Hinkle (1965), and you can learn about it most conveniently in Fransella et al. (2004). There are also two different ways in which constructs can be in a superordinate–subordinate relationship to one another. Your best way of learning more about this is to read

Kelly's original account of what he calls 'abstracting across' and 'extending' the 'cleavage' of a superordinate construct; see Kelly (1963: 57–58).

Let's keep it simple, then, for the moment. A set of constructs on any topic is part of a broader system of constructs, a system that forms a hierarchy. Some constructs are superordinate, and others subordinate, to each other, and the simple repertory grid which you learnt about in Chapter 3 simply taps into part of that hierarchy.

Constructs towards the top of the hierarchy:

- are more general in their relevance; they usually have a **wide range of convenience**;

- express personal preferences more strongly; they tend to be **more value-laden**;

- may relate to fundamental beliefs about oneself and one's place in existence; these are known as **core constructs**;

- to the extent that they are personally central in this way, are likely to be **resistant to change**.

You've encountered this issue already, during the discussion of core versus peripheral constructs in Section 5.3.3.

8.1.1 Laddering Up to Arrive at Values

When you laddered down, you asked the question 'How, in what way?' You did it in two ways: simple laddering down, as in Section 4.4.1, and pyramiding, as in Section 4.4.2.

In contrast, when you ladder up, you ask the question 'Why?' The question is asked in two stages, one of which establishes the preferred pole of a construct, and the second of which establishes why your interviewee has made this choice: what its meaning is for him or her. The procedure runs as follows.

(1) Take the first construct in your interviewee's grid. Write it down at the bottom of a fresh sheet of paper.

(2) Ask the interviewee which pole of the construct s/he prefers. This can be done in a variety of ways depending on the context and the meaning expressed by the construct:

- 'Which end of this construct do you prefer?'

- 'If the construct applied to you, which end would you rather be described by?'

- 'Which end of the construct feels nicer/good to you?'

(3) Ask the interviewee why s/he prefers that pole. Again, there is a variety of ways in which you can ask this question, and the word, 'Why?', used by itself, is best avoided. 'Why?' is a very abrupt word, if you think about it. You are not asking your interviewee to *justify themselves*, but to *explain the importance the choice has for them*. Far more preferable are the following:

- 'Why, for you, is this important?'

- 'That's interesting! What's happening here, I wonder?'

- 'What follows as the result from this particular choice? For you, I mean.'

If there isn't a clearly preferred pole, combine steps 2 and 3 into a single question that asks the interviewee about the status of the contrast being made: 'Why is this an important distinction to be making about this topic?'

(4) Write the answer down immediately above the preferred pole of the previous construct, as a word or short phrase.

(5) Identify the contrasting pole. You're identifying the interviewee's reason in the form of a second construct, superordinate to the one you started with at step 1. Since this second construct *is* a construct, it has to have two poles! Read out the reason you were given, and ask what contrast is being offered. Any one of the following would do.

- 'Now, what's the contrast for [the words written down at step 4]?'

- 'What would the other end of that construct be?'

- 'And what would you be contrasting that with?'

(6) Write the answer down above the non-preferred pole of the previous construct. You now have two constructs, the original and the superordinate one above it.

(7) Repeat steps 2 to 6 for this new, superordinate construct. Which end of the construct is preferred and why? – the personal importance; and the opposite is? Write the result down, above the previous constructs.

(8) Repeat step 7 until your interviewee can't go any further. You've arrived at a personal value.

(9) Take the next construct in your interviewee's grid. You've laddered upwards and found the topmost construct for the first construct in the original grid; now see what other personal values your interviewee has: **repeat steps 2 to 8**, starting off with the second construct of the original grid and working upwards.

(10) Do this, that is step 9, repeating steps 2 to 8, **for each of the constructs in your interviewee's original grid.** If at any step you can both see that a particular construct at step 9 leads to one of the *same* personal values you've already identified at step 8, stop what you're doing and just go on to the next construct in the grid. Remember, we're dealing with a hierarchy. We talk of constructs being in pyramidal structures; what we mean is that a *single* superordinate construct can have *several* subordinate constructs below it. And so, your interviewee is quite likely to draw on the same personal value for several of his or her original constructs. That is in the nature of personal values. They aren't specific to particular behaviour or situations, but give personal meaning to many.

And there you have it, a set of ladders, vertical structures, one for each value. The constructs at the top express your interviewee's personal values, or, at least, those values which s/he finds useful and relevant to this particular topic.

At this point, pause, and examine Tables 8.1 and 8.2, which give a worked example of steps 1 to 8 for the grid shown in Figure 2.1 (way back in Chapter 2!). Remember, you must start with the lowest construct and work upwards! Go through the procedure above, following it in the two tables.

Table 8.3 shows you the results of this procedure applied to the remaining constructs of the original grid. They're the result of steps 8 and 9, in other words. Familiarise yourself with this basic procedure before you continue. The best way is by applying it to one of your own grids.

So try Exercise 8.1 before going any further.

8.1.2 The Process of Values Elicitation

If you've done Exercise 8.1 you will have encountered some of the most important procedural issues involved in the technique of values elicitation.

Hold it. I'd rather you didn't see this subject as purely and simply a matter of technique. When you ask a person about their personal values, you touch on matters that are personally important. These may be very deep, though not necessarily in the sense that they delve into the unconscious. (As it happens, Kelly makes little use of the notion of an unconscious in the Freudian sense, in which we are motivated for reasons beyond our immediate awareness, and which plays tricks on us through various protective defence mechanisms.) But he *is* concerned about personal growth, development, and change, and he does assume that that involves a process in which we try to become more deliberate about personal beliefs that we may have taken for granted, the beliefs having been there for so long that they are bedrock. You don't touch on

Table 8.1 Basic steps in laddering upwards: the first two iterations, as applied to the first construct of Figure 2.1 in the grid on teaching methods (see Section 2.2)

Steps	Dialogue	Emergent poles	Implicit poles
7		Keeping fresh	– Dead, in a rut, safe but stale
7	'Now I want to ask you the same: assuming you still prefer the same end, "more fun and creative", why is that? What's the particular value for you of that way of preparing?' 'Why do I want to be creative? Well, everyone does, don't they? It's a way of keeping fresh.' 'And the contrast to "keeping fresh" is ...?' 'Oh, being dead, in a rut, safe but stale.'		
4; 6		More fun and more creative Other people in preparation	– Stuck in your ways; same old stuff – I can prepare this by myself
1	'Okay, let's write down your first construct. Now, which do you prefer to do: prepare material collaboratively, or by yourself?' 'Oh, I prefer to work with other people really.'		
2			
3	'Okay. Now, why's that? Why, for you, is it important to work with other people?' 'It's more fun and more creative, I guess.'		
5	'And in contrast? What's the opposite of doing something which is "fun and creative"?' 'Getting stuck in your ways; teaching the same old stuff from one course to the next.'		

Table 8.2 Completing the ladder shown in Table 8.1 by repeating step 7 until the interviewee can't go any further

Life and hope		**Death, hopelessness, despair**
Being alive, having things to look forward to	–	Stopping growing, just stagnating
Keeping fresh	–	Dead, in a rut, safe but stale
More fun and more creative	–	Stuck in your ways: same old stuff
Other people in preparation	–	**I can prepare this by myself**

This records the five iterations of step 7 by which the original construct was laddered upwards to arrive at the single personal value, 'life and hope' versus 'hopelessness and despair'.

Table 8.3 A set of personal values derived by laddering upwards from each of a set of constructs. Based on the grid shown in Figure 2.1

(Original construct no.)	**Personal value**		
1	Life and hope	–	Death, hopelessness, and despair
2	Criminal irresponsibility	–	Personal moral responsibility
3	Stagnation	–	Progress
4 and 5	Pain and suffering	–	Pleasure and enjoyment
6, 7 reversed, 8 reversed, 9	Order	–	Chaos
10	Alienation from others	–	Sensibility and affiliation

- Don't confuse this table with Table 8.2. Here, there are six distinct personal values, *each one* the result of the process exemplified in Tables 8.1 and 8.2.
- The values are written down exactly as they would have been derived by steps 9 and 10 of the laddering-up procedure. If there are some negatively evaluated poles on the left, and some positively, that is because the constructs from which the laddering started, in Figure 2.1, are also that way round.
- 'Pain and suffering versus pleasure and enjoyment' was obtained by laddering up from construct no. 4 in Figure 2.1. With construct no. 5, halfway through the laddering-up procedure, it was realised that the same value applied to that construct as well as to construct 4.
- 'Order versus chaos', likewise, lies at the top of a hierarchy whose subordinate constructs are nos 6, 7, 8, and 9 in Figure 2.1. For constructs 7 and 8, the value was derived as 'chaos versus order' rather than 'order versus chaos'.

bedrock without tremors, and if you want to shift it, there may be explosions! And even if all that you're doing is delving deep to expose that bedrock, simply to describe what's there, you should remember that what you're doing touches on some fairly personal and fundamental ontological choices for your interviewee. So I'd rather you didn't think of this simply as a matter of technique, but gave a thought to the sensitive and delicate process that is entailed.

Very well. Let's deal with the procedural issues by focusing on two matters of technique, while being careful to highlight the personal process in which we're engaged.

How Do I Know That I've Got There?

This is, perhaps, the first question that occurs to you. Exercise 8.1 has highlighted that the number of steps up the ladder is variable, and that you will sometimes be unsure when you've identified a personal value. How can you tell? There are six different ways of knowing that you are arriving at value-laden constructs.

Abstraction.   The constructs you are offered deal less and less with matters of behaviour, operational activity, and detail. As you go up the ladder, you encounter constructs which deal with the essence of existence and life. Not

good timekeeper   –   poor timekeeper

but

predictability and order   –   unpredictability and chaos

perhaps.

One way of helping the laddering process is to gently nudge your interviewee into ever greater abstraction. At step 7, for example, fairly high up the hierarchy, you might say 'Why, for you, is that the personal preference? What's the *essence* of it?'

Universality.   By their nature, personal values deal in the generalities of life. When we delve into values, we're dealing with the grand themes of existence rather than the small change of day-to-day living. You'll notice that you're moving towards the top of the hierarchy when your interviewees start talking about the world rather than their own back garden; society in general rather than the golf club in particular; life, the universe, all of creation.

Not

wide choice of products   –   poor product range

but

freedom and choice   –   slavery and constraint

for example.

And again, you can help to nudge your interviewees on towards their values by using the language of universals. At step 7, your prompt might include questions like 'What would life be like if you chose this end of the construct? What would the world look like this way, rather than the other way?', pointing to each pole in turn. Depending on your degree of rapport, you might choose to be more explicit about this: 'We're moving away from day-to-day life. Remember, we're looking to arrive at your personal values *in general* – the sort of thing that applies in many different situations and settings. What's the general issue that faces us all when we choose this end rather than the other, in your own view?'

Intimacy. You'd have to be very dense not to notice that, as you progress up the ladder, you're dealing with issues that are personal and increasingly private. In fact, one of the ways you know that you're developing skill in the laddering technique is when you find yourself feeling just a little vulnerable yourself, wondering whether you ought to be taking the interviewee through another iteration.

A lot will depend on the situation, the topic, how well you know the individual already, and how good a degree of rapport you've built up. As you'll remember from Section 5.3.1, you need to adjust what you're doing to the setting in which you do it.

Laddering is best done in private. If you're in a training setting and laddering is involved, don't *ever* ladder someone's values in front of the rest of the group unless you are an experienced trainer and are used to dealing with group and individual process issues: permissions, engagement, explicit feedback from the interviewee that what you're doing feels okay, and disengagement. If you don't know what I'm talking about, don't even think about group laddering, even if you frequently elicit basic grids in a group setting.

In the individual laddering situation, when you get the feeling that you're intruding, you have a simple choice to make: have you arrived at the personal value, or should you try just one more iteration? Don't be afraid to go on, but your answer should be the result of careful attention to the way the conversation is heading, to your best intuition, and to a deliberate checking of that intuition in all of the ways at your disposal: eye contact, gaze, and posture – all of the non-verbal as well as the verbal cues. Concede that the material is intimate; talk about what's happening; ask permission to proceed. Not 'Why's the issue of death important to you, then?' but something a wee bit less crass, depending on how the issue has arisen.

If, on balance, you feel that an exchange at this level of intimacy would be inappropriate, don't enter on another iteration. Stop at the point you've reached, and ladder no further.

Self-reference. Kelly defined as core constructs those constructs which people use to place themselves in relation to their experience. All core constructs have a relation to personal values, though not all personal values are necessarily core constructs. Nevertheless, there is sufficient overlap that you can recognise an increasing potential relevance to the interviewee's self and self-image as you proceed up the hierarchy. That's why the procedure asks about the personal choice that underlies the preference at step 3, and why intimacy is an issue, as we've discussed above. The more frequently the interviewee talks about him- or herself, the stronger the self-reference, the closer you're getting to personal values.

Self-evidence.   There is an absurdity about questioning personal values. As Donald Super once defined it in the context of occupational values measurement, a value is 'an objective sought in behaviour' (Nevill & Super, 1989). There is a tendency to take it as self-evident. If you're stating as a precept, 'Thou shalt not kill', you're in a situation in which to ask the question, 'Why?', is inappropriate! You're aware that, according to some beliefs, there are circumstances in which people do kill other people legitimately, and that military jurisprudence and religious morality seek to specify the basis for such legitimacy, but that's *not* the issue when the value itself is being enunciated. And so, to ask about a person's reasons for holding the value will seem strange, absurd, irrational, or, sometimes, just plain funny!

Acknowledging the absurdity is a good way of dealing with this. Admit that it may seem strange to examine an apparently self-evident preference, ask whether your interviewee thinks there's any more to it, and emphasise that while the preference may be obvious in general terms, you're concerned with *your interviewee's own reason* in particular.

Explicit information.   If in doubt, ask your interviewee and let them tell you! Remember that you're engaged in a collaborative activity and that, after your first iteration (steps 1–6 followed by step 7), and certainly during steps 8 and 9, your interviewee will have understood your procedure. They'll know what you're up to! And so it becomes entirely appropriate to ask whether going further, trying for a yet-more-superordinate construct, is worthwhile. 'Shall we try just one more step?' becomes, with your interviewee's permission, a shared experiment.

What Do I Do if I Can't Seem to Get There?

This is the second matter which is likely to arise. When you're engaged in steps 7 and 8, you may find that your interviewee can't provide a more superordinate construct. S/he sticks, or just keeps going round in circles, giving you answers that are synonyms to those given lower down in the ladder.

Thus, for example, dependable – undependable: 'Why do I prefer people who are dependable? Well, you can rely on them.' reliable – unreliable: 'Why, for me, is reliability important? Because if you have a reliable person, you can depend on her.'

Both of you suspect that there is, nevertheless, a superordinate value still remaining to be elucidated – one, but possibly more, upward rung in the ladder which you haven't yet identified. The constructs you're dealing with so far are not as abstract, universal, intimate, self-referential, self-evident, and explicitly identified as they might be! What to do?

- Confront the issue explicitly: ask your interviewee what's happening, and how you might both progress further up the ladder.

- Make deliberate use of the five other attributes of a personal value discussed above: as indicated earlier, in helping the interviewee to elicit the superordinate construct, use words like

  - 'essentially'

  - 'generally'

  - 'privately' or 'your own personal'

  - 'for you, personally, in particular'

  - 'I know it may be obvious, but try to spell it out!'

- As with any conversation laden with personal feelings, sharing your own feelings and experience can be a powerful way of moving onward. 'Yes, I think I can appreciate how you feel about "being left alone". When my own father died it touched me in many ways, and some, in particular, that I hadn't expected. What was the main issue for you at the time *your* loved one went?'

- Cross over and use the other side of the ladder. In other words, if you're stuck in progressing upwards from the *preferred* pole, work with the *other* pole. A general form of words to use would be along the lines of: 'You can't work out what lies behind that preference? That's okay. What about the other side? What would life be like if the other were true?' (quoting the contrasting pole of the construct at which the interviewee is stuck). Figure 8.1 illustrates this option.

A Reminder

As you can see from the foregoing, the identification of personal values in this way, beginning with the constructs provided in a repertory grid, uses a straightforward, yet very powerful, procedure that results in detailed, intimate, and personal information about your interviewee.

It doesn't take a long time. While the procedure can be done at any time, on balance and other things being equal, it's probably best done, after a 5-minute pause, in the same session as the one in which you elicit the original grid.

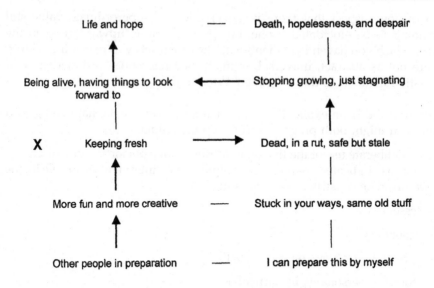

The interviewee has got stuck at **X**. Asking 'Why, for you, is it important to "keep fresh in your teaching"?' doesn't work: the interviewee finds it so self-evident to 'keep fresh' that he can't give the pole of a superordinate construct along that 'upright' of the ladder.
So, cross over and work with the contrasting pole of that 'rung' of the ladder.
'Okay, let's look at the other side. Suppose you found yourself "dead, in a rut, safe but stale". What would your existence be like? What would be the essential issue at stake?'
'It's a matter of personal growth really. I'd be getting nowhere. I'd have stopped growing and be just stagnating.'
'And crossing back to the original side of the ladder: what's the contrast to "stopping growing"?'
'Oh, that's easy! I'd be alive, and have everything to look forward to!'
'And why, for you, is that the preferable alternative?', etc.

Figure 8.1 'Crossing over' during the laddering-up process. See Tables 8.1 and 8.2

Rapport is well established, your interviewee is in a thoughtful and undistracted mood, and the constructs are fresh in his or her head.

'Other things being equal'? Well, if the session had been a long one, your interviewee not especially involved or interested, and rapport not well established, you'd close the session for the day and return for another session in due course.

In the normal course of events, though, finish the basic grid, sit back and relax, suggest one of you make a cup of tea, and then, when you're both ready again, introduce the laddering activity as a final step: something 'in which we'll explore your own personal reasons for these constructs; your own personal beliefs and values in a little more detail'.

Once you've learnt the technique and are comfortable with it, you'll find that the complete laddering procedure takes between 15 and 30 minutes, on top of the 40 to 60 minutes it takes to elicit an initial grid of around 8 to 10 constructs. It is possible to be ruminative, thoughtful, and very sensitive to the interviewee's personal feelings and privacy while moving him or her along. Eye contact is particularly helpful in pacing the laddering process. All this involves skill that takes a little while to acquire and, initially, whenever you feel you might be forcing the pace too much, slow down and give your interviewee more time for reflection.

8.2 PRIORITISING PERSONAL VALUES: RESISTANCE-TO-CHANGE TECHNIQUE

'All very well,' you might say, 'but after all this, how do I know that I've really got at my interviewee's personal values? How do I know that s/he's telling me what s/he really believes rather than what s/he would like me to believe?'

And you would be right to ask this. If you have a formal background in psychology, sociology, or behavioural studies, you will know about the **social desirability effect**. And if you are a supervisor, trainer, or manager, while you may not call it by that term, you will have come across it. You will be aware of people's tendency to express their attitudes and opinions, never mind their beliefs and values, in a socially acceptable manner.

In some circumstances, this might be a simple matter of shading expression, that is, finding a socially acceptable name for a belief. Calling a spade 'a personal digging device' rather than 'a bloody shovel', as it were. But in others, it may be a case of misinformation, a reluctance to admit that one holds an unpopular belief, or even a simple case of blatant lying about some personal value which is dear to one's own soul but to nobody else's. How might you deal with this situation? How can we be certain that the personal values we have identified are, indeed, those held by the interviewee?

The short answer is that we can't. If the interviewee doesn't wish to share his or her actual belief system with you, s/he won't. (And of course there *may* be no 'actual belief system', in the sense of a well-established underpinning structure. It may be that, for this topic in particular, existing core constructs are irrelevant, and your interviewee is just making things up as s/he goes along, feeling their way.) There is no guarantee of accuracy with the laddering technique, just as there is no guarantee of accuracy with *any* technique used in social research.

There are two main ways used by social researchers in which the social desirability effect can be handled, however, and construct laddering has its own version of both.

Firstly, one can *minimise*, as far as possible, interviewees' reasons for not reporting their actual beliefs and values. Conducting one's research and consultancy work with careful attention to ethical considerations (e.g., Russ-Eft et al., 1999), including the guarantee of such issues as confidentiality and anonymity; negotiating support for outcomes from management; and the development of a general sense of trust, and of good rapport in the face-to-face encounter are all included here. And it is surely obvious by now that all of the repertory grid technique, with its legitimation of individual perspectives and its respect for the individual's own way of construing the issues being researched, is at least as effective as, and will often be more so than, other social research methods in removing the reasons for socially desirable responding.

Secondly, one seeks to *identify the extent* to which some statements made by the interviewee are more, and less, affected by social desirability. In effect, one accepts the fact of social desirability, and works with it. Perhaps the most common approach is to identify the relative social desirability of different options, and then to ask respondents to express their preferences between options of roughly *equal* social desirability (Cronbach, 1964; Cook, 1998). By providing a sequence of comparisons in which the choices made within a set of such option pairs are aggregated, it is possible, in most cases, to identify a respondent's preference ordering over the whole set of alternatives, independent of their social desirability.

Exactly the same approach is used in the identification of personal values, especially in identifying the priorities which an interviewee gives to his or her values. It is accepted that some reported values will be less central than others, personally salient, or tied up with one's core being; and it is possible to identify this preference ordering in such a way that tends to remove the need for the individual to engage in social desirability-biased responding.

How is this done? Recall for a moment that core constructs are relatively resistant to change. The more central a belief, and the more genuinely personally value-laden a construct, the more personally important it is to see the world in that way, and the less likely an individual is to change their mind about it. And so, in order to find out which personal values are more important, and which less, one asks the interviewee to choose between values presented in such a way as to focus attention on their relative desirability. Some choices will be easy to make because the desirability, *to our interviewee*, of one option over another is clearly evident. Others will be more difficult, since the desirability of each alternative is very similar, *so far as the interviewee* is concerned. The interviewee will be prepared to compromise on some choices (indicating less-central constructs, which are more open to change), but won't on others (indicating the bedrock values: those constructs which are highly resistant to change).

The resistance-to-change technique, the procedure for identifying which personal values are more central, and which less so, and thereby describing an individual's hierarchy of personal values, is carried out in 10 steps. Let's work with an example taken from Table 8.3. A transcript of the interview procedure is given in Appendix 5. Return to it when you've read all 10 steps.

(1) Take the first two personal values identified by the laddering technique described in Section 8.1.1. Call the first personal value 'A versus contrast-A', and the second 'B versus contrast-B'. Suppose, for example, your two values are as follows:

A		contrast-A	B		contrast-B
life and hope	–	hopelessness and despair	personal moral responsibility	–	criminal irresponsibility

(2) Present your interviewee with a choice between 'A at the cost of contrast-B', or 'B at the cost of contrast-A'. Using the above example,

A		contrast-B	B		contrast-A
life and hope	at the cost of	criminal irresponsibility	personal moral responsibility	at the cost of	hopelessness and despair

Which option, 'A at the cost of contrast-B', or 'B at the cost of contrast-A', does your interviewee prefer? The choice requires the interviewee to make up their mind about how strongly they feel about each personal value. There are costs involved in each option, and so, which option has the greatest reward with the least pain?

It is helpful to present the choice as a fundamental, existential one. For example, 'I want you to imagine you are going to live out the rest of your days on an island, somewhere far away: say, in the South Pacific! I shall take you there and leave you there for ever. It's a place where you can live to the full: 'life and hope' are there! – but at the cost of a lifestyle in which people show utterly 'no responsibility' for their actions. They're 'criminally irresponsible', and you may get sucked into it! Or, alternatively, I can take you to a different island: one where people live a life of admirable 'moral responsibility' – but at the cost of an all-pervading feeling of hopelessness and despair. You have to choose one or the other: which will it be?'

(3) Record the personal value which was preferred.

(4) Now compare personal value A with the next value, C, and repeat steps 2 and 3.

A		contrast-C	C		contrast-A
life and hope	at the cost of	stagnation	progress	at the cost of	hopelessness and despair

(5) Repeat step 4, comparing value A with each of the remaining values, D, E, and so on.

(6) Now compare personal value B with the next value, C, recording the personal value which was preferred.

B		contrast-C	C		contrast-B
personal moral responsibility	at the cost of	stagnation	progress	at the cost of	criminal irresponsibility

(7) Repeat step 6, comparing value B with each of the remaining values, D, E, and so on.

(8) Repeat step 7, comparing each of the remaining values with each other: C with the remainder, D with the remainder, etc.

(9) Count the number of times that each personal value was preferred over another.

(10) Record the outcome as a hierarchy of personal values.

Table 8.4 provides you with an example of the whole procedure, working with the list of six personal values shown in Table 8.3. Notice how the personal values are expressed as each choice is presented. *Each of the two options begins with a preferred end of the personal value in question, coupled with a non-preferred end of the second personal value with which it is compared.* You're presenting the interviewee with a thought-provoking and, at times, rather difficult choice. There will be moments when s/he feels the choice is an impossible one! Your task here is to encourage the interviewee, to help him or her to think the choice through by imagining the circumstances involved, and the consequences of living with the compromise which has been adopted.

Table 8.4 Identifying the values hierarchy – the successive comparison, each with each, of the personal values shown as Table 8.3

Step	Either		at the cost of	chosen?	Or		at the cost of	chosen?
1	A and conB	Life and hope	Criminal irresponsibility	Yes	B and conA	Personal moral responsibility	Hopelessness and despair	
4	A and conC	Life and hope	Stagnation		C and conA	Progress	Hopelessness and despair	Yes
5	A and conD	Life and hope	Pain and suffering	Yes	D and conA	Pleasure and enjoyment	Hopelessness and despair	
5	A and conE	Life and hope	Chaos	Yes	E and conA	Order	Hopelessness and despair	
5	A and conF	Life and hope	Alienation from others		F and conA	Sensibility and affiliation	Hopelessness and despair	Yes
6	B and conC	Personal moral responsibility	Stagnation	Yes	C and conB	Progress	Criminal irresponsibility	
7	B and conD	Personal moral responsibility	Pain and suffering	Yes	D and conB	Pleasure and enjoyment	Criminal irresponsibility	
7	B and conE	Personal moral responsibility	Chaos	Yes	E and conB	Order	Criminal irresponsibility	
7	B and conF	Personal moral responsibility	Alienation from others	Yes	F and conB	Sensibility and affiliation	Criminal irresponsibility	
8	C and conD	Progress	Pain and suffering		D and conC	Pleasure and enjoyment	Stagnation	Yes
8	C and conE	Progress	Chaos	Yes	E and conC	Order	Stagnation	
8	C and conF	Progress	Alienation from others		F and conC	Sensibility and affiliation	Stagnation	Yes
8	D and conE	Pleasure and enjoyment	Chaos	Yes	E and conD	Order	Pain and suffering	
8	D and conF	Pleasure and enjoyment	Alienation from others		F and conD	Sensibility and affiliation	Pain and suffering	Yes
8	E and conF	Order	Alienation from others		F and conE	Sensibility and affiliation	Chaos	Yes

You should look at Appendix 5 now.

This records extracts from the transcript of the resistance-to-change interview which resulted in Tables 8.4 and 8.5. There are two things to remember about this process:

- The interviewees have to make a choice. Help them to think it through as much as you can, but *insist*, sensitively but firmly, that they choose.

- Discourage the interviewee from trying to be 'consistent' with respect to earlier choices in the procedure. The relative centrality of the personal values with respect to each other will come out in the final analysis at steps 9 and 10, when you count the preferences made. The task is difficult enough without seeking to keep track of the overall order while the comparisons are being made, and so the recommendation is that each comparison is done separately from the others.

Table 8.4, finally, shows you the outcome of steps 9 and 10 for the example of Table 8.3. The two 'chosen?' columns show whether the first or the second option of each choice was preferred. So, for example, we see that this interviewee preferred

A		**contrast-B**
life and hope	at the cost of	criminal irresponsibility

rather than

B		**contrast-A**
personal moral responsibility	at the cost of	hopelessness and despair

that is, expressed a preference for personal value A over B. This is indicated by the 'yes' in the column next to the 'life and hope at the cost of criminal irresponsibility' option in the first row of Table 8.4. Counting up the number of times each particular personal value is preferred (Table 8.5) shows the overall personal values hierarchy in Table 8.6.

For this interviewee, the fundamental personal issue is 'sensibility and affiliation versus alienation from others'. So important is the preference that he will always tend to choose sensibility and affiliation no matter what the cost might be; and so intolerable is the thought of being 'alienated from others' that he will always try to avoid a situation in which this might happen. It will be very difficult, if not impossible, to persuade him that the other issues are more important. This personal value is highly resistant to change. Similarly,

Table 8.5 Number of times each personal value is chosen in Table 8.4 (count up the 'yes' responses against each personal value)

Personal value	Times chosen
A	4
B	3
C	1
D	2
E	0
F	5

Table 8.6 The values hierarchy based on Tables 8.4 and 8.5

Personal value	The issue is	Times chosen
F	Sensibility and affiliation – alienation from others	5
A	Life and hope – hopelessness and despair	4
B	Personal moral responsibility – criminal irresponsibility	3
D	Pleasure and enjoyment – pain and suffering	2
C	Progress – stagnation	1
E	Order – chaos	0

Not all values hierarchies are as regularly ordered as this one. It's common to find two or more personal values chosen an equal number of times: you'd just write them down side by side, rather than one above the other, in the hierarchy.

subordinate constructs (those lower down in the overall construct system) that draw on this value, or are particularly representative of this value, will tend to be similarly resistant to change.

'Order versus chaos' is, in contrast, more malleable. Order was never chosen in preference to one of the other values; and the interviewee was prepared to put up with chaos in existence rather than compromising any of the other personal values. Note, this is still a personal value. Order is still preferred to chaos. It resulted from the choices made, and personal reasons given, in the original laddering exercise. But the issue carries less personal weight, and consequently, the individual may well be more open to change on matters connected with this issue.

At this point, I should point out the importance of this matter of 'resistance to change'. It's a term used very often in discussions of personal and organisational change and, typically, it is seen as something undesirable.

When the organisation has to face a complex and threatening environment, its employees are expected to be flexible and adaptable, welcoming changes in how things are done in order to cope. Employees who are reluctant to do this are seen as 'resisting change', behaviour which is greatly disapproved since it is detrimental to organisational recovery. They are thereby placed at a moral disadvantage. The change agent, in contrast (the manager or trainer who is trying to encourage them to change), is always seen as on the side of the angels, engaged in a battle with fear, reluctance, and obscurantism. S/he is advised on how best to 'overcome' resistance to change. Any basic text on organisational behaviour will supply an example (e.g., Hellriegel et al., 1995).

Yet the reasons why the individual employee might wish to 'resist' change, the possibility that they might be well informed and entirely legitimate – the consequence being that to do things differently or to think differently might be to challenge deeply held personal values built up over a lifetime of personal experience within this organisation and others – all of this is frequently not considered as a possibility. There is more on this in Jankowicz (1996).

When we identify a person's values hierarchy, we are working directly with resistance to change, without any of these moral assumptions.

That completes the basic outline of the resistance-to-change technique: a procedure which helps you to identify personal values with substantial precision, and which lessens the possibility of bias due to social desirability responding. Before leaving this section, you might want to look over Appendix 5 again, to see what was involved in using the technique.

Then work through Exercises 8.2 and 8.3.

THINGS TO DO

Exercise 8.1 Explore Your Own Personal Values

Take one of the grids which you have prepared earlier (for example, the one about 'my friends' which you elicited in Exercise 3.1). For you, what personal values underlie friendship?

You may find it helpful to take some photocopies of Figure 8.2 and use it as a worksheet, writing each original construct in at the bottom and working upwards. Obviously, there are no 'right answers' to this exercise, so I can't provide you with any direct feedback in Appendix 1. What I can do, though, is ask you some questions.

If you've done this exercise properly, the answer to each of them will be predictable. For the reasons why, see Appendix 1.14 before reading on in the chapter.

You will need one of these for each personal value you ladder. Write the result of each iteration into the spaces below, *starting from the bottom.*

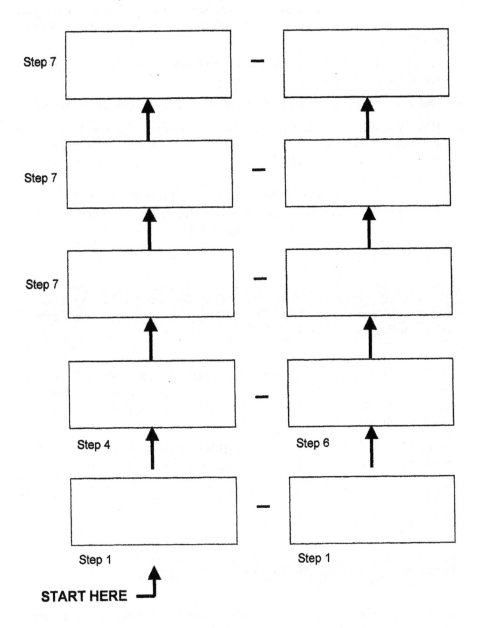

Figure 8.2 A worksheet for laddering upwards

(a) When you did this exercise, did you sometimes arrive at the topmost level without using up all of the spaces in Figure 8.2?

(b) On your way 'up' the ladders, did you sometimes get stuck at what you suspected was the same level, just saying the same thing in different words?

(c) At step 3, towards the top of any of the ladders, did it feel absurd to be asking yourself for a reason for your preference?

(d) Did you nevertheless press on and try to find a superordinate construct?

(e) When you did steps 9 and 10 to identify new personal values, did you find that you were converging on one of the values you had already identified in one of your previous ladders?

It's important that you read Appendix 1.14
now to see the reasoning involved. Then return
to Section 8.1.2.

Exercise 8.2 Which of Your Values Are Resistant to Change? (Otherwise Known as 'How Much Would You Charge the Devil for Your Soul?)

Working with the same values which you obtained as a result of Exercise 8.1 (just the ones at the top of the various ladders you prepared, remember!), compare each with each, using the format shown in the resistance-to-change procedure outlined in Section 8.2.

I can't provide you with any 'answers' to this exercise, since I don't know your values, and I have no way of knowing how you might prioritise them. However, you may glean some hints and guidelines about the procedure if you tackle the questions given in Exercise 8.3 below; these *do* have right answers!

Exercise 8.3 Working with Value Hierarchies

Address each of these questions in order, noting your response. Then check against the answers given in Appendix 1.15.

(a) You have identified two personal values:

> fair play – injustice
>
> top-down leadership – participative leadership

and you present them as follows: 'Which would you rather have, "Fair play" at the cost of "participative leadership", or "top-down leadership" at the cost of "injustice"?' Is there a problem, and if so, why?

(b) You offer your interviewee the following choice:

	A		**contrast-B**
	wisdom	at the cost of	penury and starvation
or			
	B		**contrast-A**
	comfort and survival	at the cost of	terminal stupidity

Your interviewee's response is that she can't possibly choose between the options. 'I can't bear to be thought terminally stupid, but I can't possibly make a choice that would have me starving to death! Sorry!' Which of the following responses are appropriate?

- 'That's okay. Don't worry, let's go on to the next comparison.'

- 'Tricky, isn't it? Can you think of some circumstances in a comfortable life in which you could put up with stupidity? At least you'd survive and perhaps do something about the stupidity in due course. There again, with sufficient wisdom you might be able to work out a way of surviving. Which is your preference?'

- 'No. I insist that you make a choice. The analysis will fail unless you give me a preference.'

(c) Given Table 8.7 with six choices, the interviewee has chosen the option shown **in boldface** in each case. Show the resulting personal values hierarchy.

Table 8.7 Choices made in Exercise 8.3, Question c

Either	at the cost of	or	at the cost of
Fair play	**Top-down leadership**	Participative leadership	Injustice
Fair play	**Unhappiness**	Contentment	Injustice
Fair play	Unpredictability	**Predictability**	**Injustice**
Participative leadership	Unhappiness	**Contentment**	**Top-down leadership**
Participative leadership	**Unpredictability**	Predictability	Top-down leadership
Contentment	**Unpredictability**	Predictability	Unhappiness

THINGS TO READ

Hitherto, my reading suggestions have been designed to deepen your knowledge of repertory grid technique and related theory, without necessarily providing you with different perspectives and opinions to my own. At this point, you might like to look at something different.

Mantz Yorke's classic paper of 1978 provides you with a useful refresher on some of the issues we've dealt with so far in this guide, and opens up discussion on the extent to which constructs may vary in the ways in which implicit poles relate to emergent poles. Welcome to the strange world of bent constructs!

• Yorke, D.M. (1978) 'Repertory grids in educational research: some methodological considerations'. *British Educational Research Journal* 4, 63–74.

He developed this theme in the following paper:

• Yorke, D.M. (1983) 'Straight or bent: an inquiry into rating scales in repertory grids'. *British Educational Research Journal* 9, 141–151.

Secondly, something on values.

• Horley, J. (1991) 'Values and beliefs as personal constructs'. *International Journal of Personal Construct Psychology* 4, 1–14.

provides an overview, while

• Horley, J. (2000) 'Value assessment and everyday activities'. *Journal of Constructivist Psychology* 13, 67–73.

is a short and neat paper in which real-life personal activities were used as elements, and all the personal values were supplied rather than being laddered up from a set of initially elicited constructs. Its usefulness is less as an example of personal values elicitation, and more as a short account of the stability, over time, of personal value choices.

CHAPTER 9

ALTERNATIVE WAYS OF CONSTRUING

Hitherto, we have been concentrating on single grids, showing how one or more individuals construe a particular topic, and treating each grid as a description of construing at a particular point in time. But individuals can change their minds. How can we best describe what happens when they do?

And if we compare any two individuals, their grids will, of course, be different from each other. Is there a convenient way of comparing the two?

In the first case, we deal with change, and in the second, with difference; in both, the focus is on alternative ways of construing. This chapter presents some simple grid techniques which apply in each case.

Firstly, we address personal change, and how changes in an individual's construing can be described neatly and succinctly. These procedures can be used to understand personal growth and development, whether this occurs as a result of systematic training, or simply as a consequence of the full, disorganised richness of ongoing experience. They have an application in counselling (e.g., Edmonds, 1979; Fonda, 1982; Jankowicz & Cooper, 1982) and in the personal therapeutic experience (though you will have to look elsewhere, and pre-eminently in Winter, 1992, if you're particularly interested in the clinical field).

Secondly, we outline one approach to difference in construing, the exchange grid, whose technical rationale comes from applications in individual change, but which is particularly useful when we wish to compare grids on the same topic which have been provided by two or more different individuals.

9.1 IDENTIFYING PERSONAL CHANGES IN CONSTRUING

Whenever you elicit a grid on a topic, you do so from a particular individual, in a particular place, and at a particular time. It's rather like a photograph – a snapshot of that person's views at that time and place – and all of the procedures in this guide are intended to enable you to describe your interviewee's construing at that point in time – to take and develop the photograph, as it were – as accurately as possible.

But because elicitation is an interpersonal process, there is always something of yourself in a grid. A photo of Marilyn Monroe by Bert Stern shows a rather different Marilyn to a photo by Sam Shaw, and for the same reason: portrait photography, too, is an interpersonal process. If we elicit two grids from the same person, and they differ from each other, we need to be sure that the difference is one of substance (our interviewee has changed their mind) rather than of appearance, resulting from the way we handled the interview on each of the occasions.

What we shall be doing is highlighting the differences in two snapshots taken on two separate occasions, concentrating on the differences of substance, and taking comfort from the fact that, if we're careful with our use of technique, differences due to presentation will be relatively small because the interviewer (ourselves!) is the same on both occasions, and we are doing our best to keep the presentation the same.

What kinds of changes are observable? Broadly speaking, any pair of grids elicited from the same person on two separate occasions can vary in two particular ways. Assuming that the topic stays the same,

(a) the interviewee may simply alter some of the ratings of the original grid (elements and constructs remaining as before); or

(b) some of the constructs may be different, with some new constructs added, and perhaps several of the original ones dropped. This will inevitably mean altered ratings. If some or all of the elements are also new, you would certainly expect to see new constructs as well as different ratings.

In the case of two different topics, of course, we are likely to have situation (b) rather than (a), since, as you'll remember from Section 2.1.1, it is unlikely that the range of convenience of the original constructs is so wide that they can all be used, without addition, when the topic changes.

The smaller the difference in the two grids, the easier it is to suggest a procedure, and the more straightforward the procedure will be. Let's start with the simplest case.

9.1.1 Identifying Personal Change: The Simple Change Grid

Working with identical elements and constructs is straightforward. This situation will arise if you have supplied the interviewee with their original grid, with the ratings removed, asking them to re-rate the elements using the same constructs (as part of a study of relatively short-term changes, perhaps). It *might* also occur if you elicit the second grid from scratch, using the same elements, soon after eliciting the first grid, and your interviewee finds no reason to use different constructs.

In both instances, the obvious thing to do is to focus directly on the differences between the two sets of ratings, as follows.

(1) Elicit two grids in succession from the same interviewee as outlined in Section 3.1.2. After the first grid has been completed, make a photocopy, Tipp-Exing out the ratings, and use the resulting form for the second grid. Alternatively, simply elicit the two grids in succession from scratch. In this case, note no. 2 below.

(2) Make sure that the elements and constructs are in the same position in both grids, before you start the analysis. In other words, shuffle the columns and rows of the second grid around (together with their ratings, of course!) so that the elements are in the same columns in both grids, as you look at the columns from left to right; and that the constructs are in the same rows as you read from top to bottom.

(3) Cell by cell, record the difference between the ratings in corresponding positions in the two grids. The easiest way to do this is to work with a second photocopy of the original grid, with the original ratings Tipp-Exed out. Just fill in each of the cells with *the difference between the rating in the first grid and the rating in the second grid*. (Literally: cell by cell, subtract the rating in that cell in the first grid from the rating in that cell in the second grid, putting the answer into that cell in the third grid.) At this point, you have a choice:

- Working out the absolute differences (ignoring minus signs) will provide you with an overall impression of change. Totalling the sum of differences in the change grid for each element can be informative in this regard!

- Working out the arithmetic differences (using minus signs) will make it easier to discuss the changes with your interviewee, and address the issue of why the various changes have occurred.

(4) At the bottom of each column in the change grid, sum the differences you recorded in that column, to provide a rough-and-ready indication of the overall extent to which ratings of each element have changed. (If you recorded arithmetic differences for purposes of discussion, ignore any minus signs just when you compute this total.) Table 9.1 shows an example.

(5) Consider the analysis procedures described in Chapter 5. Process analysis (Section 5.3.1) shouldn't be forgotten, even though your present procedure is focused on the numeric changes in the ratings. The way in which the second grid was completed (especially if it has been elicited rather than filled in using a photocopy), the interaction between you both, and the whole elicitation process may, on reflection, help you to interpret the numeric changes in an informative way. What was happening when the different ratings were being provided?

Eyeball analysis (Section 5.3.2) is the most relevant procedure of those outlined in Chapter 5, since it focuses attention on the ratings themselves, *and* the ways in which they are being used. Discuss the changes with your interviewee, and set them in context: why have the changes been made? Particularly, are there any changes in the supplied constructs, and why might this be?

Characterising constructs (Section 5.3.3), how are the constructs being used? Do the differences in the ratings point to constructs being used in a less propositional way? Less pre-emptively?

As you can see, all of these procedures make sense of the change by putting the purely numeric changes in context. The remainder understand the change in purely numeric terms.

(6) Consider any of the analysis procedures described in Chapter 6. The values you're working with have rather low variance (they're mainly 1s and 2s), and you may feel that the information available from the following procedures doesn't add a lot to a careful and detailed use of the analyses at step 4. But, for the record: **simple relationships** between elements (Section 6.1.1) focuses attention on which elements have changed the least, and which the most. Is there a pattern? Is there anything in common between constructs on which the ratings have changed a lot? Avoid step 7 of that procedure. **Simple relationships** between constructs (Section 6.1.2) does the same for constructs. Again, there's no need for step 7 of that procedure.

In both cases, it's important to remember that your basic data concern *change* in construing rather than construing itself. You need to be careful not to overinterpret the differences you're working with, and the best way of avoiding overinterpretation is to discuss the changes with the interviewee.

Cluster analysis (Section 6.2.2) may be useful, summarising the overall changes in a way which makes them perceptible at a glance. **Principal components analysis** (Section 6.3.2) is, in my view, best avoided. The power of

Table 9.1 Change grid analysis before and after a course on 'post-war prime ministers'

	Attlee	Churchill	Macmillan	Wilson	Thatcher	Blair	
Before the course							
Principled	2	1	2	4	4	4	Opportunist
Experienced	1	3	2	3	4	3	Inexperienced
Populist appeal	3	1	5	2	1	2	Distant from the public
Ensured a succession	3	2	1	3	4	4	Left in a hurry or likely to
Politically successful	3	3	3	2	4	4	Political failure
More effective	3	1	3	2	3	4	Less genuinely effective
After the course							
Principled	1	3	4	5	1	5	Opportunist
Experienced	2	1	2	3	4	5	Inexperienced
Populist appeal	3	2	3	2	1	2	Distant from the public
Ensured a succession	4	1	1	2	5	3	Left in a hurry or likely to
Politically successful	1	2	4	1	2	3	Political failure
More genuinely effective	2	3	1	2	2	4	Less genuinely effective
Difference grid							
Principled	1	2	2	1	3	1	Opportunist
Experienced	1	2	0	0	0	2	Inexperienced
Populist appeal	0	1	2	0	0	0	Distant from the public
Ensured a succession	1	1	0	1	1	1	Left in a hurry or likely to
Politically successful	2	1	1	1	2	1	Political failure
More effective	1	2	2	0	1	0	Less genuinely effective
Sum of differences (absolute)	6	9	7	3	7	5	

this kind of analysis comes from identifying underlying 'components', the derivation of which may be problematic (since you're dealing with data with little variance), and the meaning of which will be difficult to establish through numeric procedures alone. (Far better simply to discuss the nature of the change as under 'simple relationships between constructs' above.)

(7) Discuss all of these changes with your interviewee. In case you need reminding! In all cases, you're setting out to understand what the change means to your interviewee, why it might have occurred, and what it might lead to so far as s/he is concerned.

Table 9.1 exemplifies a common application, where the impact of a teaching programme, training course, or other intervention is being examined. At this stage, you might like to use this table to address the questions posed in Exercise 9.1.

Try Exercise 9.1 now.

9.1.2 Identifying Personal Change: The Messy Change Grid

Rather than working with two grids, each with the same elements and constructs, as above, you're working with different ones: *Messing About in Problems*, to quote the title of a fascinating book on the ways managers reflect on their thinking about practice (Eden et al., 1983).

It's probably struck you by now that situations in which the simple change grid applies are rather special. Clearly, if you ask a person to work with their original elements and constructs the second time round, you may not be giving them full scope to indicate the extent to which their views have changed. Left to themselves, they may well have chosen to provide new constructs if not new elements. Preventing this may be justifiable in a controlled study or experiment, but less so if you were investigating change in a counselling or advisory setting.

> That's right. If all that changes between two grids is the ratings on existing constructs, it's arguable that the interviewee hasn't changed in any fundamental way. S/he is telling you s/he feels differently about the topic, but the terms which apply haven't changed, and s/he isn't thinking of the world in different terms.

> Your interviewee may even change their mind about an element completely, changing a rating of '1' to a rating of '5', and thereby going from one extreme of the construct to the other, so that the opposite end of the pole applies. It is rather like a marble rolling along a slot from one end to the other, which is why this particular form of change is called 'slot-rattling'. But, in the literature on counselling, therapy, and personal growth, it is felt that this represents a relatively shallow level of change, since the old construct remains, and a person who changed their mind so as to provide an opposite rating may just as readily change their mind back again! They're still stuck in the same old grooves.

In contrast, change which involves new constructs (and indeed new elements) is generally seen as a matter of more fundamental personal alteration. Some alternatives to slot-rattling are as follows:

- Drawing on another construct easily available in the personal repertoire.

- Putting pre-verbal constructs into words and using them in the grid (you will recall the short discussion on pre-verbal constructs in Section 4.3.3).

- Considering the whole construct hierarchy, and the extent to which alternative constructs more compatible with superordinate personal values, which have not initially occurred to the interviewee, might be made available.

- Elaborating (further developing) the repertoire of constructs, and possibly reconsidering the hierarchical relationships between constructs.

- One way of extending the repertoire of elements and constructs during grid elicitation is through a process called elaboration. Note when two constructs are being used very similarly (in the sense that the ratings of all elements on these constructs are identical, or nearly so), and ask the interviewee if they can think of a new element which would receive maximally *different* ratings on each of the two constructs. Likewise, towards the end of a grid, if it is obvious that two of the elements have received identical, or very similar, ratings on all of the constructs, the interviewee might be asked to provide a new construct, on which the two elements would receive maximally different ratings. (See Jankowicz & Cooper, 1982, for further particulars of these procedures.)

- Experimenting with new forms of behaviour, both during the grid session and outside it, to suggest new ways of making sense of the new experience.

- Encouraging the application of existing constructs to situations in which they haven't previously been used, thereby increasing their range of convenience.

- Redefining the meaning and relative importance of existing constructs.

- Developing entirely new constructs which have never been in the repertoire.

All this is from Winter (1992: 240–245).

Yes. As you can see, most of these sources of change form part of the deliberate personal interventions we call, variously, guidance, counselling, and therapy. These are situations in which the individual is helped, sometimes quite energetically, to construe the topic differently! You'll need to look elsewhere for material on this subject, which is beyond the scope of this guidebook. For anyone who hasn't any formal counselling or therapy training, a good place to start would be Fonda (1982), followed by Jankowicz & Cooper (1982).

However, some of these changes can also occur spontaneously, as the interviewee decides that existing constructs are insufficient to capture his or her new experience. This is especially likely if the interviewee has decided that the old constructs are invalid; that is, that they're no longer acceptably accurate in predicting life events (Kelly, 1963: 157–160). This assumption lies at the heart of Kelly's theory. His Experience Corollary states that: 'a person's construction system varies as he successively construes the replications of events', this being seen as fundamentally a predictive, forecasting activity.

When this happens, the changes captured in a second grid can be quite complicated, and the change over the two grids rather 'messy' to analyse. The following is less of a procedure and more of a short list of initiatives by which this messiness can be handled.

(1) Elicit two grids in succession from the same interviewee. Elicit two grids in succession from scratch, using the basic procedure outlined in Section 3.1.2.

(2) Before analysis, make sure that any elements and constructs which both grids have in common are in the same position in both grids. In other words, shuffle the columns and rows of the second grid around (with their ratings, of course!) so that the elements are in the same columns in both grids, as you look at the columns from left to right, and that the constructs are in the same rows as you read from top to bottom in both grids. As the second grid is a free-form one, you will have elements and constructs left over (see Tables 9.2 and 9.3).

(3) If there are sufficient common elements and constructs to make it worthwhile, treat that portion or both grids as a simple change grid (see Section 9.1.1). Whichever of the analysis procedures from Section 9.1.1 that you decide to use, don't stop at that point, but look for links between the existing constructs and the new ones, as follows.

(4) Examine the function of the new constructs (and elements, if any), with the interviewee, putting them into context with the existing ones.

(5) Explore the process by which some of the constructs have been dropped. Steps 3, 4, and 5 are in fact different facets of the same activity, for you are trying to build a shared understanding of how, why, and how far your interviewee is thinking differently. You might find that it simplifies the task if you transfer all the constructs onto a single working grid sheet (see Table 9.3).

(6) Focus, first and foremost, on the constructs and their meaning: what's being said, and what has changed?

Additionally, to tackle steps 4 and 5, you may find it helpful to work with an organising framework: some model which will provide you with a systematic approach based on a good rationale for *how* people change their construing, and will provide a first step into theory, that is, into understanding *why* the interviewee is changing. At least three models are available in personal construct theory.

(a) The experience cycle. Construing over time consists of a cycle made up of several stages as follows: anticipation, investment, encounter, assessment, and constructive

Table 9.2 One interviewee's two grids, A1 and A2

Grid/Construct		Dr JF	Mr PMcS	Prof. AW	Ms AK	Dr LT	Dr TN	
A1.1	Clear, understandable	1	3	3	2	1	5	Difficult to follow
A1.2	Makes it interesting	1	2	3	4	1	5	Dull and boring
A1.3	Easy-going	2	5	4	1	3	4	Tense and preoccupied
A1.4	An all-rounder	2	4	5	1	4	3	Very specialised
A1.5	Lenient marker	2	2	3	1	5	4	Strict marker
A1.6	Good tutorial skills	1	2	3	2	5	4	Doesn't know how to discuss
A1.7	Good delivery	2	1	1	2	3	5	Talks too quietly and mumbles
A1.8	Makes me laugh	1	1	5	2	4	5	Rather solemn
A2.1	Can understand them easily	1	3	1	1	1	4	Difficult to follow
A2.2	Good delivery	1	1	1	1	4	5	Talks too quietly and mumbles
A2.3	Good in tutorials	1	2	1	2	4	4	Can't hold a discussion
A2.4	Makes it interesting	1	2	1	4	2	5	Dull and boring
A2.5	Relaxed	1	4	3	2	3	5	Tense, preoccupied with material
A2.6	Accessible to students	3	1	2	1	5	4	Never there to take a problem to
A2.7	Gives obscure references	3	5	4	3	2	1	Recommended texts easy to find

The topic is, 'how I feel about my lecturers'; A1 was obtained at the start of the second year and A2 at the start of the third year of a three-year degree.

Table 9.3 Single working grid sheet to summarise changes between interviewee's two grids

Grid/ Construct		Dr JF	Mr PMcS	Prof. AW	Ms AK	Dr LT	Dr TN	
A1.1 and A2.1	Clear, understandable	1,1,0	3,3,0	3,1,2	2,1,1	1,1,0	5,4,1	Difficult to follow
A1.2 and A2.4	Makes it interesting	1,1,0	2,2,0	3,1,2	4,4,0	1,2,1	5,5,0	Dull and boring
A1.3 and A2.5	Easy-going	2,1,1	5,4,1	4,3,1	1,2,1	3,3,0	4,5,1	Tense and preoccupied
A1.6 and A2.3	Good tutorial skills	1,1,0	2,2,0	3,1,2	2,2,0	5,4,1	4,4,0	Doesn't know how to discuss
A1.7 and A2.2	Good delivery	2,1,1	1,1,0	1,1,0	2,1,1	3,4,1	5,5,0	Talks too quietly and mumbles
Sum of Diffs		2	1	6	3	3	2	
A1.4	An all-rounder	2	4	5	1	4	3	Very specialised
A1.5	Lenient marker	2	2	3	1	5	4	Strict marker
A1.8	Makes me laugh	1	1	5	2	4	5	Rather solemn
A2.6	Accessible to students	3	1	2	1	5	4	Never there to take a problem to
A2.7 rev.	Recommended texts easy to find	3	1	2	3	4	5	Gives obscure references

1. The purpose is to simplify the messiness in Table 9.2. Common constructs have been shunted to the top of the table. The ratings are shown in order: grid A1, grid A2, absolute difference.

2. Where necessary (construct A2.7), the poles are reversed to show all positively evaluated poles on the left.

revision. Read more on this in Kelly (1970). If you have a background in management, you may recognise a similarity to the Kolb cycle (active experimentation, concrete experience, reflective analysis, and abstract conceptualisation); see Kolb (1984) for the basics, and Greenaway (2002) for a handy comparison of several experiential change models, Kelly's included.

(b) The creativity cycle. Fresh ways of thinking require alterations in the implicational tightness of the constructs being used to predict a situation. 'Implicational tightness' can be described as follows. Suppose you have the following two constructs about supervisors at work:

Make me feel nervous   –   I can relax in their company

Tend to distract me   –   Don't disturb my concentration

If, for you, they are implicationally tight, you'll find you can only do a good job of any task in which you're engaged by concentrating very hard when a supervisor who makes you feel nervous is looking at you.

You might find it difficult to think of alternative ways of handling this situation, so long as the tight link between these two constructs is maintained. Of course, you've developed an implicationally tight link between these two constructs for a good reason. It helps you to know what you have to do to be effective – you have to concentrate!

But the strong implicational connection gets in the way of alternative, and possibly more effective, ways of coping, unless you loosen the tightness of this link. As soon as you imagine that it may be possible *not* to be distracted by people who make you feel nervous, it becomes possible to search for new constructs.

And so the creativity cycle consists of an alternation between tight construing (in the service of effective action), loose construing (in order to search for alternatives), and renewed tight construing (efficient predictions using the revised construct set). See Winter (1992: 13–14; 258–264) on how therapists utilise this cycle.

(c) The C-P-C cycle, which stands for Circumspection, Pre-emption, and Control. The model asserts that, when making up their minds about an issue, an individual will firstly tend to engage in circumspection by looking round in their personal repertoire, and examining various propositional constructs which may be relevant to the various issues in a situation. S/he then construes pre-emptively as s/he concentrates on a single issue. Finally, s/he engages in control, that is, decides which pole of that construct to use and relate to. (You may need to refer to Section 5.3.3 at this point, to refresh your memory on propositional and pre-emptive construing.) See Winter (1992: 13–14; 247–250) for more details.

And so, 'exploring the process' becomes a matter of drawing on any of these models to structure an approach to understanding your interviewee's change. I don't want to be too prescriptive here; you should simply take your interviewee's feedback, and do what seems sensible to you both at the time. However, you might like to draw on the models by considering one or other of the following.

(6) Drawing on the C-P-C cycle, the experience cycle, and the creativity cycle, identify the kind of change which is taking place in your interviewee's construing of the topic, and act accordingly. If the issues concern a decision, you might draw on the **C-P-C** cycle as follows. Does the second grid represent an attempt to be more circumspect, pre-emptive, or controlling than in the first grid? By and large,

- if circumspect: do the new constructs cover broader ground, a greater variety of issues, than the original ones?

- if pre-emptive: are the new constructs minor variations of the other constructs in the second grid, with the ratings being rather similar? What would constructs with very different meanings, and very disparate ratings, mean in these circumstances?

- if control: are the new constructs more behaviourally specific than the ones they replace? Can you see more extreme ratings on the new constructs, reflecting a greater salience with respect to your interviewee's situation?

Perhaps the **creativity cycle** is relevant. Is the second grid produced as part of an attempt to tighten or loosen construing?

- Generally speaking, are the ratings in the second grid more closely or less closely related to each other than in the first grid? Check this out for key comparisons as follows:

- Take one of the constructs which appears in both grids (call it construct 1), a construct which seems highly related in the original grid (call it construct 2), and any construct (call it construct 3) that seems to have replaced construct 2 in the second grid. How similar are the ratings between construct 1 and construct 2 in the original grid? How similar are the ratings between construct 1 and construct 3 in the second grid? Is the second grid an attempt to loosen (lower similarity scores for the two constructs being compared) or tighten (higher similarity scores between the two constructs being compared)?

Something similar is done, in a more structured way, using just one grid form in the **Implications Grid**. The interviewee is asked, construct by construct, what changes would occur in other constructs in a grid if they changed the ratings they gave on a particular construct. Implications grids are beyond the scope of this account, but you can find more on the technique in Chapter 3 of Fransella et al. (2004).

If you have carried out a principal components analysis (see Section 6.3.1) of each of the two grids separately, you will be able to compare the variance contributions of the components in each grid, and see in gross terms to what extent the construing is loose (many components accounting for a given variance total) or tight (few components accounting for that level of variance). Alternatively, you could try one or more of the different kinds of index analysis, as mentioned in Section 5.1.1.

The **Experience Cycle** model can be drawn on if the two grids appear to be part of an ongoing process of reflective analysis: the sort of process described by authors such as Hunt (1987), Thomas & Harri-Augstein (1985), and Whitehead (1994), an activity increasingly included in the objectives of managerial doctorate programmes such as the DBA.

Questions to ask here would include the following.

- What stage in the cycle is represented by the transition between the two grids? What kinds of conformation or disconformation are involved, and what sort of revisions are being made?

- Feelings expressed during elicitation of, and strength of feeling as represented by ratings in, the second grid compared with the first would be worth exploring as you examine the investment phase. The particular difference represented by constructs dropped from the first grid, and new constructs used in the second grid, might be used to explore the assessment and constructive revision phases.

- Alternatively, if you prefer to work directly with the **Kolb cycle model**, it might be useful to see the two grids as two stages in the process of transition from concrete experience to abstract conceptualisation. This provides a direct expression of reflective analysis, and you'd concentrate on the reasons for replacing old constructs with new ones. Alternatively, you might view the two grids as a summary of the transition between abstract conceptualisation and active experimentation. If so, you might want to discuss how behaviourally explicit, and predictively robust, the constructs in the second grid were in comparison to those in the first.

At this point, you should tackle Exercise 9.2,
to get a feeling for the clear presentation
of what might originally look like a rather
messy situation.

9.2 IDENTIFYING DIFFERENCES BETWEEN PEOPLE

Cast your mind back to Sections 7.2.1 and 7.3.2. You'll recall how careful we were to ensure that the results of the content-analysis procedures described there were acceptably reliable. The reason is quite simple. When you decide on how other people's constructs should be categorised as you did there, you should do so in ways that would make sense to other people and not simply to yourself. A content analysis is meant to be used by other people, and idiosyncratic content analyses are simply less useful than content analyses which don't convey much meaning to others.

There are situations, however, when you need to capture people's idiosyncracies in order to work with them. Clearly, two single repertory grids, elicited from two different people on the same topic, is an excellent way of doing so. Having elicited two separate grids, you would go away and apply each of the procedures outlined in Chapters 5 and 6 (especially the eyeball analysis of Section 5.3.2) to each of the grids in a comparative way, noting the points of similarity and difference which made sense to yourself as investigator.

Far better, though, *to involve both interviewees in this analysis*, focusing their attention explicitly onto the similarities and differences with respect to each other's grid. One thinks of counselling and organisation development (OD) situations (such as marital/partner guidance in the former case, and team-building activities in the latter), in which the interviewees' views of one another are more informative than your own views as investigator.

> Your argument here is represented very neatly in personal construct theory. Kelly's Individuality Corollary states that 'People differ from each other in their construction of events', and, further, the Commonality Corollary reminds us that, 'to the extent that one person employs a construction of experience which is similar to that employed by another, his processes are psychologically similar to those of the other person'. In both cases, the simple comparisons between two grids which you suggest, carried out by the investigator, are indicated.
>
> However, as the Sociality Corollary has it, 'To the extent that one person construes the construction process of another, he may play a role in a social process involving the other person', and the second kind of situation which you have described is one in which it makes sense to capture the interviewee's own construing of the other interviewee's construing *directly*. Getting a partner (married or lay, domestic or occupational), or the members of a team, to work directly and explicitly *with each others' constructs* can illuminate the roles each other occupies, precisely because counselling or OD activities of these kinds deal with those relationships between people which are constrained and influenced by mutual expectations. These are pre-eminently role relationships, and the Sociality Corollary is very pertinent.

The Sociality Corollary also suggests the procedure to follow. We're concerned to identify 'the extent to which one person construes the construction processes of another'. What kinds of differences are observable?

Well, there are broadly two approaches you might take. The first, in which two people examine each other's grids on a topic of common interest, is typical of many OD team-building interventions. It simply hands over the responsibility for the comparison and analysis to the individuals concerned, with yourself acting in a general facilitating role. For want of a better word, let's call this the **simple partnering** approach. The second, the **exchange grid**, already has a name as it's a well-worn procedure. It's more structured, and investigates differences by requiring the interviewees to put themselves explicitly in each other's shoes, using each other's constructs.

9.2.1 Facilitating Mutual Exploration: Simple Partnering

Here, you would usually combine grid elicitation and analysis into one session lasting between two hours and a full day, depending on the setting and the number of people involved. In either case, the procedure has the same skeleton, and what varies is the amount of flesh you put on these procedural bones, that is, the amount of time you spend on each step. The procedure is straightforward but the results are, potentially, very rich.

(1) Negotiate a confidentiality contract. Before you start to take the group through the basic elicitation procedure, make sure that everyone knows that they will be showing their grids to each other. Assure them that the grid is a very powerful technique in that it can get beyond the 'motherhoods' and 'first approximations', but that it is completely safe, in the sense that each person remains in control of what they write on their grid sheet. If anyone doesn't wish to share something because it's too private, they can reword what they write onto the sheet, or think of something else to write.

(2) Agree a set of elements sensible to all. The topic is the same for all, and the elements are specified in the same way for all. You could:

- supply the same set of elements to everyone;

- lead a discussion in which you negotiated a set of elements through group discussion, which would then be used by everyone. This is a good way of exploring what a topic means to everyone in the group, and could itself take up to an hour, with some flip-chart work on your part as you note and agree a common set;

- elicit elements, each person providing his or her own elements under categories which are common to all.

(See Section 3.2.2 on choosing elements.) The one thing you would probably not do is to let each person choose their own elements completely freely, as this might broaden the realm of discourse beyond the point at which construct comparisons are meaningful.

(3) Agree appropriate anonymity arrangements for elements. Because they will be looking at each other's grids, you may need to get the interviewees to anonymise the elements on their grids. For example, if the topic is about 'our bosses in this firm', or 'our fellow students', the interviewees may wish to use initials in place of names – or even to resort to numbers. One technique here is to number the element spaces on the grid sheet, and ask each interviewee to jot the names which correspond to each element on a separate sheet of paper, which they show to no one. A lot depends on the exact nature of the topic, and the circumstances in which this event takes place. This isn't a difficult issue, but it is important and you need to think it through in advance.

(4) Elicit the repertory grids. As in Section 3.1.2, each person fills in their own grid sheet for themselves. You could elicit the grids in separate sessions with each interviewee, but usually, in a counselling or change setting, it helps to build social involvement and rapport if you treat this as a group session. Consider using a common qualifying phrase (see Sections 3.2.1 and 3.2.3); *don't* expend too much effort on laddering down, since you will want your interviewees to explore this mutually rather than during the initial elicitation activity.

(5) Put the interviewees into pairs, and ask each pair to swap grids. Set each member of the pair the task of 'seeing how your partner views this topic'.

- Run though the bare bones of an eyeball analysis (see Section 5.3.2) and put the main steps as headings onto a flip-chart that everyone can see.

- Emphasise that if they aren't sure of what their partner means by a construct, they should ask the partner.

- They may wish to take turns to interview each other about the other's grid, looking for points of similarity and difference in each other's construing.

- Helping each other to clarify meaning, as by laddering down initially vague constructs, is very worthwhile and may be central to this dialogue. Explain the purpose and the technique of laddering down (Section 4.4.1); encourage the use of the basic pyramiding technique (Section 4.4.2) if you want to encourage an examination of the variety of the partner's construing.

(6) Process the outcomes in a plenary session. Whether you're working with one pair of participants or many, the purpose is to generalise the outcomes from the above step, getting the interviewees to discuss and understand whatever common patterns exist, between pairs and (as appropriate) across all the pairs. Various ways of managing and extending this plenary session will occur to you, depending on your experience of facilitating other people's learning, but it would be useful to bear the following three points in mind.

- Summarise similarities and differences (perhaps by means of two simple headings on a flip-chart, getting participants to call them out as agreed between pairs). It is important to examine differences, and to negotiate a common stance towards them. Can they be minimised, debated, or eliminated, or is an explicit 'agreement to differ' required?

- Explore the background and, where possible, causes. Encourage the participants to discuss the reasons that might underlie the similarities, and especially the differences in construing, under at least two headings: are they personal, or role-related?

- Draw on personal construct theory as appropriate when handling the facilitation. Appendix 6 gives a brief summary of the formal content of the theory, and Section 5.3.3 provides you with a vocabulary, some of which may be relevant as the participants explore the different kinds of constructs they are using. The issue of values, as summarised by the notion of a core construct, may be useful in examining the questions of 'what kind of relationship would we like between us?' and 'what sort of a group/department organisation would we like to be?' You would not, on the whole, engage in any explicit value elicitation of the kind outlined in Section 8.1.1 without contracting to do so in a subsequent session of single interviews, which you had thought through carefully in advance.

(7) Agree an appropriate action plan. You would usually want to turn the material on the flip-chart into some form of implications for action, and (depending on what kind of intervention this has been) negotiate an appropriate degree of commitment to that action.

I've described the simple partnering procedure in the form of a personal/team development activity, where the interaction between the interviewees is an important part of the process. Of course, there may be situations in which the grids have to be elicited in separate sessions, with the face-to-face activity between interviewees being organised as a plenary feedback session in which you have done much of the analysis previously. There are several good accounts of the latter in Stewart & Stewart (1982).

9.2.2 Entering Another Person's World: The Exchange Grid

With this approach, the interviewees don't simply examine one another's constructs and explore the meanings *at a distance*, as it were. You put them into a situation in which they have to *actually use* one another's constructs, not simply examine them, and there are two ways in which this can happen, as you will see at step 7 of the procedure.

(1) Negotiate a confidentiality contract. Before you start to take the group through the basic elicitation procedure, make sure that everyone knows that they will be showing their grids to each other. Assure them that the grid is a very powerful technique in that it can get beyond the 'motherhoods' and 'first approximations', but that it is completely safe, in the sense that each person remains in control of what they write on their grid sheet. If any doesn't wish to share something that's too private, they can reword what they write onto the sheet, or think of something else to write.

(2) Agree a set of elements sensible to all. Usually, the topic is the same for both interviewees, and the elements are specified in the same way for both. In this case, you could:

- supply the same set of elements to everyone;

- elicit elements, each person providing his or her own elements under categories which are common to all.

(See Section 3.2.2 on choosing elements.) The first time you were doing this activity with these particular people, you wouldn't arrive at the elements through discussion, and you wouldn't let each person choose their own elements completely freely.

(3) Agree appropriate anonymity arrangements for elements. Because they will be looking at each other's grids, you may need to get the interviewees to anonymise the elements on their grids. For example, if the topic is about 'our bosses in this firm', or 'our fellow students', the interviewees may wish to use initials in place of names – or even to resort to numbers. One technique here is to number the element spaces on the grid sheet, and ask each interviewee to jot the names which correspond to each element on a separate sheet of paper, which they show to no one. A lot depends on the exact nature of the topic, and the circumstances in which this event takes place. This isn't a difficult issue, but it is important and you need to think it through in advance.

(4) Elicit the repertory grids. As in Section 3.1.2, each person fills in their own grid sheet for themselves. You could do this in separate sessions with each interviewee, or you could do this in a group setting. (You will find that facilitation is rather more structured than with the simple partnering procedure described in Section 9.2.1, incidentally, so you are unlikely to be working with many pairs of people at the same time.) Consider using a common qualifying phrase (see Sections 3.2.1 and 3.2.3); *do* spend time in laddering down, so that each grid is as specific and complete, from the interviewee's point of view, as possible. An example from one pair of interviewees is shown as Table 9.4.

(5) Photocopy each grid, and Tipp-Ex out the ratings on the photocopy. That's all you need to do. There is no need to reorder the constructs so that similar ones are in the same position, as you did in step 2 of Section 9.1.3, when you followed the messy change grid procedure.

(6) Put the interviewees into pairs, calling one person in each pair 'A', and the other 'B'; get A and B to exchange the photocopies of their own grids. (To make the instructions easier to follow, assume in this instance that A is a male and B is a female.) So Mr A works with the photocopy of Ms B's grid: he can see Ms B's elements and constructs, but not Ms B's ratings. Similarly, Ms B

Table 9.4 Two different interviewees' grids, Mr A and Ms B

Construct	Dr JF	Mr PMcS	Prof. AW	Ms AK	Dr LT	Dr TN	
A1 Clear, understandable	1	3	3	2	1	5	Difficult to follow
A2 Makes it interesting	1	2	3	4	1	5	Dull and boring
A3 Easy-going	2	5	4	1	3	4	Tense and preoccupied
A4 An all-rounder	2	4	5	1	4	3	Very specialised
A5 Lenient marker	2	2	3	1	5	4	Strict marker
A6 Good tutorial skills	1	2	3	2	5	4	Doesn't know how to discuss
A7 Good delivery	2	1	1	2	3	5	Talks too quietly and mumbles
A8 Makes me laugh	1	1	5	2	4	5	Rather solemn
B1 Concerned about the students: sees them as part of job	3	1	4	4	2	5	Doesn't give a toss about the students, just own research
B2 Confident and funny	2	1	2	2	4	5	Poor lecturer: too nervous
B3 Gives clear essay feedback	3	3	4	1	4	5	Leaves you stranded: criticisms not useful
B4 Paces the lecture to students' needs	1	1	2	3	4	5	Rushes difficult material during lectures
B5 Constantly develops material, keeps it fresh	3	2	1	5	3	4	Repetitively covers years-old material
B6 Equal and enthusiastic attention to all	1	4	2	2	5	3	Has favourites among the students
B7 Encourages questions and discussion	1	2	2	3	4	5	Belittles students' ideas and discourages their contribution

The topic is 'how I feel about my lecturers'. Both grids were obtained on the same occasion.

Table 9.5 B's attempt to reproduce A's grid

Construct		Dr JF	Mr PMcS	Prof. AW	Ms AK	Dr LT	Dr TN	
A1	Clear, understandable	1	3	3	2	1	5	Difficult to follow
A2	Makes it interesting	1	2	3	4	1	5	Dull and boring
A3	Easy-going	2	5	4	1	3	4	Tense and preoccupied
A4	An all-rounder	2	4	5	1	4	3	Very specialised
A5	Lenient marker	2	2	3	1	5	4	Strict marker
A6	Good tutorial skills	1	2	3	2	5	4	Doesn't know how to discuss
A7	Good delivery	2	1	1	2	3	5	Talks too quietly and mumbles
A8	Makes me laugh	1	1	5	2	4	5	Rather solemn
B as A1	Clear, understandable	1	1	3	4	3	5	Difficult to follow
B as A2	Makes it interesting	1	3	2	2	3	3	Dull and boring
B as A3	Easy-going	1	4	3	1	5	5	Tense and preoccupied
B as A4	An all-rounder	2	4	4	2	3	4	Very specialised
B as A5	Lenient marker	3	2	5	2	4	4	Strict marker
B as A6	Good tutorial skills	1	2	4	3	5	5	Doesn't know how to discuss
B as A6	Good delivery	1	1	2	2	3	5	Talks too quiet and mumbles
B as A8	Makes me laugh	1	1	4	2	5	5	Rather solemn

Ms B has been working with a photocopy of Mr A's grid with the ratings Tipp-Exed out, and has entered the ratings that she thinks Mr A used. Mr A's original grid is shown first, followed by B's grid as A.

works with the photocopy of Mr A's grid, seeing Mr A's elements and constructs but not the ratings.

The next step has two different possibilities.

(7a) Either: ask each interviewee to fill out the other's grid *as s/he thinks the other filled it out.* In other words, it is Mr A's task to try to reproduce the ratings which appeared in Ms B's original grid (without looking, of course!). Ms B's task to complete Mr A's grid by filling in the ratings that Ms B thinks Mr A used. Each of them has to put themselves in the other's shoes and use the other's constructs as s/he thinks the other uses them, writing in the ratings each thinks the other would have used.

(7b) Or: ask each interviewee to fill out the other's grid, *as themself.* In other words, Mr A works with Ms B's elements and constructs, but provides the ratings which Mr A *himself* would have used. Likewise, Ms B writes in *her own* ratings, but using Mr A's elements and constructs.

As you can see, the two procedures are rather different. The first is a literal attempt at thinking as the other person thinks. How well does each person understand the other? 'If I understand your understanding of the topic, I should know what you mean by each of your constructs, *and* how you use them to give meaning to each of the elements. And so I should be able to replicate the ratings that you have used.' This can get particularly penetrating if there are 'self' constructs in the grid, such as 'Myself as I am now' or 'myself as I would like to be'! How accurately can I reproduce how you think of yourself in your own terms?

The second procedure allows each individual to provide *their own* ratings – but they still have to do so with the other's constructs. 'If I understand your constructs, I should be able to use them. I should have no difficulty in providing my own ratings for those which I personally share, or am comfortable with. I may, however, struggle to provide a personal rating for those of your constructs which I don't share, or which are meaningless to me.'

There is a subtle flavour of 'can I *be you*?' in the first case, as distinct from 'what sense can I *make* of you?' in the second case. The analysis reflects this difference.

(8) Ask each interviewee A to compare B's attempt at being A with A's original grid, discussing the attempt. Then swap round, with each interviewee B comparing A's attempt at being B with B's original grid. Consider using the change grid subtraction procedure (Section 9.1.1). The point is for the 'owner' to give feedback to the other on how close the ratings were, and explore the differences. So, when it's each person's turn, the owner should address the following in the other's attempt:

- on which constructs was the other successful? Is this because the partner has similar constructs? Any other reasons?

- on which constructs was the partner less successful? Why might this be?

A change grid (as in Section 9.1.1) can, by subtracting ratings in corresponding cell positions in A's original compared with B's attempt at being A, highlight the differences if required.

The discussion in this step will be slightly different depending on which variant of exchange was used at step 7. In the former case, the initial question might be 'How successful were you in being me?' and in the second, 'Which of my constructs was it uncomfortable for you to use?'

Whichever variant is used, in situations in which the two people must work together (or, more interesting, live their lives together!), a discussion of this kind will be very fruitful. It is particularly useful if the discussion towards the end is turned in two directions.

- Firstly, that of feelings. Are the differences significant in the sense that they matter to the two partners?

- And secondly, behaviour. Are there important differences with respect to any particular elements in the grid, and what are the implications arising from the fact that the two partners have a different orientation towards those elements? Are the differences in orientation resolvable or not, and in either event, what does this imply in terms of how to behave towards the elements in question, especially if those elements are other people?

Try a quick exercise: Exercise 9.3.

9.3 IN CONCLUSION

It is very clear from this chapter that, as we consider changes and differences in construing, we have to engage with theory in rather a different way, certainly in more detail, and perhaps more profoundly, than when we were dealing with single grids. We find ourselves in the somewhat deeper waters inhabited by the change agent, whether s/he is called a personal friend giving advice (in among the shallows), a trainer-facilitator, an OD consultant, a guidance counsellor, or a clinical psychologist (in deep and murky waters indeed).

Earlier in this guidebook, we were following procedures whose significant outcome is fairly straightforward. We were working with the grid as a description, followed by an analysis whose impact on the individual depends on the extent to which the interviewee felt engaged but whose outcomes s/he can choose to forget or ignore as s/he returns to the ongoing concerns of daily life. That is true, to a degree, even of the more personally significant activities involved in the identification and prioritisation of personal values (as in the previous chapter). But now, the impact of the procedures – the particular descriptions and analyses being offered – seems to be different. Their significant outcome is more complex, and the impact is less easily ignored by the interviewees themselves.

That's not really very surprising. It's quite obvious! As soon as you start dealing with change, you confront your interviewee with more profound matters than when you engage them in descriptions of the status quo!

A single grid requires them to make fairly simple choices of which constructs might apply, and which rating best expresses the personal meanings intended. A change grid, however, is different because it requires the interviewee to confront the fact that s/he has chosen to think differently about the topic, and there is an implied pressure to give an accounting of the difference; in a sense, to justify it, if only to themselves. An exchange grid confronts the interviewee with the direct awareness, by trying them out personally, of alternative ways of making sense of the topic, and these may well be ways that had not occurred to him or her before the exchange was made. And the more important the topic might be (either personally as a result of its impact on the individual's values, or interpersonally because it requires collaboration between the two people), the more acute the internal confrontation might be.

In this case, you are asking the interviewee to consider rather more complex choices. These are the choices which Kelly called *elaborative*, those that imply the possibilities of a development or extension of his or her existing construct system. With elaborative choices, it's 'make-up-your-mind time'. Not only does the individual have to decide that the rating of elements dear to him may no longer apply, but the basis of those ratings, the constructs themselves, may have to change.

The process may well be triggered by a bit of slot-rattling, as the individual contemplates each end of a construct and decides which is preferred. But, as Kelly suggests in discussing the Choice Corollary, the choice may well be made because of the wider implications, some of which may lead to a drastic reorganisation of the whole system of constructs involved. 'Here is where inner turmoil so frequently manifests itself. Which shall a man choose, security or adventure? Shall he choose that which leads to immediate certainty or shall he choose that which may eventually give him a wider understanding?' (Kelly, 1963: 64).

Once you're dealing with issues like these, you need an organising framework within which to handle your use of the technique, and a good familiarity with the relevant theory. Something much more organised than my own short interjections becomes mandatory. Read Kelly!

And at this point, we have reached the end of the possibilities offered by a simple procedural guide. Don't forget to visit The Easy Guide to Repertory Grids website, at *www.wiley.co.uk/easyguide*

THINGS TO DO

Exercise 9.1 A Simple Change Grid Analysis

Using Table 9.1, answer the following questions:

(a) About which politician has the overall view changed the most?

(b) And the least?

(c) Why might this be?

Check your answers in Appendix 1.16.

Exercise 9.2 Handling a More Complex Change

Look again at Tables 9.2 and 9.3 and answer the following questions. The answers are in Appendix 1.17.

(a) Compare the grids shown in Tables 9.2 and 9.3. Why have some of the constructs from both grids been separated and put at the top?

(b) What are the three figures in each cell in the upper half of Table 9.3?

(c) About which staff member has the student changed his mind most?

(d) Give at least two bits of evidence for your answer to question (c) (hint: look what's happening with the constructs as well as the ratings: just slot-rattling, or something else as well?).

(e) If you knew this student was about to start his final-year dissertation in the same week as the second grid was elicited, and that his dissertation theme was in the field of specialism of Prof. AW, Dr LT, and Dr TN, does any of the three change models appear to be useful in understanding what's going on?

(f) Assuming the same circumstances as in question (e), how would you characterise the main changes?

Scribble your answers down before proceeding
to Appendix 1.17.

Exercise 9.3 An Exchange Grid

Look again at Table 9.4 and examine the two different grids about lecturers. Now turn to Table 9.5 and see what Ms B has made of Mr A's constructs and ratings. This is a *self as other* attempt; in other words, Ms B has filled in the ratings on Mr A's constructs as she thinks Mr A filled them out. Now work out the difference between the two sets of ratings following the change grid procedure (Section 9.1.1).

(a) Which lecturer has Ms B understood most similarly to Mr A?

(b) For which lecturer has Ms B least successfully understood Mr A's views?

(c) Why might this be? If you were Ms B, what sort of hunches about the reasons for difference would you want to discuss with Mr A?

Check your answers against Appendix 1.18.

THINGS TO READ

When you've a moment, fire up your web-reader and investigate the following sites. Each of them is designed with your present needs for ongoing support and resources in mind. All access URLs are correct as of the start of June 2003; should this change, a Google search under each of the italicised terms should find the new one as required.

The Site of the Book! The Easy Guide to Repertory Grids Website

If you need further examples of the various techniques described in this book, do pay a visit to

• *www.wiley.co.uk/easyguide*

The material is cross-referenced to the various sections of this book, and is pitched at several levels:

Practical Mindreading provides you with a *Vade Mecum*: companion material giving you 'more of the same' if you feel you'd like further guidance on the ground covered in this book.

The Repgrid Gateway is purely informational, acting as a portal to a growing variety of repertory grid resources. It's small at present but it is designed to grow over time.

Consultancy Services provides you with contact information about commercially charged repertory-grid based assistance should you ever require it.

The PCP Information Centre

The PCP Info Centre is an outstanding, and growing, portal to a variety of other sites devoted to personal construct psychology and repertory grid technique, run by Joern Scheer.

• *http://www.pcp-net.de/info/*

There are many very useful resources here: for example, access to a range of support networks worldwide, of which the European Personal Construct Association,

• *http://www.pcp-net.de/epca/*

the North American Personal Construct Association,

• *http://www2.newpaltz.edu/~raskinj/NAPCNmain.htm*

and the Australasian Personal Construct Group

• *http://www.bendigo.latrobe.edu.au/health/hstud/pcp/APCG.html*

will probably be the most helpful in putting you in touch with other people interested in grid technique.

• *http://www.enquirewithin.co.nz/*

The material on this site, which announces a commercial service called 'Enquire Within', is itself gratis. There is so much valuable expertise in this free material that you are well advised to look in to it.

PCP Bibliography

Gabrielle Chiari of the Italian Personal Construct Association has prepared a comprehensive bibliography of publications on Personal Construct Psychology and Psychotherapy in hard-copy form. This has now been computerised and is being maintained by Beverly Walker of the Australian Association. It is available at: *http://www.psyc.uow.edu.au/pcp/citedb/index.html*

APPENDIX 1

ANSWERS TO EXERCISES

1.1 Answers to Exercise 2.1

I can't provide exact answers since I have no way of telling what you wrote. But here are some common mistakes that it's possible to make in this exercise, and some ways of putting them right.

Table A1.1 Example answers to Exercise 2.1

Construct		Comment
Sociable	–	No! It's not a construct. It only has one end
Likes a good laugh	–	Ditto. Make sure your adjectives/ phrases come in pairs
Friendly	– Unfriendly	Okay, better. But, *in what way* 'unfriendly'?
Friendly	– Shy, slow to get to know	That's better: because the opposite fixes the meaning of the left-hand end ...
Friendly	– Aggressive and in-your-face	... compared with this example. 'Friendly' means something rather different here.
Reliable	– Unreliable	Again, this is a construct but doesn't tell us very much ...
Reliable	– A poor timekeeper	... compared with this ...
Reliable	– Difficult to trust	... or indeed this

Constructs have two poles. The meaning of 'good' depends on whether you intend to say 'good as opposed to evil' or 'good as opposed to only fair'. The first is a thundering moral judgement while the second is a comment about the quality of a student essay. The meaning of that first word, 'good', is entirely different depending on which opposite is intended.

Constructs are precise. Try to avoid opposites which are the same as the left-hand pole with the word 'not', or an equivalent, stuck on in front. Once you've decided on the *nature of the contrast*, you can get a grip on what was meant by the left-hand pole. In fact, you might want to change the word at the left to bring out the contrast better. Do so!

Recent research has suggested that using techniques which result in contrasts, as distinct from simple opposites, provides for a more complete and cognitively complex expression of a person's construct system (Caputi & Reddi, 1999).

1.2 Answers to Exercise 4.1

Table A1.2 Example answers to Exercise 4.1

Page in App. 2	Line beginning	Issue no.	The point being...
258	Now, can you tell me in what way they're reserved?	10	Getting a more detailed, operational description of a construct to avoid possible stereotyping or clichés
259	Okay, I know that this may seem a bit awkward	12	Write down the emergent pole on the left to ensure it gets the '1' end of the scale.
264	[shows the grid] Independent is a '1' and	12	Write down the emergent pole on the left to ensure it gets the '1' end of the scale.
261	How would you tell?	10	Getting a more detailed, operational description of a construct to avoid possible stereotyping or clichés
263	Looking over the ratings, it looks like all the blokes	10	Handling a construct which appears to be trivial: if in doubt, ask the interviewee and discuss it with him or her
263	[refusing to be drawn]	3	The point about a grid is to identify the interviewee's way of looking at the world, regardless of whether it matches other, more 'expert', views
264	That's all right	4	If a particular triad of elements doesn't suggest a new construct, drop it and offer another triad
266	I'll scribble that down for the moment	10	Getting a more detailed, operational description of a construct to avoid possible stereotyping or clichés: what's a 'best friend'?
266	By all means! This is about	3	The point about a grid is to identify the interviewee's way of looking at the world, regardless of whether it matches other, more 'expert', views
266	Oh no: the 'three-at-a-time' bit is just	2	You only give the elements in triads in order to elicit constructs which are different from the preceding ones. If another way of presenting elements brings this about, that's fine!
266	Okay. Now look, what I'd like to do	8	Handling several constructs which come out 'in a rush': are they different enough from each other, or just different aspects?
268	I was going to say 'predictable–unpredictable'	7	Interviewee, as well as interviewer, wants to be sure the construct isn't repeating an earlier one
268	That's fine. Now let's do the ratings on each of	11	Rate the triad first if the construct was elicited with a triad; otherwise, just go along the row from left to right
268	Well, actually, you're not doing too badly	6	Encourage and reassure the interviewee when s/he's flagging, or worried that 'there aren't enough different constructs'

1.3 Answers to Exercise 4.2

First question:

Q: Is it easier to pyramid lots of subordinate constructs from a construct the interviewee feels is important to him or her?

A. I've really no idea: it depends on what the construct was, and what the grid from which you took it was about. I'd love to know what your interviewee's constructs were, though!

However, it is possible to say a little. Very broadly speaking, constructs which are more personally relevant, those which relate to personal values, and especially those which are involved in your interviewee's understanding of him- or herself are likely to have a large number of subordinate constructs. If the topic of the grid was relatively impersonal (such as 'cars I have owned'), this would be less likely to occur.

Anyway, I've got you thinking about the relative importance of constructs. Good! That'll be useful in Chapter 7. And you practised laddering technique as well.

Second question

Q: How would you characterise the constructs? What sort of constructs are they?

A: Again, I can't tell, not knowing the topic and not being able to see the constructs.

However, I asked you to make a judgement of your own about someone else's constructs, despite all I've said in Chapters 3 and 4 about the interviewee being the one whose judgements matter. And I have you wondering what I'm looking for when I ask you to 'characterise constructs': what sort of thing I'm on about.

Do constructs come in different varieties? Can one be analytic about them, independently of what the interviewee might think of them?

Fine. It's time to look at Chapter 5, which is about the analysis of single repertory grids.

1.4 Answers to Exercise 5.2

Each answer is keyed to the transcript in Appendix 2 so that you can check the answer for yourself.

(a) What the interviewee is thinking about:

- How did the interviewer negotiate the topic with the interviewee?

  By saying he wanted to understand the way in which he viewed his friends.

  [App. 2, p. 257, paragraph beginning 'Okay, so we have eight people you know ...']

- What was the qualifying statement?

  The qualifying statement used was 'in terms of how you think of them as friends'

  [App. 2, p. 257, paragraph beginning 'Okay, whoa, hold on a bit!']

(b) How the interviewee represented the topic:

- What were the elements?

- Eight named friends

  [App. 2, p. 257, paragraph beginning 'Okay, so we have eight people you know ...']

- How were they agreed?

  The interviewer suggested that a range of friends be used.

  [App. 2, p. 257, paragraph beginning 'Topic: My Friends']

(c) How does the interviewee think?

- What are the constructs?

  They're as shown in the final table.

  [App. 2, p. 270]

  Note both poles of the constructs, and how the interviewee has been helped to refine the meaning by laddering down (for example, 'reserved, hold back till they're introduced – friendly and approachable' was changed to 'reserved, hold back till they're introduced – outgoing, will approach others first'.

  [App 2, p. 258, paragraph beginning 'Now, can you tell me in what way ...'])

  Read over all of them. And form an impression of what kinds of construct they are (you will be given some guidelines on construct categorisation in Section 5.3.3).

(d) What does the interviewee think?

- What kind of scale is used, and how would you characterise the ratings?

It's a 5-point scale.

[App. 2, p. 259, paragraph beginning 'Now, suppose that what we have here is a rating scale.']

The ratings are unremarkable: no rows or columns with a preponderance of the same value; each construct has at least one '1' and one '5'. So there seems to be no particular bias or emphasis obvious in an eyeball inspection. (In contrast, imagine if one of the constructs had received ratings of just 1 and 5!)

(e) Look at the supplied elements and constructs

- At an initial glance, which element seems as though it received the most similar ratings to the supplied element?

There are no supplied elements in this grid.

Similarly, form a quick impression of which construct seems to have received the most similar ratings to the supplied construct.

The supplied construct is 'best friends – don't get on with (each other)'. At a quick glance, it would seem to have received very similar ratings to construct 'on the same wavelength, react similarly, more predictable – more difficult to predict': the two constructs differ by one rating point, and that's in the rating given to element CD. It looks as though this interviewee defines friendship in terms of predictability, being 'on the same wavelength', in particular.

[App. 2, p. 270]

(f) Draw your conclusions

- What are the main points, bearing in mind any process analysis you have already conducted?

There's lots of things you can say here, and they'd depend on your recall of what happened during elicitation! Some of the more obvious things are as follows:

The interviewee was open and quick on the uptake, though things needed clarifying, such as the directionality of the scale [App. 2, p. 259, paragraph beginning 'Okay, I know this may seem a bit awkward, but the scale goes from ...'].

It wasn't hard work: steady effort, but not a matter of 'pulling teeth' and with occasional touches of humour [App. 2, p. 262, paragraph beginning 'Ah, KL! He's the couch potato's couch potato! ...'].

Some of the constructs were generated relatively quickly, with the interviewer jotting them down and then going back over them to obtain ratings ('on the same wavelength'; 'easy/a good laugh'; 'same background as myself'; 'honest, reliable, dependable') [App. 2, p. 267]. With the exception of the construct 'easy/a good laugh' the pattern of ratings appears to be rather similar on each of these constructs [App. 2, p. 268]: is this a 'friendship' cluster? This is something to check in greater detail when doing a more statistical analysis (see Section 6.2).

GH appears to be rather special (receiving the largest number of ratings of '1' on scales which all have their preferred end with a value of '1' rather than '5') and KL the least liked (receiving the largest number of '5' ratings likewise) [App. 2, p. 270] Well, fair enough: GH is the interviewee's girlfriend [App. 2, p. 263, paragraph beginning: 'GH is my girlfriend....'].

Now return to Chapter 5 and continue at Section 5.3.3.

1.5 Answers to Exercise 5.3

(a) *Core*: you can't really tell which of the constructs express personal values or are otherwise sufficiently private as to express core constructs; you'd need to do some laddering upwards to answer this question. The following constructs might be good ones to try laddering in this way:

Independent, self-sufficient   –   A conformist, group-dependent

More predictable   –   More difficult to predict

Open and emotionally honest   –   Secretive, pull the wool over your eyes

(b) *Propositional*: there's just the one which you could regard as propositional:

No siblings   –   Many siblings

and in your analysis you might want to explore to what extent other constructs (such as 'reserved – outgoing'; perhaps 'open – secretive') are related, as you explore your interviewee's thinking, especially if you were doing a study of what having siblings, as opposed to being an only child, meant to your interviewees. You could characterise:

Best friends   –   Don't get on with

as 'constellatory', since friendship is a construct around which most people build quite complex, rich and close associations. If you glance back at Appendix 2 (the transcript of this grid interview), page 266, you'll see how many associated constructs tumbled out when the interviewer invited the interviewee to be a bit more specific about what he meant by 'best friends'; and if you look at the ratings given to 'best friends' and

> On the same wavelength   –   Difficult to predict
> Easy/a good laugh   –   Have to be careful with them

in particular, you'll see how similar they are.

(c) *Affective*: there are several of these, which isn't all that significant given the topic of the grid!

> Open and emotionally honest   –   Secretive, pull the wool over your eyes re feelings
> Easy/a good laugh   –   Have to be careful with them

(d) *Evaluative*: these are often the affective ones, in the sense that feelings involve preference judgements and hence evaluations. However, it's interesting to notice one construct in this grid in which the interviewee makes an evaluative statement without particularly expressing an emotion:

> Good schooling, like an old   –   Weaker schooling: inner-city
> grammar school   comprehensive

(e) *Attributional*: there's no particularly attributional construct here. None that make statements attributing causes or reasons to the actions or behaviour of the people who make up the elements of this grid.

Now go back to the very end of Section 5.3.3 and finish off the chapter.

1.6 Answers to Exercise 6.1

(a) The basic sums of differences between elements are shown in Table A1.3.

(b) The smallest sum of differences is 4, for T1 and T3; and the largest sum of differences is 20, for T1 and T4. The first pair are indeed the most similarly rated, and the latter, the least similarly rated.

(c) The trainer construed by the interviewee as most similar to herself is T3: the sum of differences is 7, the lowest of all the matches with the Self element.

Table A1.3 A simple element analysis of the grid shown as Table 6.15

1	T1	T2	T3	T4	Self	5
Prepares thoroughly	5	2	5	3	2	Seat-of-pants speaker
Energetic, moves about	1	2	1	5	1	Just stands there stolidly
Intellectual	3	1	3	5	2	Pedestrian
Language articulate, precise, and concise	5	1	4	2	3	Language shambolic, appeals to intuition
Makes it seem so obvious and clear	3	1	2	5	3	You have to work to understand his point
Tells jokes	1	5	2	4	3	Takes it all very seriously
Overall, enjoyed his courses	1	3	2	5	2	Overall, didn't enjoy his courses

Simple element analysis

Sums of differences

T1 against	–	18	4	20	9
T2 against		–	14	16	9
T3 against			–	18	7
T4 against				–	15

Okay! Now return to Section 6.1.1.

1.7 Answers to Exercise 6.2

Table A1.4 A simple element analysis of the grid shown as Table 6.16

1	PC	Mac G3	iMac G4	eMac	Ideal	5
Looks boxy and 'standard'	1	2	5	4	5	The looks are to die for
Large range of software	1	2	4	2	1	Smaller range of software
Slow performer	1	3	5	2	5	Fast
Easy to set up	5	1	1	2	1	Difficult to set up
Good build quality	5	2	1	3	1	Flimsy build
Easy to upgrade	2	3	1	1	1	Upgrade is a dealer job
Difficult to move	1	1	4	5	5	Transportable

Simple element analysis

	PC	Mac G3	iMac G4	eMac	Ideal
Sums of differences					
PC against	–	12	23	15	21
Mac G3 against		–	13	11	13
iMac G4 against			–	10	4
eMac against				–	8
Ideal against					–

(a) The clear favourite to buy, if the constructs were equally important to you and there were no other elements or constructs to consider, would be the iMac G4 computer. A wise choice as of mid-2003.

(b) The least favoured computer is the PC. It compares poorly against the Ideal because it looks dreadful, has a poor build quality, is difficult to set up, performs slowly, and is difficult to move. It has a lot of software available for it, though, and is fairly easy to upgrade if you're prepared to bolt on various cards. All right, I prefer Macs, I admit it.

Fine. Now return to Section 6.1.1.

1.8 Answers to Exercise 6.3

The % similarities you calculated should look like those in Table A1.5.

Table A1.5 A simple element analysis of the grid shown as Table 6.16 with element % similarity scores

1	PC	Mac G3	iMac G4	eMac	Ideal	5
Looks boxy and 'standard'	1	2	5	4	5	The looks are to die for
Large range of software	1	2	4	2	1	Smaller range of software
Slow performer	1	3	5	2	5	Fast
Easy to set up	5	1	1	2	1	Difficult to set up
Good build quality	5	2	1	3	1	Flimsy build
Easy to upgrade	2	3	1	1	1	Upgrade is a dealer job
Difficult to move	1	1	4	5	5	Transportable

Simple element analysis

	PC	Mac G3	iMac G4	eMac	Ideal
% similarity scores					
PC against	–	57.14	17.86	46.43	25.00
Mac G3 against		–	53.57	60.71	53.57
iMac G4 against			–	64.29	85.71
eMac against				–	71.43
Ideal against					–

(c) The element which shows the smallest difference from the ideal in Table 6.16 should indeed have the highest % similarity score. All you've done is to turn element differences into % similarities. The extent of relationship should be preserved however you measure it!

Table A1.6 An extract from a grid on 'Computers I might buy', together with construct difference scores, completed

	1	PC	Mac G3	iMac G4	eMac	Ideal	5		Against C1	Against C2	Against C3	Against C4	Against C5	Against C6	Against C7
									Simple construct analysis UNREVERSED						
C1	Looks boxy and 'standard'	1 (5)	2 (4)	5 (1)	4 (2)	5 (1)	The looks are to die for	R	–	7	3	15	13	13	3
C2	Large range of software	1 (5)	2 (4)	4 (2)	2 (4)	1 (5)	Smaller range of software	E	9	–	6	8	8	6	8
C3	Slow performer	1 (5)	3 (3)	5 (1)	2 (4)	5	Fast	V	13	10	–	14	14	10	6
C4	Easy to set up	5 (1)	1 (5)	1 (5)	2 (4)	1 (5)	Difficult to set up	E	3	10	4	–	2	6	14
C5	Good build quality	5 (1)	2 (4)	1 (5)	3 (3)	1 (5)	Flimsy build	S	3	8	2	16	–	6	14
C6	Easy to upgrade	2 (4)	3 (3)	1 (5)	1 (5)	1 (5)	Upgrade is a dealer job	E	5	12	6	14	12	–	14
C7	Difficult to move	1	1	4	5	5	Transportable	D	17	10	14	6	6	6	–

Excellent. Now back to Section 6.1.2 to learn
about relationships between constructs.

1.9 Answers to Exercise 6.4

Please see Table A1.6.

(c) It looks as though two pairs of constructs are particularly highly matched:

'easy to set up – difficult to set up' and 'good build quality – flimsy build' have a sum of differences of only 2. Flimsily built computers are also seen as difficult to set up. However, if you look at the reversals, C3 reversed has rather similar ratings to C5 unreversed: the sum of differences is also 2. In other words, there's a high match between 'fast – slow performer' and 'good build quality – flimsy build'.

The interviewee tends to see computers which have a good build quality as easy to set up; he also sees them as fast performers.

Now return to Section 6.1.2, step 7.

1.10 Answers to Exercise 6.5

Please see Table A1.7.

Now return to Section 6.1.3.

1.11 Answers to Exercise 6.6

(a) In Figure 6.3, which construct lies closest to the axis representing a principal component?

Construct D lies closest to the vertical line representing the second principal component. Just! Constructs C, D, E, and F lie rather close as well, varying only in the amount of variance associated with that component: C the most, D the least.

(b) Which construct shows the least variance along its component?

Construct D.

(c) And which the most?

Construct A, along the first principal component (the horizontal axis).

(d) If element 6 represented myself, element 5 my partner, and element 3 my ideal self, which of us is closest to that ideal?

My partner lies closer, in a straight line, to my ideal self than I do. (Element 5 is closer on the page to element 3 than element 6.) Perhaps that's why I like my partner: she represents the kinds of things I admire and would aspire to in myself!

Table A1.7 Grid interview with the manager of the clothing section of a department store, examining the simple relationship between constructs, showing reversals (% similarity scores), completed

1	(left pole)	Jane	Ann	Billie	Ian	Alma	May	5 (right pole)		Simple construct analysis UNREVERSED					
										Against Con 1	Against Con 2	Against Con 3	Against Con 4	Against Con 5	Against Con 6
Con 1	Learns the new models quickly	5 (1)	1 (5)	1 (5)	1 (5)	4 (2)	2 (4)	Takes a while to learn the features of new lines	R E	–	16.67	–50.00	91.67	33.33	66.67
Con 2	Too forward in pushing a sale: tends to put customers off	3 (3)	4 (2)	3 (3)	1 (5)	2 (4)	1 (5)	Good balance between active selling and just being helpful	V	0	–	16.67	25.00	0	0
Con 3	Could be more interested in after sales	1 (5)	5 (1)	4 (2)	4 (2)	1 (5)	3 (3)	After sales (alterations, other bespoke elements) well handled	E R	66.67	0	–	–41.67	0	–16.67
Con 4	Awareness of sizes, colours, availability	5 (1)	1 (5)	2 (4)	1 (5)	4 (2)	2 (4)	Availability and choice knowledge poor	S	–58.33	8.33	75.00	–	41.67	75.00
Con 5	Pleasant and easy-going	3 (3)	1 (5)	2 (4)	5 (1)	4 (2)	3 (3)	Takes it all very seriously	E	0	66.67	50.00	8.33	–	66.67
Con 6	Overall, an effective salesperson	5 (1)	1 (5)	2 (2)	4 (4)	4 (4)	2 (2)	Overall, a less effective salesperson	D	–33.33	33.33	66.67	–25.00	–16.67	–

What would have to change to bring me closer to my ideal self? Well, whatever it is that the constructs and components represent! I'd have to move down on the second component and from left to right on the first to move closer to element 3. Hold on to that notion of movement and change, and

Return to Section 6.3.1 where you left off.

1.12 Answers to Exercise 7.1

Not so much a set of answers, but rather, a set of five categories (**in boldface**) and allocations of constructs to those categories which I, as your collaborator, have devised.

Reliability and character

Consistent quality – quality inconsistent

Unreliable – always reliable

A long finish – little if any finish

Ready for immediate drinking – will benefit from laying down

Needs to rest and air – drinkable straight on opening

The eye

Cloudy – clear

Old and brown – young and fresh

Deep colour – colour rather shallow

The nose

Yeasty – clear of yeast

Chocolate overtones – citrus overtones

Fruity – grassy

Heady – light

The palate

Sweet – dry

Robust with tannin – gentle, without tannin roughness

Smooth – petillant

Musty and stale – fresh and bright

Scented and flowery – deep and heavy

Cost

Expensive – cheap

Over-priced – A bargain

Make a reliability table. Lay out these categories along the top of a sheet of paper; enter your own categories for this exercise as a column on the left of the sheet of paper; and then enter each construct (or just its number for brevity's sake) into the appropriate place in the table, mine as they are above, yours as you decided them, all following the procedures described in Section 7.2.1, steps 4.2 and 4.3. The result should look something like Tables 7.2 and 7.3. Where do we differ? What adjustments might we negotiate to increase our reliability? I make no pretence at expertise in wine tasting! The categories are my own invention. But there should be enough here to help you to practise the content analysis steps described in Section 7.2.

Now return to Section 7.2.2.

1.13 Answers to Exercise 7.3

This is what each of your grids should look like after you have prepared them for Honey's content-analysis procedure, steps 1 to 5. The particular example shown is the grid from person no. 8, as given in Figure A1.1.

You need to check:

(a) that you have worked out correctly the values of the sums of differences, % similarity scores, unreversed and reversed;

(b) that you have chosen the larger of each possibility, unreversed or reversed. In other words, you should have circled:

construct 1 unreversed

construct 2 unreversed

construct 3 unreversed

construct 4 reversed 'knows the right questions to ask to check progress' matches with 'overall greater expertise', while 'you can talk your way around him and get away with murder' matches with 'overall less expertise'

construct 5 reversed, same rationale as above

construct 6 unreversed;

(c) that you have identified the high, intermediate, and low % similarity scores as shown. If you were to order the constructs in terms of the % similarities, in other words, they'd look like this:

Topic: Expertise in Project Managers

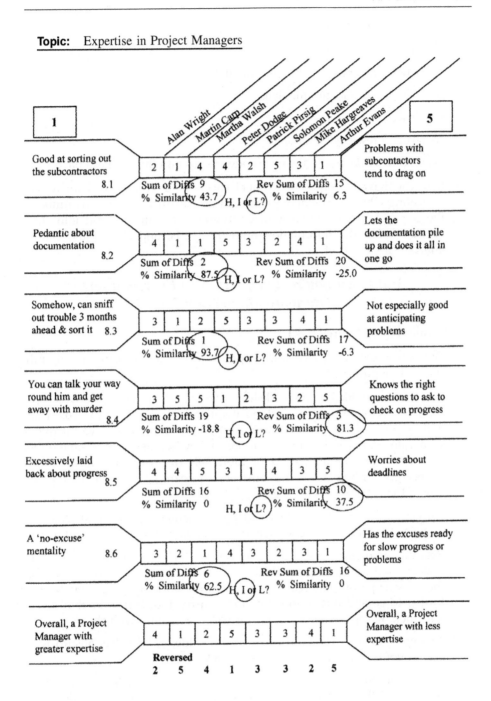

Figure A1.1 Answers to exercise with Honey's technique

construct 3: 93.7%, high

construct 2: 87.5%, high

construct 4 reversed: 81.2%, intermediate

construct 6: 62.5%, intermediate

construct 1: 43.7%, low

construct 5 reversed: 37.5%, low;

(Your constructs won't always divide evenly into thirds; these have.)

(d) that you haven't forgotten to label each of the constructs with a code indicating which respondent provided this construct, and which number in the sequence of elicitation it is. Once you've cut up the grid into strips or transferred the information onto file cards, and started the content analysis, it's too late!

And when you're done, return to the remaining few words in Section 7.4.

1.14 Answers to Exercise 8.1

(a) Did you sometimes arrive at the topmost level without using up all of the spaces in Figure 8.2?

Yes, that's very likely. The worksheet offers you five spaces into which you can write in the result of each step 7 iteration as you ladder upwards. There will be times when you find you can't go any further, and you arrive at your value in fewer than five iterations. (Likewise, there will be times when you need more iterations: six or more sets of boxes! In which case, of course, just scribble down the construct, squeezing it in above the topmost box in the Figure 8.2 worksheet.)

(b) On your way 'up' the ladders, did you sometimes get stuck at what you suspected was the same level, just saying the same thing in different words?

Yes, that frequently happens. You get the feeling that you're repeating yourself and not getting any higher up the ladder of abstraction, towards the most superordinate construct. This may be a sign that you *have* no further to go and this is your topmost construct; or it may be that you've got stuck. Return to Section 8.1.2 for ways of dealing with this.

(c) At step 3 towards the top of any of the ladders, did it feel absurd to be asking yourself for a reason for your preference?

Yes, I wouldn't be surprised if this happened. Value-laden constructs are self-evident things, and to question them seems absurd ('But *why* do you prefer "having fun" to "being bored"? Oh, come on!')

(d) Did you nevertheless press on and try to find a superordinate construct?

Yes, you should. It's worth persevering to see whether there isn't a still-more-superordinate preference being expressed. (Different people give themselves different reasons for wanting to have fun, after all.)

(e) When you did steps 9 and 10 to identify new personal values, did you find that you were converging on one of the values you had already identified in one of your previous ladders?

Yes, you'd expect this to happen, at least sometimes. Constructs are organised into hierarchies that are pyramidal, in which subordinate constructs may be different expressions of the same superordinate construct. The same value can find expression in different ways. It isn't always the case, of course.

Now return to Exercise 8.1.

1.15 Answers to Exercise 8.3

(a) Given the two personal values,

Fair play   –   Injustice

Top-down leadership   –   Participative leadership

to present them as a choice between 'fair play' and 'top-down leadership' is to remove the implicational dilemma. Assuming that most people prefer participative leadership to top-down leadership, there's no contest between the options you are presenting to the interviewee, and no challenge to values that would encourage him or her to make a *preference* choice between the two values. Regardless of how the two values are written down, in offering the choice as 'A at the cost of contrast-B', or 'B at the cost of contrast-A', *always make sure that you put the preferred end of the personal value at A and B*, and the non-preferred end of the personal value at the contrasting end. Because of the way in which you laddered up to arrive at the personal value, you will *always* know which is the preferred end of each of the two personal values!

So the choice in this instance should be presented as:

A		**contrast-B**
fair play	at the cost of	top-down leadership

or

B		**contrast-A**
participative leadership	at the cost of	injustice

(b) Needless to say, the second option is the preferred one.

You *do* have to get a preference for each of the personal value pairings, and the technique will fail unless you do so. The first option is out.

But so is the third one. Ultimately, in grid work, what you're doing has to make sense to your interviewee, and they can't be browbeaten into going along with you.

They can, however, be cajoled, so long as you go about it the right way! Try to help them think their position through, with a little imagination and attention to the possibilities in each option.

Hence the second option is the right one.

It would be wrong, though, if you stopped at the end of the third sentence. This offers the interviewee a way out of the dilemma which, if she is getting tired or frustrated, she might accept because she sees a reason behind it. The last sentence is required in order to point out that the other option is *also* open to reasoning. This keeps the dilemma in being, but provides more information according to which she can choose a rationale which reflects her value preferences.

(c) The four different values were chosen as shown in Table A1.8.

Table A1.8 The values hierarchy for Table 8.7, Question c

	Personal values	Times chosen
Fair play – injustice	Contentment – unhappiness	2
Participative leadership – top-down leadership	Predictability – unpredictability	1

Fair play and contentment were each chosen twice: so far as this example goes, they are the most resistant to change, and hence the most central, to this interviewee. The type of leadership and the predictability of life, while still there as values, are somewhat less resistant to change, and thereby more peripheral in comparison to the first two.

1.16 Answers to Exercise 9.1

(a) The change grid shows absolute differences, so it's worth looking at the bottom row, which shows the sums of differences for each element. It looks as though the interviewee's views of Churchill have changed the most: the sum of differences is 9.

The changes which contribute particularly to this total are on the constructs, 'principled – unprincipled', 'experienced – inexperienced', and 'more effective – less effective'; after the course, he is regarded as being more experienced than he was before the course, and seen as rather less effective.

(b) Again in the bottom row, the politician about whom there has been the least change is Wilson.

(c) It's impossible to tell, without discussing the new ratings with the interviewee. It may be possible to glean something from the direction of changes if you look at the two basic grids (the 'before' and 'after' grids), and note the direction of the differences.

So, for example, the interviewee's views of Blair may be changing to a more extreme position, towards an assessment of 'inexperienced', in the light of information gained on the course about the length of time all of these politicians were active since first elected to Parliament – Blair became prime minister rather more quickly than the others. And it may be that the ratings on 'ensured the succession' and 'political success' have moved towards neutrality as a result of learning a little about how such factors *are* predicted by political commentators!

But you would really *have* to discuss this with the interviewee to be sure.

In point of fact, discussion with this interviewee showed that his initial constructs about Churchill had been particularly influenced by his previous knowledge of Churchill's role as a leader in World War II. The course provided a wider perspective on Churchill's performance by reminding him of Churchill's periods of relative obscurity between the two world wars, and his declining effectiveness in the post-war period. The speculations about Blair were partially confirmed.

Now return to Section 9.1.2.

1.17 Answers to Exercise 9.2

(a) The constructs which have been separated and placed at the top of Table 9.3 are those which are common to both of the grids in Table 9.2. (Notice how minor variations in wording are ignored; if in doubt, ask the interviewee!) The remaining constructs are listed below. The reason this has been done is to make the analysis of the change less messy than working directly with the two grids in Table 9.2.

(b) The three figures in each cell are, in order, the rating of that element on that construct in the first grid, its rating on the same construct in the second grid, and the absolute difference between these two ratings (that is, the difference ignoring minus signs). You can't do this for all the constructs, but you can do it for those constructs which are common to both grids, as you did in the change grid (see Section 9.1.2 and Exercise 9.1), which has identical elements and identical constructs before and after.

(c) That would appear to be Prof. AW.

(d) One reason for saying this is the sum of differences: a total of 6 over the five constructs common to both grids, which is the largest difference sum. This summarises the 'slot-rattling' that's occurred in the interviewee's views.

The second reason goes beyond slot-rattling, and looks at changes in the actual constructs used. Constructs A1.4, A1.5, and A1.8 have been dropped. For one reason or another, the interviewee no longer finds them predictive. Similarly, he has chosen to think of his lecturers in terms of two new constructs, A2.6 and A2.7. Notice how, as a result, Prof. AW's ratings on these constructs have moved from a rather negative evaluative stance, to a more positive evaluative stance, than in the case of all the other lecturers.

(e) Which model to choose? Whichever seems to you to be most useful!

The student is about to make a choice of dissertation tutor.

What might the **C-P-C cycle** suggest? You might notice that he has reduced the number of constructs in the second grid, and the two new ones, together with the ones that were dropped, seem to reflect a refocusing on supervisor skills directly relevant to working on a dissertation. This is certainly not 'circumspection'; he is beginning to make his mind up.

He is drawing on what he knows about the tutorial supervision process and looking for particular skills; in terms of the **experience cycle**, he is 'anticipating' what working with these tutors will be like, considering what kinds of 'investment' are required. Provided he gets over his nervousness with respect to the Prof., it looks as though he can live with him better than he can with either Dr LT or Dr TN. Does he need to have another short meeting ('encounter'!) with all three, or does the second grid already represent his 'constructive revision'?

(f) As we saw in (d) above, his views of Prof. AW, on the common constructs, have certainly changed drastically since the first grid, in a direction which seems to be favourable towards a supervisor–student relationship. He's more focused (no longer finds a lecturer's gifts as an entertainer to be a useful way of thinking!) and is looking for someone who is easily accessible and doesn't require the student to pay for a lot of inter-library loans in order to access the recommended texts required for the dissertation. He seems to realise that he can live with the Prof. (finds him more interesting and easier to understand than before), and realises he has better tutorial skills than he first thought.

Now return to Section 9.2.

1.18 Answers to Exercise 9.3

(a) If you do a quick change grid comparing Ms B as Mr A with Mr A's original, you can see that the sum of differences is lowest for the first lecturer, Dr JF. When it comes to this lecturer, Ms B understands Mr A's views well here.

(b) Likewise, Ms B has been least successful in reproducing Mr A's views of Dr LT: a sum of differences of 9.

(c) The difference between Ms B's ratings as Mr A seems to arise from the first three constructs, among them being

> Clear, understandable   –   Difficult to follow

and

> Makes it interesting   –   Dull and boring

Ms B hasn't realized just how 'clear and understandable' Mr A felt Dr LT to be, and how interesting he felt Dr LT's presentation of the material to be. Could this be (see Table 9.4, lower half) because Ms B's own assessment of Dr LT places him at the less favourable end on such constructs as

> Paces the lecture to   –   Rushes difficult material
> students' needs   during lectures

and

> Constantly develops   –   Repetitively covers years-old
> material, keeps it fresh   material

and this makes it difficult for her to appreciate how 'clear and understandable' he might appear to Mr A? How Mr A can see this lecturer as someone who can make material interesting?

The kind of questions that Ms B might put to Mr A might include

- How can someone who uses previous years' material (and you know Dr JF does a bit of that!) – be thought of as interesting?

● I find that Dr JF rushes over stuff that we don't quite understand: to me, that makes him difficult to follow! What is it that makes him so understandable for you?

In discussion, Mr A might discover that Ms B does see Dr JF as fairly concerned about the students and appeal to that. If so, the challenge for Ms B might be to discount her feeling that Dr JF only does that to the students he views with excessive favouritism (see Ms B's construct B6). And so on.

And finally, return to Section 9.3.

APPENDIX 2

EXTRACTS FROM THE TRANSCRIPT OF A GRID SESSION

This grid is the kind you'd produce when doing Exercise 3.1. It's provided here in order to:

(a) give you a point of comparison when doing your own first grid

(b) provide material for Exercise 4.1.

The grid is presented bit by bit, as the constructs are elicited. The interview*ER*'s and the Interview*EE*'s utterances are labelled 'ER' and 'EE', respectively.

Topic: My Friends

Elements: eight named friends, represented here by their initials. It has been suggested to EE that he include a range of friendships, from close, through 'just acquainted, so-so', to include one person he doesn't particularly like.

ER: Okay, so we have eight people you know, friends of yours to a smaller or greater degree. Now, I want you to let me know what you think about them – how you see them and perhaps what feelings you have towards them. Anything, really, that you think is relevant if I want to understand how you view your friends.

EE: Well, that's a lot, really. I mean, some are new and some are old, four, no, five of them are males, AB has red hair, how do you?...and then this one...

ER: Okay, whoa, hold on a bit! That's great, er, let's find things out bit by bit, and think it through systematically. Actually, a good way of doing that is to compare them in threes. Now, if I were to say to you: (person) AB: CD: GH: which two of these people are alike in some way, and different from the third, in terms of how you think of them as friends?

EE: I find this a bit confusing. AB and CD don't see a lot of each other...er, but, they'd be more likely to meet when GH is around, since CD and GH are sharing a house with some other people and...not sure what you mean.

ER: Well, think of them as the separate people they are. Now, as individuals, is there a characteristic which, say, AB and CD have which GH doesn't? Or some characteristic which has AB and GH as alike, with CD being different? Forget about whether they're house-sharing, for the time being. As individuals, AB, CD, and GH?

EE: Well, AB and CD are both a bit reserved; GH isn't. On the other hand, CD and GH are very good at sports but AB isn't at all sporty. Is that what you mean? Then there's when I first met them...

ER: Yes, that's just the sort of thing I mean. Hold on while I get the first one down.

✓	AB	CD	GH	KL	MN	OP	QR	ST	✗
Reserved									

ER: So AB and CD are alike because they're reserved, whereas, in contrast, GH is...?

EE: Oh, I'd say she's outgoing, you know, friendly and approachable.

✓	AB	CD	GH	KL	MN	OP	QR	ST	✗
Reserved	✓	✓	✗						Friendly and approachable

ER: Now, can you tell me in what way they're reserved? I mean, what would I notice about them that I wouldn't about GH?

EE: It's not that they're shy – well, I suppose CD is a *bit* shy; no, it's about how 'forward' they are. If you met them for the first time at a party they'd sort of wait until you introduced them; GH, well, she'd be across the room shaking hands straightaway!

ER: So if I have this as [writes in and shows *EE*]:

✓	AB	CD	GH	KL	MN	OP	QR	ST	✗
Reserved, hold back till they're introduced	✓	✓							~~Friendly and approachable~~ Outgoing, will approach others first

EE: Yes, that's right.

ER: Now, suppose that what we have here is a rating scale. A 5-point scale. The words I have on the left, 'reserved, hold back', is the '1' end of the scale, and the words on the right, 'outgoing, will approach', are the '5' end of the scale. I want you to rate each of these three people on this scale. Give each of them a number, 1, 2, 3, 4, or 5, to say which end of the scale they're nearest to. So: how would you rate AB?

EE: Well, I've said, rather reserved; give him a '4' and CD a '5' cos he's more reserved?

ER: Okay, I know this may seem a bit awkward, but the scale goes from 'reserved equals "1" to 'outgoing equals "5"'. Forget which one's 'bigger' or 'has more of'; it's the direction, nearer to the left or nearer to the right, that we want. The words on the left [shows grid] stand for the '1' end of the scale – if someone is very reserved, they'd get a '1'; a bit reserved would be a '2'; not at all reserved, but in fact very outgoing, would be a '5', d'you see?

EE: Right, if that's what you want, then CD gets a '1' and AB gets a '2', reserved, but not as much as CD.

ER: And in contrast, GH?

EE; Oh, yes, definitely very outgoing; give her a '5'.

1 ✓	AB	CD	GH	KL	MN	OP	QR	ST	5 ✗
Reserved, hold back till they're introduced	✓2	✓1	5✗						~~Friendly and approachable~~ Outgoing, will approach others first

ER: And what about the others? How would you rate KL on this scale?

EE: Ah. Well, pretty outgoing, really. A '5', maybe a '4'?

ER: Is he as outgoing as GH or less so?

EE: Oh, I'd say less – a '4'.

1	AB	CD	GH	KL	MN	OP	QR	ST	5
Reserved, hold back till they're introduced	✓2	✓1	5	4					~~Friendly and approachable~~ Outgoing, will approach others first

ER: And MN?

EE: More like AB, really; a '2' I'd say.

ER: What about OP?

EE: Oh. Well, I've got a problem here. Have you a '10' on the scale?! OP is very forward, much more so than GH!

ER: No, but we can give him a '5', that's the most outgoing...

1	AB	CD	GH	KL	MN	OP	QR	ST	5
Reserved, hold back till they're introduced	√2	√1	5	4	2	5			~~Friendly and approachable~~ Outgoing, will approach others first

ER: ...but we may have to move GH along a bit; she's less outgoing than OP, so give her a '4'?

EE: I see what you mean. Yes, okay, a '4' for GH, and then OP is a '5'. But KL is less outgoing than either of them – change it to a '3'?

ER: Yes, that sounds okay, if that sums up how you see them in terms of reserved versus outgoing. Here we are [shows]:

1	AB	CD	GH	KL	MN	OP	QR	ST	5
Reserved, hold back till they're introduced	√2	√1	4	3	2	5			~~Friendly and approachable~~ Outgoing, will approach others first

EE: That's fine. On that basis, QR is a '3' as well. ST, now, she's different. More like AB, really.

ER: Reserved, but not as reserved as CD?

EE: Yes, that's right. A '2'.

1	AB	CD	GH	KL	MN	OP	QR	ST	5
Reserved, hold back till they're introduced	√2	√1	4	3	2	5	3	2	~~Friendly and approachable~~ Outgoing, will approach others first

ER: Good! That's your first construct – one way you have of thinking about your friends and friendship. You said something earlier about being sporty? Is that something you have in mind when you think about friends?

EE: Yes, I enjoy being fit myself, and though not all my friends are interested, I do tend to notice how healthy or otherwise they are!

ER: So is this about being fit and healthy, or being interested in sports?

EE: Well, I suppose it's to do with how they feel about keeping fit. I mean, you can be a couch potato who watches football on TV, you could call that 'sporty', but it's not what I have in mind. Yes, look, that's what it is: whether you get a buzz off them; or whether, sure, they care to stay alive but they're just...amiable, maybe, but slobs!

ER: What if we were to say 'care about their health' as opposed to 'health doesn't matter to them'?

EE: Not really, everyone cares about their health! No, it's more to do with making an effort to be fit and healthy.

1	AB	CD	GH	KL	MN	OP	QR	ST	5
Reserved, hold back till they're introduced	✓2	✓1	4	3	2	5	3	2	~~Friendly and approachable~~ Outgoing, will approach others first
Makes an effort to be fit and healthy									

ER: As opposed to?

EE: As opposed to not being particularly bothered.

ER: How would you tell?

EE: Oh, you know, activity: goes for a swim, makes an effort, joined a gym, you could say the sort of person who'd have their own personal trainer if they could afford it.

ER: And the opposite?

EE: It's definitely to do with not making any special effort to look after himself. Or herself.

1	AB	CD	GH	KL	MN	OP	QR	ST	5
Reserved, hold back till they're introduced	√2	√1	4	3	2	5	3	2	~~Friendly and approachable~~ Outgoing, will approach others first
Makes an effort to be fit and healthy: active; swim, gym (personal trainer type!)									Makes no special effort to look after themselves

ER: So there we have it [shows grid]. A new rating scale: 'makes an effort' (with all the other things that we've said about making an effort) is the '1' end of the scale; 'makes no special effort' is the '5' end of the scale. How would you rate AB?

EE: Oh, not particularly sporty; I'd say a '4', not especially interested. CD's into being fit, and GH, yes, she's pretty much a fitness freak, even more so.

1	AB	CD	GH	KL	MN	OP	QR	ST	5
Reserved, hold back till they're introduced	√2	√1	4	3	2	5	3	2	~~Friendly and approachable~~ Outgoing, will approach others first
Makes an effort to be fit and healthy: active; swim, gym (personal trainer type!)	4	2	1						Makes no special effort to look after themselves

ER: There you are, And the others, going along the row?

EE: Ah, KL! He's the couch potato's couch potato! MN, yes, she's healthy and talks about it a lot; she's into alternative medicine too. OP, neither, really; I'd give her a '3'. It's just not an issue with her; she says she's happy enough to rest on her laurels now that she's given up smoking! QR, yes, another slob, though not as gross as KL. That leaves ST, who's moderately interested. A '2'? No, that would be like CD; better say '3'.

1	AB	CD	GH	KL	MN	OP	QR	ST	5
Reserved, hold back till they're introduced	√2	√1	4	3	2	5	3	2	~~Friendly and approachable~~ Outgoing, will approach others first
Makes an effort to be fit and healthy: active; swim, gym (personal trainer type!)	4	2	1	5	1	3	4	3	Makes no special effort to look after themselves

EE: Looking over the ratings, it looks like all the blokes are slobs, yeah!...no, that's not true, CD isn't. Does their sex matter? Should we put that in or is it a bit trivial?

ER: Well, we're talking about *your* friendships here, and how you think about them. Is their sex relevant to you? You tell me!

EE: GH is my girlfriend. Well, I'm not especially a 'man's man', I enjoy getting on with either! No, leave it out.

ER: All right, so we look for another construct, another way in which you think of friends and friendship. Suppose I ask you to think about KL, MN, and OP. Which two of these are alike, in some way to do with friendship, and thereby different from the third?

EE: KL's a slob, no, we've said that...oh, okay. KL worries what you think about him; the other two don't. Well, not that he worries, but other people's opinions matter to him. MN and OP are more independent, don't need to rely on other people so much.

ER: Hm. You were saying earlier that OP is 'very forward', like GH?

EE; Yes, she likes other people, but she doesn't need other people. MN's the same. KL reminds me of that psychological test, what was it? Gave you a score on whether you were 'group-dependent, a sound follower'...? Which makes me wonder: what if my way of thinking is just, you know, wrong, not as an expert on people would see it?

ER: [refusing to be drawn] Oh, well, never mind about all those psychologists – it's *your* constructs we're interested in. So, you're saying that MN and OP are alike because they're independent and don't rely on being part of a group, whereas KL needs to be 'of' a group, as well as in it, as it were?

EE: Yes, that puts it rather well; give him '1'. He's more of a conformist really; they're more self-sufficient, both the same: give them a...Sorry, which way round is it?

ER: [shows the grid] Independent is a '1' and conformist is a '5'.

1	AB	CD	GH	KL	MN	OP	QR	ST	5
Reserved, hold back till they're introduced	✓2	✓1	4	3	2	5	3	2	~~Friendly and approachable~~ Outgoing, will approach others first
Makes an effort to be fit and healthy: active; swim, gym (personal trainer type!)	4	2	1	5	1	3	4	3	Makes no special effort to look after themselves
Independent, self-sufficient	1	2	2	5	✓1	✓1	3	4	A conformist, group-dependent, 'of' a group as well as 'in' a group

ER: And the others?

EE: This is an easy one. AB and CD are both independent types, 1 and 2; GH comes alive when she's with other people but no, I wouldn't say she's clingy – give her a 2. That leaves QR – he's sort of half-way – and ST. She's fairly groupy, give her a '4', I think.

ER: Now here's another comparison. AB, QR, and ST.

EE: Let's see now. QR and ST are alike because...AB is reserved and their own person, while they're...This is difficult, I'm stuck on the other constructs with these three people...

ER: Is there a way that QR and AB are alike as opposed to ST?

EE: No. I just can't see anything.

ER: That's all right. Try comparing these three: GH, MN, and ST.

EE: GH and MN are...no, I was going to say single children, and ST is part of a large family. Is that the same as being independent as distinct from group-dependent, I wonder?

ER: You tell me!

EE: Well, it's not true about KL: he's a single child, but group-dependent. This isn't exactly the same as the previous one, really.

ER: And it'll be very interesting to see how far you do see the two characteristics (independent/only child, group-dependent/from a large family) as similar – we can measure that in the analysis. Go ahead. 'No other brothers or sisters' is the '1' end of the scale; 'many brothers and sisters' is the '5' end of the scale. The more siblings, the larger the rating.

EE: GH and MN are only children, so is KL; ST, in contrast, has three older brothers, poor girl; and OP has two brothers and two sisters! What does that look like on your sheet?

ER: [shows]. Not quite the same ratings. What about AB and CD?

EE: No, not really. AB has a sister, CD has two, QR is one of a pair of twins – give her a '2', the same as 'AB'. Is that all of them now?

ER: Yes, that's right.

1	AB	CD	GH	KL	MN	OP	QR	ST	5
Reserved, hold back till they're introduced	✓2	✓1	4	3	2	5	3	2	~~Friendly and approachable~~ Outgoing, will approach others first
Makes an effort to be fit and healthy: active; swim, gym (personal trainer type!)	4	2	1	5	1	3	4	3	Makes no special effort to look after themselves
Independent, self-sufficient	1	2	2	5	✓1	✓1	3	4	A conformist, group-dependent, 'of' a group as well as 'in' a group
No siblings	2	3	✓1	✓1	1	5	2	4	Many siblings

EE: Now, what would you say about AB, KL, and ST? Which two of these are similar, but different from the third, in terms of friendship as you think of friendship?

ER: Oh, in terms of sheer liking them. AB and ST are my best friends, apart from my girlfriend GH. KL I don't particularly get on with.

1	AB	CD	GH	KL	MN	OP	QR	ST	5
Reserved, hold back till they're introduced	√2	√1	4	3	2	5	3	2	~~Friendly and approachable~~ Outgoing, will approach others first
Makes an effort to be fit and healthy: active; swim, gym (personal trainer type!)	4	2	1	5	1	3	4	3	Make no special effort to look after themselves
Independent, self-sufficient	1	2	2	5	√1	√1	3	4	A conformist, group-dependent, 'of' a group as well as 'in' a group
No siblings	2	3	√1	√1	1	5	2	4	Many siblings
Best friends	✓							✓	Don't get on with

EE: I'll scribble that down for the moment; but could you say a bit more about them? What do you look for in a best friend as distinct from someone who you don't particularly get on with?

ER: Lots, really. They don't have to think like me, but we have to be on the same wavelength; then they have to be easy to be with, you know, a good laugh. And for me, being from the same background helps. I know it shouldn't, but can I put it down?

EE: By all means! This is about what you think, not what you should think. I appreciate your honesty.

ER: [Laughs] And that's another thing. I look for honesty from my friends. Reliability, someone you can depend on.

EE: Okay. Now, look, what I'd like to do at this stage is to flag up 'best friends' versus 'don't get on with', since that summarises the purpose of the whole grid; and then quickly tease out the other characteristics you've just mentioned. We'll leave 'best friends' just like that, and view the whole of the grid as defining what that particular construct means for you.

EE: Well, these were all a bit 'top-of-my-head', you know; shouldn't I do the three-at-a-time bit – make sure I'm doing it properly?

ER: Oh, no: the 'three-at-a-time' bit is just to get you to come up with fresh constructs each time; if you can spin out a set just like that without the 'three-at-a-time' routine, that's fine! And when you start rating each of the friends, I'll make sure that you think it through so it's not just off the top of your head! Now, here's what you've just said [scribbles quickly, and shows]:

1	AB	CD	GH	KL	MN	OP	QR	ST	5
Reserved, hold back till they're introduced	✓2	✓1	4	3	2	5	3	2	~~Friendly and approachable~~ Outgoing, will approach others first
Makes an effort to be fit and healthy: active; swim, gym (personal trainer type!)	4	2	1	5	1	3	4	3	Makes no special effort to look after themselves
Independent, self-sufficient	1	2	2	5	✓1	✓1	3	4	A conformist, group-dependent, 'of' a group as well as 'in' a group
No siblings	2	3	✓1	✓1	1	5	2	4	Many siblings
~~Best friends~~ BEST FRIENDS	✓							✓	~~Don't get on with~~ DON'T GET ON WITH
On the same wavelength									
Easy/a good laugh									
Same background as myself									
Honest, reliable, dependable									

ER: Now before we do anything else, you need to tell me whether I've understood you. 'On the same wavelength': you said that that isn't how similarly you think...

EE: No, it's more to do with reacting the same way, seeing the funny side at the same time; how predictable they are, really, in their reactions.

ER: And easy to be with? Just that, as distinct from minding your ps and qs with them?

EE: Exactly. That leaves 'same background'. Well, you know, parents being similar people, same sort of schools, all that. Can you just say, 'I know what you mean', and leave it at that?

ER: Yes, of course, if that's your preference. But what about 'honest, reliable, dependable'? One in particular, or are they all the same? What single word or idea would you put down as the opposite?

EE: I was going to say 'predictable – unpredictable', but I've already said that. All right, let's say open and emotionally honest, as distinct from secretive, pulling the wool over your eyes as far as feelings are concerned.

ER: That's fine. Now let's do the ratings on each of these constructs, one by one. Leave the overall 'best friends' one for the moment. [Fills in the ratings as EE calls them out.]

1	AB	CD	GH	KL	MN	OP	QR	ST	5
Reserved, hold back till they're introduced	√2	√1	4	3	2	5	3	2	~~Friendly and approachable~~ Outgoing, will approach others first
Makes an effort to be fit and healthy: active; swim, gym (personal trainer type!)	4	2	1	5	1	3	4	3	Makes no special effort to look after themselves
Independent, self-sufficient	1	2	2	5	1	1	3	4	A conformist, group-dependent, 'of' a group as well as 'in' a group
No siblings	2	3	1	1	1	5	2	4	Many siblings
~~Best friends~~ BEST FRIENDS	✓	✓							~~Don't get on with~~ DON'T GET ON WITH
On the same wavelength, react similarly, more predictable XXX	1	3	1	5	4	1	3	2	More difficult to predict XXX
Easy/a good laugh	2	5	1	4	4	1	3	2	Have to be careful round them
Same background as myself XXXX	1	2	2	5	4	2	4	3	Different background XXXX
~~Honest, reliable, dependable~~ Open and emotionally honest XX	1	3	1	5	3	2	3	2	Secretive, pull the wool over your eyes re feelings XX

ER: Now then. Let's get a little distance for moment. Try another triplet, and remember, a new construct: something unrelated as far as possible to the ones we've already talked about. Try AB, ST, and MN.

EE: It's very difficult to avoid repeating myself. I don't have a very varied way of thinking, do I? It's all the same!

ER: Well, actually, you're not doing too badly. It's extraordinary, really, how very well, thank you, we manage to do with relatively few really different ways of looking at the world! Now, does anything occur?

EE: No...oh well, I suppose there's education: AB and MN had a very good schooling, conventionally, while ST wasn't 'academic', left school early, and has had a tough time of it. And before you ask, by 'good schooling' I mean something like the old grammar schools, as distinct from a big, inner-city comprehensive.

1	AB	CD	GH	KL	MN	OP	QR	ST	5
Reserved, hold back till they're introduced	✓2	✓1	4	3	2	5	3	2	~~Friendly and approachable~~ Outgoing, will approach others first
Makes an effort to be fit and healthy: active; swim, gym (personal trainer type!)	4	2	1	5	1	3	4	3	Makes no special effort to look after themselves
Independent, self-sufficient	1	2	2	5	✓1	✓1	3	4	A conformist, group-dependent, 'of' a group as well as 'in' a group
No siblings	2	3	✓1	✓1	1	5	2	4	Many siblings
~~Best friends~~ BEST FRIENDS	✓	✓							~~Don't get on with~~ DON'T GET ON WITH
On the same wavelength, react similarly, more predictable ✗✗✗	1	3	1	5	4	1	3	2	More difficult to predict ✗✗✗
Easy/a good laugh	2	5	1	4	4	1	3	2	Have to be careful round them
Same background as myself	1	2	2	5	4	2	4	3	Different background
~~Honest, reliable, dependable~~ Open and emotionally honest	1	3	1	5	3	2	3	2	Secretive, pull the wool over your eyes re feelings
Good schooling, like an old grammar school	✓1	3	1	2	✓1	4	2	5	Weaker schooling: big, inner-city comp.

ER: That's fine. And the ratings? [fills them in as EE reports them.] This has been a very detailed session and we've both worked very hard! Finally, my usual catch-all question. Working with friends, three at a time mostly, is a very effective way of identifying people's constructs, but it is an unusual way of talking about friendships, and I'd hate to have the technique get in the way of the meaning! And so, let me ask you: looking at these people as a group, is there any construct that is crying out for expression but hasn't yet had an opportunity to be spoken, because the way we were going about it got in its way?

EE: No. Looking at them carefully, I have to say...nothing else occurs to me.

ER: That's fine. And now, just one last thing. I'm going to cover over the ratings, and ask you to make an overall assessment of these eight people. Overall, summarising it all, and as a general feeling: how would you rate each of them on a scale that goes from 'best friends' = '1', to 'don't get on with' = '5'?...Many thanks!

The final grid is shown below.

1	AB	CD	GH	KL	MN	OP	QR	ST	5
Reserved, hold back till they're introduced	√2	√1	4	3	2	5	3	2	~~Friendly and approachable~~ Outgoing, will approach others first
Makes an effort to be fit and healthy: active; swim, gym (personal trainer type!)	4	2	1	5	1	3	4	3	Makes no special effort to look after themselves
Independent, self-sufficient	1	2	2	5	√1	√1	3	4	A conformist, group-dependent, 'of' a group as well as 'in' a group
No siblings	2	3	√1	√1	1	5	2	4	Many siblings
~~Best friends BEST FRIENDS~~	√	√							~~Don't get on with DON'T GET ON WITH~~
On the same wave-length, react similarly, more predictable ✗✗✗	1	3	1	5	4	1	3	2	More difficult to predict ✗✗✗
Easy/a good laugh	2	5	1	4	4	1	3	2	Have to be careful round them
Same background as myself	1	2	2	5	4	2	4	3	Different background
~~Honest, reliable, dependable~~ Open and emotionally honest	1	3	1	5	3	2	3	2	Secretive, pull the wool over your eyes re feelings
Good schooling, like an old grammar school	√1	3	1	2	√1	4	2	5	Weaker schooling: inner-city comp.
BEST FRIENDS	1	2	1	5	4	1	3	2	DON'T GET ON WITH

APPENDIX 3

ELEMENT % SIMILARITY SCORES

	Number of constructs in grid						
Sum of diffs	10	9	8	7	6	5	4
40	0						
39	2.50						
38	5.00						
37	7.50						
36	10.00	0					
35	12.50	2.78					
34	15.00	5.56					
33	17.50	89.33					
32	20.00	11.11	0				
31	22.50	13.89	3.13				
30	25.00	16.67	6.25				
29	27.50	19.44	9.38				
28	30.00	22.22	12.50	0			
27	32.50	25.00	15.63	3.57			
26	35.00	27.78	18.75	7.14			
25	37.50	30.56	21.88	10.71			
24	40.00	33.33	25.00	14.29	0		
23	42.50	36.11	28.13	17.86	4.17		
22	45.00	38.89	31.25	21.43	8.33		
21	47.50	41.67	34.38	25.00	12.50		
20	50.00	44.44	37.50	28.57	16.67	0	
19	52.50	47.22	40.63	32.14	20.83	5.00	
18	55.00	55.00	43.75	35.71	25.00	10.00	
17	57.50	52.78	46.88	39.29	29.17	15.00	
16	60.00	55.56	50.00	42.86	33.33	20.00	0
15	62.50	58.33	53.13	46.43	37.50	25.00	6.25
14	65.00	61.11	56.25	50.00	41.67	30.00	12.50
13	67.50	63.89	59.38	53.57	45.83	35.00	18.75
12	70.00	66.67	62.50	57.14	50.00	40.00	25.00
11	72.50	69.44	65.63	60.71	54.17	45.00	31.25
10	75.00	72.22	68.75	64.29	58.33	50.00	37.50
9	77.50	75.00	71.88	67.86	62.50	55.00	43.75
8	80.00	77.78	75.00	71.43	66.67	60.00	50.00
7	82.50	80.56	78.13	75.00	70.83	65.00	56.25
6	85.00	83.33	81.25	78.57	75.00	70.00	62.50
5	87.50	86.11	84.38	82.14	79.17	75.00	68.75
4	90.00	88.89	87.50	85.71	83.33	80.00	75.00
3	92.50	91.67	90.63	89.29	87.50	85.00	81.25
2	95.00	94.44	93.75	92.86	91.67	90.00	87.50
1	97.50	97.22	96.88	96.43	95.83	95.00	93.75
0	100.00	100.00	100.00	100.00	100.00	100.00	100.00

APPENDIX 4

CONSTRUCT % SIMILARITY SCORES

Sum of diffs.	No. of elements in grid						
	10	9	8	7	6	5	4
40	−100.00						
39	−95.00						
38	−90.00						
37	−85.00						
36	−80.00	−100.00					
35	−75.00	−94.44					
34	−70.00	−88.89					
33	−65.00	−83.33					
32	−60.00	−77.78	−100.00				
31	−55.00	−72.22	−93.75				
30	−50.00	−66.67	−87.50				
29	−45.00	−61.11	−81.25				
28	−40.00	−55.56	−75.00	−100.00			
27	−35.00	−50.00	−68.75	−92.86			
26	−30.00	−44.44	−62.50	−85.71			
25	−25.00	−38.89	−56.25	−78.57			
24	−20.00	−33.33	−50.00	−71.43	−100.00		
23	−15.00	−27.78	−43.75	−64.29	−91.67		
22	−10.00	−22.22	−37.50	−57.14	−83.33		
21	−5.00	−16.67	−31.25	−50.00	−75.00		
20	0.00	−11.11	−25.00	−42.86	−66.67	−100.00	
19	5.00	−5.56	−18.75	−35.71	−58.33	−90.00	
18	10.00	0.00	−12.50	−28.57	−50.00	−80.00	
17	15.00	5.56	−6.25	−21.43	−41.67	−70.00	
16	20.00	11.11	0.00	−14.29	−33.33	−60.00	−100.00
15	25.00	16.67	6.25	−7.14	−25.00	−50.00	−87.50
14	30.00	22.22	12.50	0.00	−16.67	−40.00	−75.00
13	35.00	27.78	18.75	7.14	−8.33	−30.00	−62.50
12	40.00	33.33	25.00	14.29	0.00	−20.00	−50.00
11	45.00	38.89	31.25	21.43	8.33	−10.00	−37.50
10	50.00	44.44	37.50	28.57	16.67	0.00	−25.00
9	55.00	50.00	43.75	35.71	25.00	10.00	−12.50
8	60.00	55.56	50.00	42.86	33.33	20.00	0.00
7	65.00	61.11	56.25	50.00	41.67	30.00	12.50
6	70.00	66.67	62.50	57.14	50.00	40.00	25.00
5	75.00	72.22	68.75	64.29	58.33	50.00	37.50
4	80.00	77.78	75.00	71.43	66.67	60.00	50.00
3	85.00	83.33	81.25	78.57	75.00	70.00	62.50
2	90.00	88.89	87.50	85.71	83.33	80.00	75.00
1	95.00	94.44	93.75	92.86	91.67	90.00	87.50
0	100.00	100.00	100.00	100.00	100.00	100.00	100.00

APPENDIX 5

EXTRACTS FROM THE TRANSCRIPT OF A RESISTANCE-TO-CHANGE SESSION

See the procedure shown in Section 8.1.3. Table 8.4 shows the successive comparisons made in following that procedure, and Tables 8.5 and 8.6 show the result. It's the kind of process to expect when you do Exercise 8.3. The interviewER's and interviewEE's utterances are labelled 'ER' and 'EE', respectively.

ER: So now we know some of your personal values: the ones which you draw on in construing this topic. Let's see how you prioritise them. Yes, they're all personal beliefs, important to you...but some are more strongly held than others. I'd like to explore with you which ones are bedrock, and which are, you know, important but less fundamental. Let's start with your first pair of values:

Life and hope   –   Hopelessness and despair

and

Personal moral responsibility   –   Criminal irresponsibility

Now, I want you to imagine that I'm taking you away to a beautiful tropical island, somewhere in the south Pacific: somewhere where you'll spend the rest of your days. Actually, there are two possible islands. On the first one, you'll live as part of a society where there is 'life and hope', *but* at the cost of 'criminal irresponsibility'. Shall I leave you to live there? Or shall we sail on to the second island, where you can live a life of complete 'personal moral responsibility', *but* you will certainly encounter great 'hopelessness and despair'. Which will you choose?

EE: No, sorry! I want life and hope and personal moral responsibility. Not the other stuff!

ER: I'm sure you do! But this choice is a tough one, and you have to take it! Either 'life and hope', but having to put up with 'criminal irresponsibility', or you can have the 'personal responsibility' you want, but there's a price: 'hopelessness and despair'. Which is it to be?

EE: Aww. Well, I have to have hope. I couldn't bear to live out my days in utter despair.

ER: And you agree to put up with a level of irresponsibility you see as criminal?

EE: Yes, if I must, I must. If I have hope, I can always trust that things might change . . .

ER: Okay: that's a preference for life and hope [places a 'yes' against personal value A]. Now here's another possibility. Suppose the choice was a different one, involving your two values

Life and hope   –   Hopelessness and despair

and

Progress   –   Stagnation

You can live out your days with a feeling of 'life and hope', but in a society in which there is stagnation; or you can choose 'progress', but at the cost of 'hopelessness and despair'. Which would you prefer?

EE: Oh. The first one sounds impossibly frustrating: what's the point of living a life in which all your hopes result in nothing but stagnation? If I can make progress I can't be hopeless and despairing *all* of the time! Yes, I'll take the second option.

ER: Right: that's your third personal value, progress, preferred over your first, life and hope, despite the costs attached [places a 'yes' against personal value B]. Now we compare the first and the fourth. This time your choice is as follows. On your first island, you would have all the 'life and hope' you wanted, but at the cost of 'pain and suffering'. Alternatively, you could live a life lacking all suffering: a life of 'pleasure and enjoyment', *but* there would be 'hopelessness and despair' to put up with. Which would you choose?

EE: Well, I guess I would put up with pain and suffering. It's possible to take your mind off your troubles if you have a sense of hope.

ER: Ah, hold on . . . that's a choice of 'life and hope' rather than 'pleasure and enjoyment'?

EE: That's right.

ER: [places a 'yes' against personal value A]. Now, what about the following? You can have 'life and hope', *but* the cost is a disordered society: you live in 'chaos', and are a part of it. Alternatively, you have all the 'order' that you might crave, but at the cost of 'hopelessness and despair'. Which is it to be? Remember, for the rest of your days . . .

EE: Order is important to me... There again, it would be a rather sterile existence, order amidst hopelessness and despair. No, I think I prefer 'life and hope' at the cost of 'chaos'. While there's hope, there's some sort of life!

ER: [Another 'yes' is placed against personal value A, 'life and hope'. So far, this value has been preferred three times, with just one occasion on which another value was preferred to it.] And finally, with this personal value. Your choice is 'life and hope', but the cost you have to pay is that you're 'alienated from other people'. Or, you can have all the 'sensibility and affiliation' with other people that your heart might desire, but you experience 'hopelessness and despair'.

EE: That's awful. Can I skip this one?

ER: No, I'm afraid you can't! It has to be one or the other.

EE: But it's a contradiction! How can I have any sort of hope if I'm alienated from other people? It's an impossible combination! Sorry, but I can't.

ER: My heart goes out to you! Look on it this way, though. Can you imagine hope with alienation, at all?

EE: No. People matter to me. There would be no hope whatsoever if we were alienated.

ER: And can you imagine any circumstances in which sensibility and affiliation could be combined with hopelessness and despair?

EE: Well, yes, I suppose I could. I would cling on to other people as a way of handling the despair.

ER: So you have to have sensibility and affiliation... you're resigned to giving up hope?

EE: I suppose so.

ER: [places a tick against personal value F, 'sensibility and affiliation']. Now, the choice changes slightly. We're going to examine your second personal value, and see how it compares against the others.

> Personal moral responsibility   –   Criminal irresponsibility

compared, firstly, with

> Progress   –   Stagnation

That gives us this sort of choice. Option one. You live out a life of 'personal moral responsibility' but at a cost of 'stagnation'. Alternatively, option two: you live in circumstances in which 'progress' is possible and, indeed, occurs, but where people are 'criminally irresponsible', and you get sucked into it too. Which will you choose?

EE: Well, no, personal moral responsibility matters. 'Progress' is a problematic notion sometimes. There are times when one can live with a bit of stagnation if one can avoid irresponsibility. Yes: it has to be the first option.

ER: [places a 'yes' against personal value B, 'personal moral responsibility']. And the second comparison with this personal value, 'personal moral responsibility' at the cost of 'pain and suffering', or 'criminal irresponsibility' but you live a life of 'pleasure and enjoyment'.

EE: I must sound very puritan to you...but this one's easy. Irresponsible pleasure is tempting...but no, the choice is personal moral responsibility even though there may be some pain attached.

ER: [marks personal value B, 'personal moral responsibility', with a tick, and continues]. Okay. Though we're still working with your second personal value, we've made a lot of comparisons already, and when we've finished this one, we'll be halfway done. This time it's 'personal moral responsibility' at the cost of 'chaos', or 'stability and order' but you have to put up with 'criminal irresponsibility'...

And so it continues. Notice how, having completed the first five comparisons ('life and hope' against all the rest), you don't have to make any further comparison that includes 'life and hope' when you're focusing on any of the other personal values. All of them have already been compared with 'life and hope'.

When you've finished all the comparisons, add up the 'yes' responses against each personal value as in Table 8.5, and write them down in order, as in Table 8.6.

You'll find that, as your interviewees get used to the task, and find ways of thinking about the circumstances in which they are asked to make a choice, they can adjust...trim...alter the ways they think about the personal values, compromising them to a greater or smaller degree. And that is the point of this procedure, of course. There are some personal values which are very resistant to change. Your interviewee *will not budge*! And there are others which are...more malleable. Notice, though, that this is a relative issue. All of the values you're working with have been identified *as* personal values in the laddering exercise which precedes the present forced-choice procedure.

APPENDIX 6

THE FORMAL CONTENT OF KELLY'S PERSONAL CONSTRUCT THEORY

Table A6.1 summarises the basic assertions of the theory (Kelly, 1952/1991). The corollaries are presented in a different order than Kelly's, but in his own words. I then provide a brief comment or gloss on each one.

Table A6.1 The fundamental postulate and the corollaries

Fundamental postulate	A person's processes are psychologically channelised by the ways in which he anticipates events.	The world out there is real; the world in here is equally real. Psychologically, people operate by building internal representations of the phenomena they experience. They do so in order actively to predict what will happen next. This activity has the same epistemological status as the activity of the 'scientist' when s/he seeks to understand and explain nature.
Construction corollary	A person anticipates events by construing their replications.	People develop these internal representations by recognising regularities and recurring patterns in their experience, which they represent internally by means of contrasts called 'constructs'.
Dichotomy corollary	A person's construct system is composed of a finite number of dichotomous constructs.	Constructs are reference axes, not concepts; so, to understand someone's meaning, you need to know 'both ends', that is, the *implicit pole* as well as the *expressed pole*, of the construct. Thus, 'good' as opposed to 'inadequate' expresses a different meaning to 'good' as opposed to 'evil'.
Range corollary	A construct is convenient for the anticipation of a finite range of events only.	Unlike a concept, which applies to everything it encompasses, a construct is limited to a *focus of convenience* found useful by the person using it. It's not used for all things in all circumstances.

(continued)

Table A6.1 (*Continued*)

Modulation corollary	The variation in a person's construction system is limited by the permeability of the constructs within whose range of convenience the variants lie.	Some constructs are more permeable (can accommodate many new events within their *range of convenience*); for example, 'good–bad'. Others are less permeable (apply to only a few); for example, 'fluorescent–incandescent'.
Organisation corollary	Each person characteristically evolves for his convenience in anticipating events, a construction system embracing ordinal relationships between constructs.	Regarded as a data structure, the internal representations we call constructs are organised as a hierarchic system. Some constructs are more central and have the nature of personal values, subsuming other, more specific constructs.
Fragmentation corollary	A person may successively employ a variety of construction systems which are inferentially incompatible with each other.	While there is a tendency towards consistency between different parts of the system – especially between core constructs (personal values) and their subordinate constructs – this consistency isn't total; it may vary according to circumstances and events as the individual interprets them.
Experience corollary	A person's construction system varies as he successively construes the replications of events.	Constructs represent 'working hypotheses' about what will happen next. If they, or their implications, aren't effective in prediction, they are open to amendment in the light of those events, though people differ in the extent to which they are prepared to make, or even notice, a possible need for, such amendment.
Choice corollary	A person chooses for himself that alternative in a dichotomised construct through which he anticipates the greatest possibility for the elaboration of his system.	We often express preferences for one pole of each construct as opposed to another. If the whole system is to be effective in anticipating events, it makes sense for us to develop a preference which allows us to 'grow' the system in a way which increases the accuracy of our predictions and anticipations.
Individuality corollary	People differ from each other in their construction of events.	Different people develop their own meanings – their own constructs – for the same events, and this is what gives them their individuality and distinct personhood.

(*continued*)

Table A6.1 (*Continued*)

Commonality corollary	To the extent that one person employs a construction of experience which is similar to that employed by another, his processes are psycho- logically similar to those of the other person.	People are similar to the extent that they construe (see the meaning in) events similarly (and not because they encounter similar events, nor because they behave in the same way).
Sociality corollary	To the extent that one person construes the construction process of another, he may play a role in a social process involving the other person.	We enter into effective role relation- ships with other people (for example, boss–subordinate; parent–child; husband–wife) to the extent that we are aware of, and can understand, some of the other person's constructs (and not because the two sets of constructs are the same, nor because society has defined roles for us).

APPENDIX 7

AIDE-MÉMOIRE/SUMMARY OF GRID PROCEDURES

This appendix presents the various procedures outlined throughout the chapters in one place for easy reference while you're learning them. With practice, you'll be able to depart from them, and know the good reasons why you're departing from them. Initially, though, each procedure is available in outline form for reference. You'll need to check back to the full presentation occasionally, since some of the outlines are very sparse.

Basic Repertory Grid Elicitation

Section 3.1.2

(1) Agree a topic.

(2) Agree a set of elements.

(3) Explain that you wish to find out how your respondent thinks about the elements.

(4) Taking three elements, ask your respondent, 'Which two of these are *the same* in some way, and *different* from the third?'

(5) Ask your respondent why: 'What do the two have in common, as opposed to the third?'

(6) Check that you understand what contrast is being expressed.

(7) Present the construct as a rating scale.

(8) Ask your respondent to rate each of the three elements on this scale, writing the ratings into the grid as s/he states them.

(9) Now ask the respondent to rate each of the remaining elements on this construct.

(10) Your task is to elicit as many different constructs as the person might hold about the topic. So, repeat steps 4 to 8, asking for a fresh construct each time, until your respondent can't offer any new ones.

Laddering Down

Section 4.4.1

Laddering down is used at stage 6 of the basic grid elicitation procedure.

6b Put a *'how'* question to the interviewee about the emergent pole of the original construct.

- Write the answer down below the emergent pole.
- Put a 'how' question to the interviewee about the implicit pole.
- Write down the answer below the implicit pole.
- Stop at that point, or repeat the *'how'* question in more detail still, about the construct you've just written down.
- Apply the remaining steps of the basic grid procedure to the final construct you arrive at.

Pyramiding

Section 4.4.2

Pyramiding is used as an alternative to laddering down at stage 6 of the basic grid elicitation procedure.

6b Put a *'how'* question to the interviewee.

- Write the answer down below the emergent pole of the original construct.
- Ask what is the opposite or contrasting pole of the construct you wrote down above, and write *it* down.
- Go back to the implicit pole of the original construct and ask a 'how' question to the interviewee about it.
- Write the answer down below the implicit pole of the original construct.
- Ask what is the opposite or contrasting pole of the construct you wrote down above, and write *it* down.
- Stop at that point, or repeat the *'how'* question in more detail still, about the constructs you've just written down, noting the emergent poles, and asking in each case what their opposite is.
- Apply the remaining steps of the basic grid procedure to *all* of the constructs you arrive at.

Eyeball Analysis

Section 5.3.2

Eyeball analysis is used as a preliminary to any other analysis technique.

- What is the interviewee thinking about?
- How has the interviewee represented the topic?
- *How* does s/he think: what are the constructs?
- *What* does s/he think: how have the elements been rated on the constructs?
- Examine the supplied elements and constructs and their ratings.
- Draw conclusions.

Characterising Constructs

Section 5.3.3

The following four numbered steps apply in adopting a systematic approach to analysing the following kinds of constructs: core versus peripheral; propositional versus constellatory; constructs used pre-emptively; affective, behavioural, evaluative, and attributional.

(1) Identify constructs which appear to have that characteristic.

(2) Assess the proportion with that characteristic among the others in the whole grid.

(3) Ascribe significance to this proportion, in context.

(4) Examine relationships: how do these particular constructs relate to other constructs?

The particular way in which relationships are assessed varies depending on which sort of construct is being dealt with: see Section 5.3.3.

Simple Relationships Between Elements

Section 6.1.1

This is a suggested approach to the use of element difference sums and % similarity scores.

(1) Calculate differences in ratings of the first pair of elements on the first construct.

(2) Sum down the page over the remaining constructs and note the total.

(3) Repeat for all pairs of elements.

(4) Compare the sums of differences, especially the smallest and largest.

(5) Discuss these relationships with the interviewee.

(6) Examine relationships with supplied elements, if any.

(7) Ensure comparability with other grids by turning the difference scores into % similarity scores.

Use the formula:

$$\text{element \% similarity} = 100 - (\{SD/[(LR-1) \times C]\} \times 100)$$

where SD is the sum of differences, LR is the largest rating possible on the scale, and C is the number of constructs in the grid; or refer to the table in Appendix 3.

Simple Relationships Between Constructs

Section 6.1.2

This is the analogous procedure for constructs.

(1) Calculate the differences in the ratings of the first element on the first pair of constructs.

(2) Sum across the page for the remaining elements.

(3a) Repeat for all pairs of constructs.

(3b) Repeat step 3a for all pairs of constructs with one set of ratings reversed.

(4) Find the smallest sum of differences among all the comparisons you've made, unreversed and reversed.

(5) Discuss these relationships with the interviewee.

(6) Examine relationships with supplied constructs, if any.

(7) Ensure comparability with other grids by turning the difference scores into % similarity scores.

Use the following formula:

$$\text{construct \% similarity} = 100 - (\{SD/[(LR-1) \times E]\} \times 200)$$

where SD is the sum of differences, LR is the largest rating possible on the scale, and E is the number of elements in the grid; or refer to the table in Appendix 4.

Cluster Analysis: Elements

Section 6.2.2

Follow the example shown in Table 6.11 and Figure 6.2.

This is one possible approach for making sense of the output from a cluster-analysis package.

(1) Examine the elements, and notice which elements have been reordered.

(2) Examine the shape of the element dendrogram.

(3) Identify construct similarities and differences.

(4) What does this mean in terms of the way in which your interviewee is thinking?

(5) Find the highest % similarity score.

(6) Examine the remaining scores.

Cluster Analysis: Constructs

Section 6.2.2

See also the example shown in Table 6.12 and Figure 6.2.

This is the corresponding procedure for constructs.

(1) Examine the constructs: notice how they have been reordered.

(2) Look at the shape of the construct dendrogram.

(3) Identify element similarities and differences.

(4) What does this mean? Discuss the implications with your interviewee.

(5) Find the highest % similarity score.

(6) Examine the remaining scores.

Principal Components Analysis

Section 6.3.2

Here's just one procedure for making sense of the output of a principal components analysis package. There are many others, depending on what you're looking for, but it's one I find convenient.

(1) Determine how many components you'll need to work with: how many do you need to account for 80% of the variance?

(2) Examine the shape of the lines representing the constructs: how tightly are they spread?

(3) Identify any similarities in the meaning of the constructs which make up each 'sheaf':

- by inspection

- by examining their relationship to any supplied construct.

(4) Note the position of any meaningful groupings with respect to the two principal components: the vertical axis and the horizontal axis.

(5) Check your interpretations with the interviewee. *Resist the temptation to pronounce about them.*

Content Analysis: Bootstrapping – Core-Categorisation Procedure

Section 7.2.1

This is the core procedure which is used as steps 1 and 2 of the content-analysis procedures which follow. Each item being categorised is compared with each of the others.

(1) If an item is in some way like the first item, the two are placed together under a single category.

(2) If an item is different to the first item, they're put into separate categories.

(3) Remaining items are compared with each of the categories and allocated to the appropriate one if an appropriate category exists.

(4) A new category is created if required; when a new category is created, the possibility that existing categories need to be redefined (combined, or broken up, with their items reallocated accordingly) is considered.

(5) This process continues until all the items have been classified.

(6) However, any unclassifiable items are placed in a small category marked 'miscellaneous'.

(7) No more than 5% of the total is regarded as such.

Content Analysis: Bootstrapping – Generic Content-Analysis Procedure

Section 7.2.1

Here's the full process. It should incorporate the reliability procedures shown below.

(1) Identify the categories.

(2) Allocate the constructs to the categories, following the core-categorisation procedure, steps 1 to 7 above.

(3) Tabulate the result.

(4) Establish the reliability of the category system (using the procedure shown below).

(5) Summarise the table; first, the meaning of the category headings.

(6) Summarise the table: next, find examples of each category heading.

(7) Summarise the table; finally, the frequency under the category headings.

(8) Complete any differential analysis which your investigation requires.

(9) Complete any statistical tests on this differential analysis as required.

Content Analysis: Bootstrapping – Reliability

Section 7.2.1

This is for inclusion at stage 4 of the above procedure. These steps improve the reliability of the content analysis, and measure the degree of reliability achieved, for reporting purposes. The former is essential and the latter advisable.

(4) Establish the reliability of the category system.

    (4.1) Involve a colleague: ask a colleague to repeat steps 1 to 3 independently.

(4.2) Identify the categories you both agree on, and those you disagree on.

(4.3) Record your joint allocation of constructs.

(4.4) Measure the extent of agreement between you.

- Index A: the number of constructs lying along the diagonal for the categories you have both agreed on as a percentage of all the constructs in the *whole* table.

- Index B: the number of constructs lying along the diagonal for the categories you have both agreed on as a percentage of the constructs allocated to the categories you have both agreed on.

(4.5) Negotiate over the meaning of the categories.

(4.6) Finalise a revised category system with acceptably high reliability.

(4.7) Report the final reliability figure:

- agreement on all the category definitions, and 90% successful allocation (or, if you're using a reliability coefficient, 0.80 or above).

Content Analysis: Honey's Procedure

Section 7.3.2

(1) Obtain ratings on a supplied 'overall' construct.

(2) Compute sums of differences for each construct against the 'overall' construct, using the procedure shown earlier, 'simple relationships between constructs' (see Section 6.1.2).

(3) Ensure comparability with other grids, turning sums of differences into % similarity index.

(4) Take the individual's personal metric into account: annotate each construct with the H-I-L index.

(5) Label each construct with these two indices.

(6) Identify the categories.

(7) Allocate constructs to categories, following the core-categorisation procedure (see above).

(8) Tabulate the result.

(9) Establish the reliability of the category system (Section 7.2.1, steps 4.1–4.7).

(10) Summarise the table: first, the meaning of the category headings.

(11) Summarise the table: find examples of each category heading.

    (11.1) Within each category, order the constructs from top to bottom with respect to their % similarity scores.

    (11.2) Looking at all the constructs within a category, identify personally salient constructs (referring to the H-I-L indices) on which there is consensus in the group.

    (11.3) If there are subthemes within a category, group them according to the meaning being expressed.

(12) Summarise the table: state the frequency under the category headings.

(13) Complete any differential analysis which your investigation requires.

(14) Complete any statistical tests on this differential analysis, as before.

Laddering Up to Arrive at Values

Section 8.1.1

(1) Take the first construct in the grid.

(2) Ask the interviewee which pole s/he prefers.

(3) Ask the interviewee to describe the basis for this preference.

(4) Note the answer immediately above the preferred pole of the original construct, as a new construct.

(5) Identify the contrasting pole of that new construct.

(6) Note it, above the implicit (non-preferred) pole of the original construct.

(7) Repeat steps 2 to 6 for this new superordinate construct.

(8) Repeat step 7 until the interviewee can't go any further.

(9) Take the next construct in the original grid; repeat steps 2 to 8 for it.

(10) Do step 9 for each of the remaining constructs in the original grid.

Recognising a Personal Value

Section 8.1.2

In deciding when to end the laddering procedure, note that a personal value is characterised by several of the following attributes:

- abstraction
- universality
- intimacy
- self-reference
- self-evidence
- explicit information (that is, ask the interviewee!).

Prioritising Personal Values: The Resistance-to-Change Technique

Section 8.2

(1) Take the first two personal values identified by the laddering technique (Section 8.1.1), calling them A–Contrast A and B–Contrast B.

(2) Present the interviewee with a choice of A at the cost of Contrast B, or B at the cost of Contrast A.

(3) Record the personal value which is preferred.

(4) Compare value A with the next value, C, following the above two steps.

(5) Repeat step 4, comparing value A with each of the remaining values.

(6) Now compare value B with the next value, C.

(7) Repeat step 6, comparing value B with each of the remaining values.

(8) Repeat step 7, comparing each of the remaining values with each other.

(9) Count the number of times that each personal value was preferred over another.

(10) Record the outcome as a hierarchy of personal values.

Identifying Personal Change: The Simple Change Grid

Section 9.1.1

Where elements and constructs are identical in two grids from the same person,

(1) Elicit two grids in succession from the same interviewee, with the same elements and constructs.

(2) Ensure that elements and constructs are written in the same position in both grids.

(3) Cell by cell, record the difference between the ratings in corresponding positions in the two grids, using either the absolute value (ignoring minus signs) or the arithmetic value of the difference.

(4) At the bottom of each column of the change grid, sum the differences in that column.

(5) Consider a process analysis (Section 5.3.1), do an eyeball analysis (Section 5.3.2), and characterise constructs (Section 5.3.3) in the change grid.

(6) Consider any of the analysis procedures described in Chapter 6, though

   (a) simple relationships between elements

   (b) simple relationships between constructs

   (c) cluster analysis

   are likely to be more useful than principal components analysis.

(7) Discuss all these changes with the interviewee.

Identifying Personal Change: The Messy Change Grid

Section 9.1.2

Where elements and constructs differ in two grids from the same person,

(1) Elicit two grids in succession from the same interviewee.

(2) Before analysis, make sure that any elements and constructs which both grids have in common are in the same position in both grids.

(3) If there are sufficient common elements and constructs to make it worthwhile, treat that portion of both grids as a change grid (see above, and Section 9.1.1).

(4) Examine the function of the new constructs (and elements, if any) with the interviewee.

(5) Explore the process by which some of the constructs have been dropped; focus, first and foremost, on the constructs and their meaning: what's being said, and what has changed?

(6) Drawing on the C-P-C cycle, the Experience Cycle, and the Creativity Cycle, change models, identify the kind of change which is taking place in your interviewee's construing of the topic, and act accordingly.

Facilitating Mutual Exploration: Simple Partnering

Section 9.2.1

This is suitable for work in a group.

(1) Negotiate a confidentiality contract.

(2) Agree a set of elements sensible to all.

(3) Agree appropriate anonymity arrangements for elements.

(4) Elicit the repertory grids.

(5) Put the interviewees into pairs, and ask each pair to swap grids, discussing similarities and differences in their pairs. Eyeball analysis (Section 5.3.2) and laddering down (Section 4.4.1), or pyramiding (Section 4.4.2) is likely to be useful here.

(6) Process the outcomes in a plenary session.

(7) Agree an appropriate action plan.

Entering Another Person's World: The Exchange Grid

Section 9.2.2

(1) Negotiate a confidentiality contract.

(2) Agree a set of elements sensible to all.

(3) Agree appropriate anonymity arrangements for elements.

(4) Elicit the repertory grids.

(5) Photocopy each grid, and Tipp-Ex out the ratings on the photocopy.

(6) Put the interviewees into pairs, calling one person in each pair 'A', and the other 'B'. Get A and B to exchange *the photocopies* of their own grids.

(7) Either ask each interviewee to fill out the other's grid *as s/he thinks the other filled it out*, or ask each interviewee to fill out the other's grid *as themselves*.

(8) Ask each interviewee A to compare B's attempt at being A with A's original grid, discussing the attempt. Then swap round, with each interviewee B comparing A's attempt at being B with B's original grid. Use the simple change grid subtraction procedure (Section 9.1.1).

GLOSSARY

Cluster Analysis: a statistical technique for highlighting the pattern of relationships in a repertory grid by grouping elements (and then constructs) on the basis of the similarity of individual ratings. Produces outputs which are, arguably, more client-friendly than those provided by a principal components analysis, *q.v.* p. 118.

Construct: one of the four components of a repertory grid; an attribute which an individual uses to make sense of his or her experience. Expressed as two contrasted poles; constitutes a choice about that experience or a preference with respect to that experience, p. 10.

Content Analysis: the only feasible way of aggregating the information present in a large set of repertory grids, by collecting and categorising the different meanings of constructs present in the set. Honey's technique makes use of some of the information available in the ratings as well, pp. 146, 169.

Constructivism: the epistemological position which asserts that the significance and usefulness (not 'truth') of a proposition is established by an agreement between individuals about the meaning of the observations they make. The main concern is therefore for the extent of shared assumptions and the reliability of observations made in order to understand what is going on, p. 44. Contrast with *Positivism, q.v.*

Core Construct: a construct which is central to the individual, around which s/he builds his or her personal identity and its place in the wider scheme of existence. All core constructs have a relationship to an individual's values, though not all personal values are core constructs, p. 83.

Corollary: a proposition which supplements a fundamental statement. In Kelly's personal construct theory (see Appendix 6) there are 11 of them, all amplifying his fundamental postulate about human psychological functioning, p. 59.

C-P-C Cycle: one of three models for describing change in construing, and particularly those which relate to decision making. People change their minds by engaging in Circumspection, Pre-emption, and Control, in that order, pp. 219–220.

Creativity Cycle: another of the three models for describing change in construing; views the creative process as one in which implicational connections between constructs are successively loosened and tightened, p. 219.

Dendrogram: a diagram, which looks like a tree, whose branches represent the relationships between adjacent elements (or adjacent constructs) as produced in a cluster analysis, pp. 121, 122.

Elaborative Choice: a decision among alternative ways of construing a situation which results in permanent changes in a person's construct system, p. 231.

Element: one of the four components of a repertory grid; an example of, sampling of, instance of, or occurrence within, a given *Topic*, p. 13.

Emergent Pole: that part of a construct to which the individual explicitly refers; for example, the meaning of 'tense' when the individual is using the construct 'tense versus relaxed' and talks about being tense. In triadic grid elicitation it is normally identified as the characteristic which two of the triad of elements have in common, and is written down on the left of the grid-sheet, p. 48. Contrast with *Implicit Pole, q.v.*

Experience Cycle: one of three models for describing change in construing; consists of stages of Anticipation, Investment, Encounter, Assessment and Constructive Revisions. Managers and business students will recognise the similarity to Kolb's Cycle, p. 219.

Implicit Pole: that part of a construct which is left tacit by the individual; for example, the meaning of 'relaxed' when the individual is using the construct 'tense versus relaxed' and talks about being tense. In triadic elicitation it is normally identified as the contrast – the characteristic pertaining to the odd one out of the elements, and is written down on the right of the grid sheet, p. 48. Contrast with *Emergent Pole, q.v.*

Negotiation of Meaning: the process underlying construct elicitation by which you arrive at a precise understanding of the individual's personal meaning, p. 11.

Ontological Choices: decisions made by individuals, in line with their personal values, through which their priorities in life and existence are expressed. What's *your* bottom line? Are justice and the rule of law important, or should human frailty be allowed for? Are business organisations run for their employees, their shareholders or their customers? Is education fundamentally about preparing people to make a contribution to society, or is it basically about personal growth and development? Each of these alternatives represents an ontological choice, p. 191.

Personal Repertoire: the totality of constructs which a particular individual uses, p. 12.

Positivism: the epistemological position which asserts that the truth of a proposition can be established by facts which exist independently of the observer, waiting to be discovered and to be put into use. The main concern is therefore for the validity and reliability of observations made in order to explain what is going on, p. 44. Contrast with *Constructivism, q.v.*

Principal Components Analysis: a statistical technique for highlighting the pattern or relationships in a repertory grid, by identifying hypothetical underlying components on the basis of patterns of variability in the ratings. Outputs are, arguably, less client-friendly than those produced by a cluster analysis, *q.v.*, but more useful in identifying 'what needs to change' in a counselling or guidance application, pp. 127–130.

Range of Convenience: the set of various realms of discourse within which a particular construct can be usefully applied. Constructs like 'Comfortable–Painful' have a wide range of convenience (you can use them in a wide variety of contexts), while those like 'Incandescent–Luminescent' have a very narrow range of convenience (you can't use them to talk about much, other than light sources), p. 12.

Ratings: one of the four components of a repertory grid; a number on a scale applied to each element on each construct, by which an individual expresses a meaning, pp. 13–14.

Realm of Discourse: the general field of personal knowledge within which the *Topic* of a grid is situated, p. 12.

Resistance-to-Change Technique: a way of helping a person to decide on their value priorities: those which represent ontological bedrock, and those over which s/he's prepared to compromise a little bit, p. 197.

Social Desirability Effect: the tendency for people to express their attitudes, opinions, beliefs, and values in a socially acceptable manner. When working with personal values, *Resistance-to-Change Technique, q.v.*, can control the effect to some extent, p. 197.

Topic: one of the four components of a repertory grid; the subject-matter of a particular repertory grid, pp. 12–13.

REFERENCES

Adams-Webber, J. (1989) 'Some reflections on the "meaning" of repertory grid responses'. *International Journal of Personal Construct Psychology* 2, 77–92.

Bales, K.F. (1950) *Interaction Process Analysis: A Method for the Study of Small Groups.* Cambridge, MA: Addison-Wesley.

Berger, P.L. & Luckmann, T. (1976) *The Social Nature of Reality.* Harmondsworth: Penguin.

Boose, J.H. (1985) 'A knowledge acquisition program for expert systems based on personal construct psychology'. *International Journal of Man–Machine Studies* 23, 495–525.

Brown, L.D. & Kaplan, R.E. (1981) 'Participative research in a factory' in P. Reason & J. Rowan (eds), *Human Inquiry: A Sourcebook of New Paradigm Research* (pp. 303–314). Chichester: Wiley.

Burleson, B.R., Kunkel, A.W. & Szolwinski, J.B. (1997) 'Similarity in cognitive complexity and attraction to friends and lovers: experimental and correlational studies'. *Journal of Contructivist Psychology* 10, 221–248.

Burr, V. & Butt, T. (1992) *An Invitation to Personal Construct Psychology.* London: Whurr.

Caputi, P. & Reddi, P. (1999) 'A comparison of triadic and dyadic methods of personal construct elicitation'. *Journal of Constructivist Psychology* 12, 253–263.

Cohen, J. (1968) 'Weighted kappa: nominal scale agreement with provision for scaled disagreement or partial credit'. *Psychological Bulletin* 70, 213–220.

Collett, P. (1979) 'The repertory grid in psychological research' in G.P. Ginsburg (ed.), *Emerging Strategies in Social Psychological Research.* Chichester: Wiley.

Cook, M. (1998) *Personnel Selection.* London: Wiley.

Cromwell, R. & Caldwell, D.F. (1962) 'A comparison of ratings based on personal constructs of self and others'. *Journal of Clinical Psychology* 18, 43–46.

Cronbach, L.J. (1964) *Essentials of Psychological Testing,* London: Harper & Row.

Davis, H., Stroud, A. & Green, L. (1989) 'Child characterization sketch'. *International Journal of Personal Construct Psychology* 2, 323–337.

Duck, S. (1973) *Personal Relationships and Personal Constructs: A Study of Friendship Formation.* London: Wiley.

Eden, C., Jones, S. & Sims, D. (1983) *Messing About in Problems.* Oxford: Pergamon Press.

Edmonds, T. (1979) 'Applying personal construct theory in occupational guidance'. *British Journal of Guidance and Counselling* 7, 225–233.

Epting, F.R., Probert, J.S. & Pittman, S.D. (1993) 'Alternative strategies for construct elicitation: experimenting with experience'. *International Journal of Personal Construct Psychology* 6, 79–98.

Feixas, G., Geldschläger, H. & Neimeyer, R.A. (2002) 'Content analysis of personal constructs'. *Journal of Constructivist Psychology* 15, 1–19.

Flanagan, J.C. (1954) 'The critical incident technique'. *Psychological Bulletin* 51, 237–258.

Fonda, N. (1982) 'Using repertory grids in counselling' in V. Stewart & A. Stewart (eds), *Business Applications of Repertory Grid* (pp. 116–141). London: McGraw-Hill.

Fransella, F., Bell, R. & Bannister, D. (2004) *A Manual of Repertory Grid Technique*. 2nd edn. London: Routledge.

Gaines, B. & Shaw, M. (1993) 'Knowledge acquisition tools based on personal construct psychology'. *Knowledge Engineering Review* 8, 49–85.

Greenaway, R. (2002) 'Experiential learning cycles'. *www http://reviewing.co.uk/research/learning.cycles.htm*, accessed 30 December 2002.

Harré, R. (1981) 'The positivist-empiricist approach and its alternative' in P. Reason & J. Rowan (eds), *Human Inquiry: A Sourcebook of New Paradigm Research* (pp. 3–17). Chichester: Wiley.

Harter, S.L., Erbes, C.R. & Hart, C.C. (2001) 'Use of the role construct repertory grid to assess the personal constructions of sexual abuse survivors'. Paper given at the Ninth Biennial Conference, North American Personal Construct Network, State University of New York at New Paltz.

Hellriegel, D., Slocum, J.W. Jr. & Woodman, R.W. (1995) *Organizational Behavior*. Minneapolis, MN: West Publishing.

Hill, R.A. (1995) 'Content analysis for creating and depicting aggregated personal construct derived cognitive maps' in R.A. Neimeyer & G.J. Neimeyer (eds), *Advances in Personal Construct Psychology* (pp. 101–132). Greenwich, CN: JAI Press.

Hinkle, D.N. (1965) 'The Change in Personal Constructs from the Viewpoint of a Theory of Implications', PhD thesis, Ohio University.

Hisrich, R.D. & Jankowicz, A.D. (1990) 'Intuition in venture capital decisions: an exploratory study using a new technique'. *Journal of Business Venturing* 5, 49–62.

Holsti, O.R. (1968) 'Content analysis' in G. Lindzey & E. Aronson (eds), *The Handbook of Social Psychology*, vol. 2. *Research Methods*. London: Addison-Wesley.

Honey, P. (1979) 'The repertory grid in action'. *Industrial and Commercial Training* 11, 452–459.

Horley, J. (1991) 'Values and beliefs as personal constructs'. *International Journal of Personal Construct Psychology* 4, 1–14.

Horley, J. (2000) 'Value assessment and everyday activities'. *Journal of Constructivist Psychology* 13, 67–73.

Humphreys, P. & McFadden, W. (1980) 'Experiences with MAUD: Aiding decision structuring versus bootstrapping the decision maker'. *Acta Psychologica* 45, 51–69.

Hunt, D.E. (1987) *Beginning with Ourselves: In Practice, Theory, and Human Affairs*. Cambridge, MA: Brookline Books.

Jankowicz, A.D. (1987a) 'Whatever became of George Kelly? Applications and implications'. *American Psychologist* 42, 481–487.

Jankowicz, A.D. (1987b) 'Intuition in small business lending decisions'. *Journal of Small Business Management* 25, 45–52.

Jankowicz, A.D. (1990) 'Applications of personal construct psychology in business practice' in G.J. Neimeyer & R.A. Neimeyer (eds), *Advances in Personal Construct Psychology*, vol. 1 (pp. 257–287). Greenwich, CN: JAI Press.

Jankowicz, A.D. (1996a) 'On "resistance to change": in the post-command economies, and elsewhere' in M. Lee, H. Letiche, R. Crawshaw & M. Thomas (eds), *Management Education in the New Europe: Boundaries and Complexity* (pp. 139–162). London: International Thomson Business Press.

Jankowicz, A.D. (1996b) 'Personal values among public sector employees: a methodological study'. Paper given at the 3rd Conference of the European Personal Construct Association, Reading, UK, April.

Jankowicz, A.D. (2000a) *Business Research Projects*. 3rd edn. London: Thomson.

Jankowicz, A.D. (2000b) 'Self-reference in the identification of personal values: is there a functional limit constraining a hierarchy of constructs?' in J.M. Fisher & N. Cornelius (eds), *Challenging the Boundaries: PCP Perspectives for the New Millennium*, Proceedings of the 5th Conference of the European Personal Construct Association (pp. 109–119). Malta, April.

Jankowicz, A.D. (2001) 'Why does subjectivity make us nervous? Making the tacit explicit'. *Journal of Intellectual Capital* 2, 61–73.

Jankowicz, A.D. & Cooper, K. (1982) 'The use of focused repertory grids in counselling'. *British Journal of Guidance and Counselling* 10, 136–150.

Jankowicz, A.D. & Thomas, L.F. (1982/1983) 'The FOCUS cluster-analysis algorithm in human resource development'. *Personnel Review* 11, 15–22; erratum: 1983, 12, 22.

Jones, H. (1998) 'Bringing two worlds together: personal and management development in the NHS'. *Human Resource Development International* 1, 341–356.

Kaczmarek, P. & Jankowicz, A.D. (1991) 'American students' perceptions of counselor approachability: professional implications'. *International Journal for the Advancement of Counseling* 14, 313–324.

Kelly, G.A. (1955/1991) *The Psychology of Personal Constructs*. 2nd edn. London: Routledge.

Kelly, G.A. (1963) *A Theory of Personality: The Psychology of Personal Constructs*, London: Norton.

Kelly, G.A. (1970) 'A brief introduction to personal construct theory' in D. Bannister (ed.), *Perspectives in Personal Construct Theory* (pp. 1–30). London: Academic Press.

Kolb, D. (1984) *Experiential Learning: Experience as the Source of Learning and Development*. Englewood Cliffs, NJ: Prentice-Hall.

Landfield, A.W. (1968) 'The extremity rating revisited within the context of personal construct theory'. *British Journal of Social and Clinical Psychology* 7, 135–139.

Landfield, A.W. (1971) *Personal Construct Systems in Psychotherapy*. Chicago: Rand McNally.

Landfield, A.W. & Cannell, J.E. (1988) 'Ways of assessing functionally independent construction, meaningfulness, and construction in hierarchy' in J.C.S. Mancuso & M.L.G. Shaw (eds), *Cognition and Personal Structure: Computer Access and Analysis* (pp. 67–89). New York: Praeger.

Leitner, L.M. & Pfenninger, D.T. (1994) 'Sociality and optimal functioning'. *Journal of Constructivist Psychology* 7, 119–135.

MacMillan, I., Zemann, C.L. & SubbaNarashimha, P.M. (1987) 'Criteria distinguishing successful from unsuccessful ventures in the venture screening process'. *Journal of Business Venturing* 2, 123–137.

Mair, M. (1989) 'Kelly, Bannister, and a story-telling psychology'. *International Journal of Personal Construct Psychology* 2, 1–14.

Mair, M. (1990) 'Telling psychological tales'. *International Journal of Personal Construct Psychology* 3, 121–135.

Neimeyer, G.J. & Neimeyer, R.A. (1985) 'Relational trajectories: a personal construct contribution'. *Journal of Social and Personal Relationships* 2, 325–349.

Neimeyer, R.A. (1981) 'The structure and meaningfulness of tacit construing' in H. Bonarius, R. Holland & S. Rosenberg (eds), *Personal Construct Psychology: Recent Advances in Theory and Practice* (pp. 105–119). London: Macmillan.

Neimeyer, R.A. (1983) 'The development of personal construct psychology' in J.R. Adams-Webber & J. Mancuso (eds), *Applications of Personal Construct Theory* (pp. 155–172). London: Academic Press.

Neimeyer, R.A. (1985) *The Development of Personal Construct Psychology*. Lincoln, NB: University of Nebraska Press.

Neuendorf, K.A. (2002) *The Content Analysis Guidebook*. London: Sage.

Nevill, D.D. & Super, D.E. (1989) *The Values Scale: Application and Research*, Palo Alto, CA: Consulting Psychologists Press.

O'Cinneide, B. (1986) *The Case for Irish Enterprise*. Dublin: Enterprise Publications.

Perrault, W.D.J. & Leigh, L.E. (1989) 'Reliability of nominal data based on qualitative judgements'. *Journal of Marketing Research* 26, 135–148.

Pervin, L. (1973) 'On construing our constructs: a review of Bannister and Fransella's *Inquiring Man*'. *Contemporary Psychology* 18, 110–112.

Riemann, R. (1990) 'The bipolarity of personal constructs'. *International Journal of Personal Construct Psychology* 3, 149–165.

Russ-Eft, D., Burns, J.Z., Dean, P.J., Hatcher, T., Otte, F.L. & Preskill, H. (1999) *Standards on Ethics and Integrity*. Report to Academy of Human Resource Development, January.

Salmon, P. (1976) 'Grid measure with child subjects' in P. Slater (ed.), *Explorations of Interpersonal Space*. New York: Wiley.

Saussure, F. de (1915/1983) *Course in General Linguistics*. London: Duckworth.

Scheer, J. (2003) 'Computer programmes for grids'. *http://www.pcp-net.de/info/comp-prog.html*, accessed 8 January 2003.

Selltiz, C.S., Wrightsman, L.S. & Cook, S.W. (1981) *Research Methods in Social Relations*. London: Holt, Rinehart & Winston.

Sewell, K.W., Adams-Webber, J., Mitterer, J. & Cromwell, R.L. (1992) 'Computerised repertory grids: review of the literature'. *International Journal of Personal Construct Psychology* 5, 1–23.

Shaw, M.L.G. (1980) *On Becoming a Personal Scientist*. London: Academic Press.

Stewart, V. & Stewart, A. (1982) *Business Applications of Repertory Grid*. London: McGraw-Hill.

Thomas, L.F. & Shaw, M.L.G. (1976) *FOCUS Manual*. Centre for the Study of Human Learning, Brunel University.

Thomas, L.F. (1977) *User's Guide to the FOCUS Programme*. Uxbridge: Centre for the Study of Human Learning, Brunel University.

Thomas, L.F. & Harri-Augstein, S. (1985) *Self-Organised Learning*. London: Routledge and Kegan Paul.

Tyebjee, T.T. & Bruno, A.V. (1984) 'A model of venture capital investment activity'. *Management Science* 30, 1051–1066.

Viney, L.L. & Westbrook, M.T. (1976) 'Cognitive anxiety: a method of content analysis of verbal samples'. *Journal of Personality Assessment* 40, 140–150.

Watson, W., Ponthieu, L. & Doster, J. (1995) 'Business owner-managers' descriptions of entrepreneurship: a content analysis'. *Journal of Constructivist Psychology* 8, 33–51.

Whitehead, J. (1994) 'How do I improve the quality of my management? A participatory action research approach'. *Management Learning* 25, 137–153.

Winter, D. (1992) *Personal Construct Psychology in Clinical Practice*. London: Routledge.

Yorke, D.M. (1978) 'Repertory grids in educational research: some methodological considerations'. *British Educational Research Journal* 4, 63–74.

Yorke, D.M. (1983) 'Straight or bent: an inquiry into rating scales in repertory grids'. *British Educational Research Journal* 9, 141–151.

Yorke, M. (1989) 'The intolerable wrestle: words, numbers, and meanings'. *International Journal of Personal Construct Psychology*, 2, 65–76.

INDEX OF NAMES AND
FIRST-NAMED AUTHORS

SUBJECT INDEX

Page references in **bold** refer to figures and tables.
'Ex' indicates that the entry preceding is part of an exercise

Lightning Source UK Ltd.
Milton Keynes UK
UKOW07f2142080118
315759UK00004B/83/P